The UK
Air Fryer
Book for Beginners

This Great Air Fryer Cookbook Will Help You Create Healthy and Delicious Food
that Your Family and Friends Will Love

Matilda Singh

CONTENT

Introduction

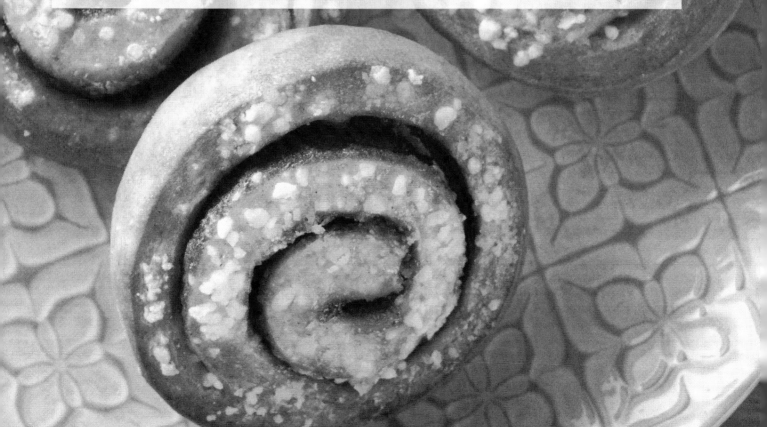

Air fryers are becoming more and more popular as people realize how convenient and easy they are to use. If you're thinking about getting an air fryer, or you've just gotten one, you may be wondering what to do with it. Luckily, there are plenty of air fryer cookbooks out there that can help you make the most of your air fryer. One of the great things about air fryers is that they can be used to make all kinds of food, from appetizers to main courses to desserts. An air fryer cookbook can help you figure out what kinds of food can be cooked in an air fryer and how to cook them. An air fryer is a kitchen appliance that cooks food by circulating hot air around it. It is similar to a convection oven in that it cooks food quickly and evenly. However, an air fryer uses less oil than a traditional fryer, making it a healthier option. Air fryers come in a variety of sizes, but most are small enough to fit on a countertop. They typically have a basket or tray that holds the food, as well as a control panel with a timer and temperature settings. Air fryers work by circulating hot air around the food. The air is heated by an element, and the food is cooked by the circulating hot air. This method of cooking is similar to convection cooking, and it results in food that is cooked evenly and quickly. Air fryers are a healthier alternative to traditional fryers because they use less oil. The food is still cooked in hot air, but the amount of oil used is significantly less.

Fundamentals of an Air Fryer

An air fryer is a kitchen appliance that uses hot air to cook food. The food is placed in a basket or tray, and hot air is circulated to it, cooking the food. Air fryers can be used to cook a variety of foods, including chicken, fish, vegetables, and even desserts. One of the great things about air fryers is that they can help you to create healthy meals. This is because air fryers cook food with little to no oil. This means that you can reduce the amount of fat and calories in your meals. Air fryers can also be used to reheat leftovers or pre-cooked foods. If you're looking for a versatile and healthy way to cook your food, then an air fryer is a great option. Be sure to check out all the different features and capabilities of air fryers before you purchase one so that you can find the perfect one for your needs. If you're like most people, you probably think of an air fryer as a healthier alternative to a deep fryer. But what exactly is an air fryer, and how does it work? An air fryer is a small appliance that uses circulating hot air to cook food. The food is cooked in a basket or tray that is placed in the air fryer. The hot air circulates the food, cooking it evenly on all sides. Most air fryers have temperature control and a timer, so you can set it to

cook your food for the desired amount of time. Once the food is cooked, it is typically removed from the air fryer and served. So, how does an air fryer work? Air fryers work by circulating hot air around the food. The hot air is generated by a heating element, and it circulates the food in the basket or tray.

What is an Air Fryer?

An air fryer is a kitchen appliance that cooks food by circulating hot air around it. It is similar to a convection oven, but it uses less energy and can cook food faster. Air fryers are becoming increasingly popular, as they can be used to make a variety of healthy and delicious meals. Air fryers work by circulating hot air around the food, using a fan. This circulates the hot air evenly so that the food cooks evenly. Air fryers can be used to cook a variety of foods, including chicken, fish, vegetables, and even desserts. One of the benefits of using an air fryer is that it can help to reduce the amount of fat in your food. When food is cooked in an air fryer, the fat is drawn out of the food and into the air. This means that you can cook food

that is healthier for you, as there will be less fat in the food. There are two main types of air fryers – countertop and toaster oven style. Countertop air fryers are the most popular type. They're small and compact and can be stored on the counter or in a cupboard. They typically have a capacity of 2-5 quarts and come with a variety of features, such as digital controls, timers, and automatic shut-off. Toaster oven styles are larger and can be placed on the counter or mounted under a cabinet. They typically have a capacity of 6-8 quarts and offer more features. When it comes to kitchen appliances, the air fryer is a relatively new kid on the block. But that doesn't mean that people aren't already wondering whether or not it's a healthy option. So, is an air fryer healthy? The short answer is yes; air fryers are generally a healthy option. They can help you cook food with less oil, and as a result, less fat. Of course, as with any cooking method, there are some things to keep in mind. For example, if you're air frying frozen foods, you'll want to check the label to make sure they don't contain any unhealthy additives. And, as with any cooking method, it's important to not overdo it. Moderation is key! All in all, though, air fryers are a perfectly healthy option for your cooking needs. So go ahead and enjoy!

Structure

When looking at the structure of an air fryer, it is important to first understand how an air fryer works. An air fryer uses hot air to cook food. The hot air circulates the food, cooking it evenly. Most air fryers have a basket that holds the food. The basket is placed in the air fryer and the lid is closed. The air fryer will have a timer that you set. Once the timer goes off, the air fryer will turn off and your food will be cooked. Some air fryers also have temperature control. This allows you to set the temperature at that you want the air fryer to cook. The higher

the temperature, the faster the food will cook. Air fryers come in a variety of sizes. The size of the air fryer will determine how much food you can cook at one time. If you are cooking for a family, you will want to get a larger air fryer.

Functions

An air fryer can be used to fry, bake, or roast food. The device works by circulating hot air around the food, which cooks it in a similar way to traditional deep frying. Air fryers are typically more energy-efficient than deep fryers, and they can also be used to cook food more quickly. Air fryers can be used to cook a variety of foods, including chicken, fish, vegetables, and even some desserts. Air fryers are amazing little devices that can do so much more than just fry food. In addition to being able to fry food, air fryers can also bake, grill, and roast food. This makes them versatile kitchen appliances that can be used for a variety of different dishes.

Baking

Baking in an air fryer is a great way to get the taste and texture of traditional baked goods without all the fat and calories. Air fryers work by circulating hot air around the food, so they cook food faster and more evenly than other methods. To bake in an air fryer, start by preheating the appliance to the correct temperature. Then, place your food in the air fryer basket and cook for the recommended time. When the food is done, carefully remove it from the basket and enjoy! Air fryers are perfect for baking all kinds of foods. Try air-frying your favorite recipes for cookies, cakes, pies, and more. You can even use your air fryer to make healthy versions of your favorite comfort foods. So, get creative in the kitchen and enjoy all the delicious possibilities that air fryers have to offer!

Roasting

If you haven't tried roasting in your air fryer, you're missing out! Roasting in your air fryer is a quick and easy way to get perfectly cooked food every time. Here are a few tips to help you get started:

1.Preheat your air fryer to the correct temperature. This will vary depending on what you're cooking, but a good rule of thumb is to preheat to 400 degrees Fahrenheit.

2.Place your food in the air fryer basket and make sure it's evenly spread out. This will help ensure even cooking.

3.Cook for the recommended time. Again, this will vary depending on what you're cooking, but a general rule is to cook for 10 minutes per inch of food.

4.Let your food rest for a few minutes before serving. This will help it to retain its juices and flavor.

5.Enjoy!

Grilling

Grilling in the air fryer is one of the best ways to cook food. It is quick, easy, and healthy. You can use any type of air fryer, but we recommend using a grill pan or a griddle pan. If you are using a grill pan, preheat the pan on medium heat for about 10 minutes. Then, place the food on the pan and cook for 3-5 minutes per side. If you are using a griddle pan, preheat the pan on medium heat for about 5 minutes. Then, place the food on the pan and cook for 2-3 minutes per side. Air fryers are great for grilling because they cook the food evenly. There is no need to flip the food over, and you don't have to worry about the food sticking to the pan. When grilling in the air fryer, make sure to use oil or cooking spray to prevent the food from sticking.

Frying

Frying in an air fryer is a great way to cook food without all the added oil and fat. Air fryers work by circulating hot air around the food, which cooks it quickly and evenly. This makes for a healthier alternative to traditional frying methods. There are a few things to keep in mind when frying in an air fryer. First, be sure to preheat the air fryer before adding any food. This will help ensure that the food cooks evenly. Second, add a small amount of oil to the air fryer basket before adding the food. This will help to prevent sticking and ensure that the food cooks evenly. Finally, be sure to cook the food in small batches. Overcrowding the air fryer basket will result in uneven cooking. Air frying is a great way to enjoy your favorite fried foods without all the unhealthy aspects. By following these tips, you can ensure that your food comes out delicious and crispy every time.

Operating Buttons

Power ON Button: The first thing you'll need to do is plug in your air fryer. You can simply do it by power button

Temperature Button: When you'll need to choose your desired cooking temperature. This can be done by pressing the "temperature" button on the air fryer.

Start Button: Once you've selected your cooking temperature, you'll need to press the "start" button.

Power OFF Button: When your food will be cooked to perfection! All you need to do now is press the "off" button and enjoy your delicious meal.

Benefits of Using an Air Fryer

An air fryer is a kitchen appliance that allows you to cook food using little to no oil. This means that you can enjoy your favorite fried foods without all of the unhealthy fat and calories. Additionally, air fryers cook food quickly and evenly, so you can enjoy perfectly cooked meals in a fraction of the time. If you haven't jumped on the air fryer bandwagon yet, you're missing out! Here are some benefits of using an air fryer that will make you want to run out and buy one immediately.

1.Air fryers cook food evenly and quickly.

2.You can cook a variety of foods in an air fryer, from chicken and fish to vegetables and even desserts.

3.Air fryers require little to no oil, making them a healthier option than traditional frying methods.

4.Air fryers are compact and take up minimal counter space.

5.Air fryers are relatively easy to use and clean.

6.Air fryers can save you money in the long run since you won't have to use as much oil.

7.Air fryers are perfect for small households or couples who don't want to cook large meals.

8.Air fryers are easy to use and clean, making them a hassle-free option for busy weeknights.

9.Air fryers are compact and take up minimal counter space, making them ideal for small kitchens.

10.Air fryers are relatively affordable, making them a great option for budget-conscious cooks.

11.Air fryers are available in a variety of sizes, so you can choose the perfect model for your family.

12.Air fryers come with a variety of features, so you can find the perfect one to suit your needs.

One of the advantages of using an air fryer is that it can help to reduce the amount of fat in your food. This is because the food is cooked in hot air, rather than being submerged in oil. Another advantage of air fryers is that they are generally very easy to use. Most air fryers come with simple controls that allow you to set the cooking temperature and time.

Step By Step Air Frying

Air frying is a healthier alternative to deep frying as it uses less oil and can still produce crispy food. If you're new to air frying, here is a step-by-step guide on how to do it.

1.Choose your food. Air frying works best with small, evenly-sized pieces of food that have a high surface area to volume ratio like chicken wings, French fries, or mozzarella sticks.

2.Preheat your air fryer. Most air fryers have a preheat function, so be sure to use it before you start cooking. This will help ensure that your food cooks evenly.

3.Coat your food in oil. This step is optional, but if you want your food to be extra crispy, you can coat it in a thin layer of oil before cooking.

4.Place your food in the air fryer basket.

5.Cook for the recommended time, flipping the food halfway through cooking.

6.Remove the food from the air fryer and enjoy!

Straight from the Store

If you're in the market for an air fryer, you may be wondering what straight from the Store has to offer. Here's a quick overview of the company and its products. Straight from the Store is a family-owned business that has been selling air fryers for over 10 years. The company is based in the Netherlands and ships worldwide. Straight from the Store offers a wide range of air fryers, including both small and large models.

The company also sells a variety of accessories, such as an air fryer cookbook and an air fryer rack. Prices for Straight from the Store air fryers start at around £49. However, the company offers discounts for multiple purchases and offers free shipping on orders over £82. If you're looking for an air fryer, straight from the Store is a great option. The company offers a wide selection of air fryers, competitive prices, and free shipping on orders over £82.

Air fryers under £82

Air fryers have been all the rage in recent years. But what are they? How much do they cost? An air fryer is a small appliance that uses hot air to cook food. It works by circulating hot air around the food, which cooks it quickly and evenly. So, do you need an air fryer? If you like to cook fried foods, then an air fryer can be a great addition to your kitchen. It can help you make healthier versions of your favorite fried foods. And it can be a lot of fun to experiment with different recipes. If you're not sure if an air fryer is right for you, then check out some reviews online. There are plenty of people who have written about their experiences with air fryers. As for how much air fryers cost, they can range from about £49 to £164. It really on the features and brand that you choose. Air fryers are becoming increasingly popular as people look for ways to eat healthier. While most air fryers on the market are quite expensive, there are a few models that are under £82. The GoWISE USA 3.7-Quart Air Fryer is one of the most popular air fryers under £82. It has a simple design and is easy to use. The GoWISE air fryer comes with a recipe book, so you can get started cooking right away. The Chefman TurboFry 3.5 Liter Air Fryer is another popular option. It is slightly larger than the GoWISE air fryer, but it has a lot of the same features. It also comes with a recipe book to help you get started. The Philips HD9220/28 Air fryer is a high-end option that is still under £82. It has a digital display and comes with a recipe book.

Cleaning and Caring of Your Air Fryer

Cleaning

If you've ever used an air fryer, you know how convenient they are. But what you may not know is that they're also really easy to clean—and you don't even need any special cleaners. Here's how to clean your air fryer in just a few simple steps. First, unplug your air fryer and empty any food or oil. Next, remove the basket or pan and wash it in your sink with hot, soapy water. If your air fryer has a removable drip tray, be sure to wash that as well. Once the basket and drip tray are clean, it's time to clean the inside of the air fryer. The easiest way to do this is to wipe it down with a damp cloth. If there are any stubborn stains, you can try scrubbing them with a soft-bristled brush. Once you've cleaned the inside and outside of your air fryer, it's time to dry everything off. It's a quick and easy way to cook a delicious meal. But, if you're not careful, it can also be a bit of a pain to clean. Here are a few tips to help make cleaning your air fryer a breeze:

1 Don't let food build up. It's important to clean your air fryer after each use before the food has a chance to harden and become difficult to remove.

2 Use hot water and soap. If you have stubborn food stuck to the basket, soak it in hot water and dish soap for a few minutes before scrubbing.

3 Use a soft sponge. Don't use anything abrasive on the non-stick coating of your air fryer. A soft sponge or cloth is all you need.

4 Don't forget to clean the lid. The lid of your air fryer can get pretty greasy.

Caring

It is important to always read the manual that comes with your air fryer. This will ensure that you are using it correctly and safely. Be sure to clean your air fryer regularly. This helps to ensure that food doesn't stick to the basket and that it cooks evenly. Most air fryers have removable baskets that can be washed in the dishwasher. Be careful of what you cook in your air fryer. Some foods, like breaded chicken, can cause the breading to come off and get stuck in the air fryer. This can then cause the food to stick and be difficult to clean. If you have any questions or concerns about your air fryer, be sure to contact the manufacturer. It is important to keep your air fryer

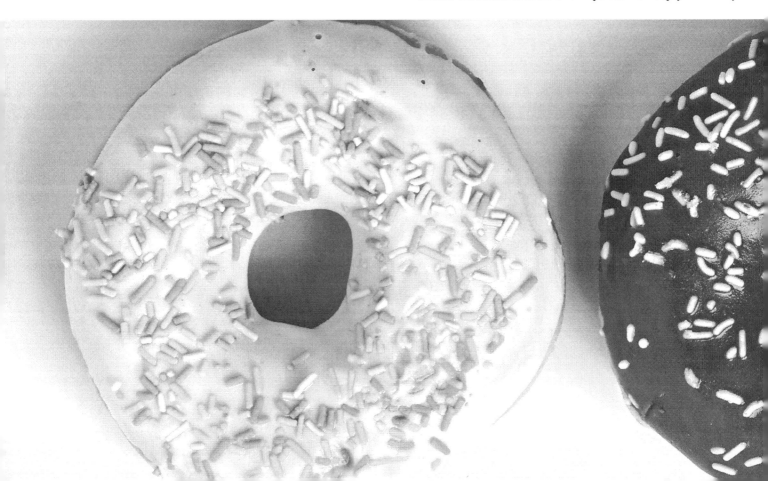

clean so that your food comes out tasting its best. Here are a few tips on how to care for your air fryer:

♦ Before cooking, wipe the inside and outside of the air fryer basket with a damp cloth.

♦ After cooking, unplug the air fryer and allow it to cool before cleaning. Wipe the inside and outside of the basket with a damp cloth.

♦ Once a week, remove the basket and shake any loose crumbs into the garbage. Wash the basket in warm, soapy water, rinse and dry thoroughly.

♦ If your air fryer has a removable drawer, wash it in warm, soapy water, rinse and dry it thoroughly.

♦ Never submerge the air fryer in water.

Frequently Asked Questions and Notes

If you're like most people, you probably have a lot of questions about your air fryer. Here are some of the most frequently asked questions about air fryers, along with the answers.

1.What is an air fryer?

An air fryer is a kitchen appliance that uses hot air to cook food. The food is placed in a basket or tray, and hot air is circulated to it, cooking the food.

2.How does an air fryer work?

Air fryers work by circulating hot air around the food, cooking it evenly. The hot air is generated by a heating element, and the food is cooked in a basket or tray.

3.What can you cook in an air fryer?

You can cook just about anything in an air fryer, from chicken and fish to vegetables and even desserts.

4.What are the benefits of using an air fryer?

Air fryers have several benefits, including:

♦ They can cook food faster than traditional methods.

♦ They can cook food more evenly, resulting in less burnt or overcooked food.

♦ They can be used to cook a variety of foods, including meat, vegetables, and even desserts.

5.What are the different types of air fryers?

There are two main types of air fryers – countertop and toaster oven style.

If you're like me, you love your air fryer. It's a quick and easy way to cook up a delicious meal with minimal effort. But there are a few things to keep in mind when you're using your air fryer, especially when it comes to taking notes. Here are a few tips for taking notes while using your air fryer:

♦ Make sure to write down the cooking time. This is especially important if you're cooking multiple items in the air fryer. You don't want to overcook or undercook anything, so it's important to keep track of the cook times.

♦ Note the temperature. Again, this is important for ensuring that your food is cooked properly.

♦ Keep an eye on the food. Even if you're using a timer, it's still a good idea to check on the food periodically to make sure it's cooking properly.

♦ Take note of any adjustments you make.

• 4-Week Diet Plan •

Week 1

Day 1:
Breakfast: Omelet with Parmesan
Lunch: Tomato Bites with Pecan Sauce
Snack: Cheese Apple Rollups
Dinner: Spicy Asian Turkey
Dessert: Cinnamon Cocoa Muffins

Day 2:
Breakfast: Bacon Egg Cups
Lunch: Cheesy Cauliflower and Broccoli
Snack: Asian Five-Spice Chicken Wings
Dinner: Spiced Roast Pork
Dessert: Cream Egg Custard

Day 3:
Breakfast: Cheese Beef Pizza
Lunch: Spinach and Tomato Omelette
Snack: Crispy Avocado Fries
Dinner: Smoked Beef Patties
Dessert: Coffee Cake Muffins

Day 4:
Breakfast: Soft Ham Muffins
Lunch: Broccoli with Tomato Sauce
Snack: Tasty Bagel Chips
Dinner: Cheese Cod Fillets
Dessert: Easy Lime Bars

Day 5:
Breakfast: Baked Avocado Egg Boat
Lunch: Herbed Broccoli with Cheese
Snack: Buffalo Cheese Chicken Bites
Dinner: Simple Basil Prawns
Dessert: Courgette Bread

Day 6:
Breakfast: Chicken Cauliflower Casserole
Lunch: Garlicky Onion-Stuffed Mushrooms
Snack: Crispy Cheddar Cheese Wafers
Dinner: Crispy Pork Chops
Dessert: Poppy Seed Muffins

Day 7:
Breakfast: Quick Mascarpone Omelet
Lunch: Croquettes of Fried Squash
Snack: Cheese Crab Toasts
Dinner: Herbed Spicy Chicken Drumsticks
Dessert: Flavoured Vanilla Scones

Week 2

Day 1:
Breakfast: Baked Cod and Eggs
Lunch: Spicy Cauliflower Balls
Snack: Crispy Apple Wedges
Dinner: Pork and Mushroom Cheeseburgers
Dessert: Baked Nutmeg Donuts

Day 2:
Breakfast: Spicy Chicken Omelet
Lunch: Cheesy Tomatoes
Snack: Cumin Aubergine Fries
Dinner: Spicy Cod Pan
Dessert: Lime Almond Pie

Day 3:
Breakfast: Chicken Frittata with Goat Cheese
Lunch: Herbed Peppers and Onion with Mayo
Snack: Almond Banana Sticks
Dinner: Authentic Pork Kebabs
Dessert: Raspberry Tart

Day 4:
Breakfast: Apricot and Oat Bars
Lunch: Delicious Oyster Mushroom Omelet
Snack: Crispy Peaches
Dinner: Japanese-Style Flank Steak
Dessert: Fluffy Turmeric Cookies

Day 5:
Breakfast: Banana Cinnamon Bread
Lunch: Creamy Egg with Swiss Chard
Snack: Garlic Chicken Wings
Dinner: Tasty Lime Chicken Thighs
Dessert: Simple Mint Pie

Day 6:
Breakfast: Veggie Sausage Wraps
Lunch: Easy Broccoli with Sesame Seeds
Snack: Berry Granola
Dinner: Parmesan Tuna Boats
Dessert: Coconut Saffron Cookies

Day 7:
Breakfast: Cinnamon Doughnut Bites
Lunch: Cheese Cauliflower Bites
Snack: Hummus Olive Tacos
Dinner: Tangy Pork Bolognese
Dessert: Coconut Cheese Balls

Week 3

Day 1:
Breakfast: Spicy Baked Eggs
Lunch: Sausage and Mushroom Casserole
Snack: Simple Cheese Sandwich
Dinner: Herbed Chicken with Roma Tomatoes
Dessert: Sweet Sage Muffins

Day 2:
Breakfast: Courgette and Chocolate Muffins
Lunch: Cheesy Egg and Veggie Salad
Snack: Italian Rice Balls with Olives
Dinner: Cheese Turkey Burgers with Bacon
Dessert: Raspberry Jam

Day 3:
Breakfast: Cheese Chicken Rolls
Lunch: Crispy Asparagus Fries
Snack: Cheese Stuffed Peppers
Dinner: Pork Sausage with Eggs and Peppers
Dessert: Coconut Vanilla Shortcake

Day 4:
Breakfast: Leftover Beef and Kale Omelet
Lunch: Crispy Air Fried Vegetables
Snack: Tasty Muffuletta Sliders
Dinner: Roast Beef with Jalapeño Peppers
Dessert: Easy Raspberry Cream

Day 5:
Breakfast: Coconut Muesli Bites
Lunch: Cauliflower Quiche
Snack: Bacon Rumaki
Dinner: Prawns in Italian Style
Dessert: Low-Carb Hot Chocolate

Day 6:
Breakfast: Scones with Sweet Lemon Glaze
Lunch: Brussels Sprouts and Pancetta Salad
Snack: Prawns Pirogues
Dinner: Lemon Crawfish
Dessert: Almond milk Pie

Day 7:
Breakfast: Morning Sandwiches with Avocado
Lunch: Healthy Spinach and Cauliflower Bowl
Snack: Fried String Beans
Dinner: Mexican Cheese Steak
Dessert: Muffins with Pumpkin Spice

Week 4

Day 1:
Breakfast: Coconut Omelet with Nutmeg
Lunch: Sweet Potatoes Glazed in Tamarind
Snack: Cheese Ham Stuffed Mushrooms
Dinner: Turkey Mushroom Meatloaf
Dessert: Homemade Butter Cookies

Day 2:
Breakfast: Cheesy Kale and Egg Mix
Lunch: Fried Pickles
Snack: Tasty Kale Chips
Dinner: Lemony Pork Skewers
Dessert: Almond Chia Balls

Day 3:
Breakfast: Air Fryer Mozzarella Balls
Lunch: Roasted Cauliflower with Pepper Jack Cheese
Snack: Pickle Poppers Wrapped in Bacon
Dinner: Beef Kebab with Baby Rocket
Dessert: Coconut Cream Cups

Day 4:
Breakfast: Baked Swiss Chard and Eggs
Lunch: Omelet with cheese and mixed greens
Snack: Sour Pork Belly Strips
Dinner: Scallops with Rosemary
Dessert: Lemon Cream Pudding

Day 5:
Breakfast: Breakfast Granola Squares with Raisins
Lunch: Fried Asparagus with Cheese
Snack: Blooming Onion
Dinner: BBQ Skirt Steak with Herb
Dessert: Courgette with Sweet Cream Cheese

Day 6:
Breakfast: Kale frittata with Onion
Lunch: Spicy Veggie Fritters
Snack: Cheese Calamari Rings
Dinner: Sweet and Sour Mussels
Dessert: Almond Cookies

Day 7:
Breakfast: Fragrant Snapper with Cheese
Lunch: Veggies with Yogurt Tahini Sauce
Snack: Cheddar Cheese Crisps
Dinner: Chicken Lettuce Tacos
Dessert: Coconut Muffins

Chapter 1 Breakfast Recipes

Baked Mozzarella Jalapenos

Prep time: 5 minutes | Cook time: 30 minutes | Serves: 6

120g shredded mozzarella	6 beaten eggs	1 teaspoon softened coconut oil	pepper
2 sliced jalapenos	60g coconut cream	½ teaspoon crushed black	

1. Combine all of the ingredients in the baking dish and mix thoroughly to combine. 2. After that, place the baking pan in the air fryer and cook the food for 30 minutes at 175°C.
Per Serving: Calories 206; Fat 13.9g; Sodium 244mg; Carbs 6g; Fibre 4.6g; Sugar 2.36g; Protein 15.6g

Courgette Latkes with Swiss Chard

Prep time: 10 minutes | Cook time: 8 minutes | Serves: 4

2 grated courgettes	1 teaspoon garlic powder	50g chopped Swiss chard	25g grated Parmesan
2 tablespoons coconut flour	1 beaten egg	1 teaspoon chili flakes	

1. Combine the courgette, coconut flour, garlic powder, egg, Swiss chard, chili flakes, and parmesan in a mixing bowl. 2. Prepare the tiny latkes and place them in the air fryer that has been set to 185°C. 3. Prepare the latkes on each side for 4 minutes.
Per Serving: Calories 68; Fat 2.9g; Sodium 165mg; Carbs 4.9g; Fibre 0.7g; Sugar 0.69g; Protein 5.76g

Chicken and Veggie Salad

Prep time: 15 minutes | Cook time: 10 minutes | Serves:4

135g boiled and chopped asparagus	1 teaspoon of garlic powder	1 tablespoon of apple cider vinegar	1 teaspoon each of avocado and olive oil
150g chopped Swiss chard	1 tablespoon of chopped almonds	200g of chicken fillet	

1. Roughly chop the chicken fillet and combine it with the apple cider vinegar, garlic powder, and olive oil. 2. Cook the chicken in the air fryer at 190°C for 10 minutes. 3. After that, thoroughly combine the cooked chicken with the remaining ingredients.
Per Serving: Calories 205; Fat 8.94g; Sodium 449mg; Carbs 22.3g; Fibre 2.5g; Sugar 3.25g; Protein 9.6g

Omelet with Parmesan

Prep time: 5 minutes | Cook time: 20 minutes | Serves: 4

50g Parmesan, grated	½ teaspoon chili flakes	60ml coconut cream	
5 eggs, beaten	½ teaspoon dried parsley	½ teaspoon coconut oil	

1. Set the air fryer to 180°C and coat the basket with coconut oil. 2. Next, combine coconut cream, Parmesan, chili flakes, and dry parsley. 3. Place the omelet in the air fryer and cook for 20 minutes.
Per Serving: Calories 270; Fat 18.5g; Sodium 301mg; Carbs 8.12g; Fibre 0.5g; Sugar 1.05g; Protein 17.4g

Cheese and Prawns Dip

Prep time: 10 minutes | Cook time: 25 minutes | Serves:8

200g of peeled and deveined prawns	60ml chicken stock	Red pepper flakes in the amount of half	120ml sour cream
2 teaspoons melted butter	2 teaspoons of lemon juice, fresh	100g of room-temperature cream cheese	4 tablespoons of mayonnaise
2 minced garlic cloves	Salt and black pepper, to taste		

1. Set the Air Fryer to 200°C to begin preheating. Melted butter should be used to grease a baking dish's bottom and sides. 2. In the baking dish, combine the prawns, garlic, chicken stock, lemon juice, salt, black pepper, and red pepper flakes. 3. Bake for 10 minutes after transferring the baking dish to the frying basket. Fill your food processor with the mixture, and then pulse it until it is roughly chopped. 4. Add the mayonnaise, sour cream, and cream cheese. 5. Add the mozzarella cheese on top and bake in the prepared Air Fryer at 180°C for 6 to 7 minutes or until the cheese is bubbling. 6. If desired, serve right away with breadsticks.
Per Serving: Calories 160; Fat 9.9g; Sodium 222 mg; Carbs 2.93g; Fibre 0.3g; Sugar 1.04g; Protein 15.02g

Fragrant Snapper with Cheese

Prep time: 10 minutes | Cook time: 25 minutes | Serves:4

2 tablespoons Olive oil	675g of snapper fillets	1 cayenne pepper teaspoon	50ml of white wine
1 finely sliced shallot	Sea salt and black pepper, to	A half-teaspoon of dried basil	100g of shredded Gruyere
2 minced garlic cloves	taste	120g of tomato puree	cheese

1. Heat 1 tablespoon of olive oil at a medium-high temperature in a pot. The shallot and garlic should now be cooked until fragrant and soft. 2. Heat the air fryer to 185°C. 3. 1 tablespoon of olive oil should be used to grease a casserole dish. In the casserole dish, put the snapper fillet. Add salt, black pepper, and cayenne pepper for seasoning. Add the mixture of sautéed shallots. 4. Add the basil, tomato puree, and wine to the casserole dish. Cook for 10 minutes in an Air Fryer that has been heated. 5. Add the cheese shavings on top and simmer for an additional 7 minutes. Serve right away.
Per Serving: Calories 291; Fat 19.89g; Sodium 358mg; Carbs 6.3g; Fibre 1.2g; Sugar 3.14g; Protein 45.96g

Baked Eggs with Cauliflower Rice

Prep time: 10 minutes | Cook time: 30 minutes | Serves:4

455g of rice from cauliflower	1 tablespoon melted butter,	6 eggs	
1 diced onion	freshly ground black pepper,	100g of shredded cheddar	
6 pieces of seared bacon	and sea salt, as desired	cheese	

1. In a casserole dish that has been lightly buttered, put the cauliflower rice and onion. Add the seared bacon. Add salt and pepper to the cauliflower rice before drizzling the melted butter over it. 2. Bake for 10 minutes at 200°C in the prepared Air Fryer. 3. Reduce the heat to 175°C. 4. Make six indents for the eggs; crack one egg into each indent, bake for 10 minutes, flipping the pan once or twice. 5. Add cheese, then bake for an additional five minutes. Enjoy!
Per Serving: Calories 488; Fat 36.35g; Sodium 809mg; Carbs 15.13g; Fibre 2.9g; Sugar 7.86g; Protein 26.1g

Quick Mascarpone Omelet

Prep time:8 minutes | Cook time: 10 minutes | Serves:6

8 beaten eggs	60g mascarpone	1 teaspoon black pepper	½ teaspoon coconut oil

1. Combine eggs, mascarpone, and freshly ground pepper. 2. Next, use coconut oil to lubricate the air fryer basket. 3. Include the egg mixture, and then cook the omelet at 195°C for 10 minutes.
Per Serving: Calories 180; Fat 13.2g; Sodium 137mg; Carbs 2.06g; Fibre 0.1g; Sugar 1.25g; Protein 12.11g

Bacon Egg Cups

Prep time: 10 minutes | Cook time: 14 minutes | Serves: 6

6 eggs	6 pieces of bacon	1 teaspoon coconut oil	1 teaspoon parmesan

1. Place the bacon slices inside the ramekins that have been greased with coconut oil. 2. In the air fryer, cook the bacon for 2 minutes on each side at 185°C. 3. After that, break the eggs on top of the bacon and top them with parmesan. 4. Bake the eggs at 190°C for 10 minutes.
Per Serving: Calories 245; Fat 20.1g; Sodium 224mg; Carbs 1.2g; Fibre 0g; Sugar 0.87g; Protein 12.2g

Savoury Cheese Buns

Prep time: 10 minutes | Cook time: 12 minutes | Serves:2

2 tablespoons of coconut flour	1 teaspoon of mascarpone	2 beaten eggs	
¼ teaspoon of baking powder	1 teaspoon of melted coconut	1 teaspoon of avocado oil	
1 teaspoon of erythritol	oil	30g of grated mozzarella	

1. In a mixing bowl, combine all ingredients and knead the dough. 2. Prepare the miniature buns, then put them in the air fryer. 3. Bake the buns for 12 minutes at 190°C, or until golden brown.
Per Serving: Calories 192; Fat 14.17g; Sodium 224mg; Carbs 2.37g; Fibre 0.4g; Sugar 1.25g; Protein 13.56g

Cheese Chicken Rolls

Prep time: 10 minutes | Cook time: 30 minutes | Serves:6

2 well-whisked eggs	3 chicken breasts, cut in half lengthwise	2 tablespoons paprika sweet	15g fresh coriander, chopped
100g of parmesan cheese, grated	1½ tablespoons finely chopped fresh chives	½ teaspoon of whole-grain mustard	⅓ teaspoon of freshly ground black pepper, or more amounts as desired
1½ tablespoons of virgin olive oil	300g of mozzarella cheese	½ teaspoon of cumin powder	
		⅓ teaspoon of sea salt, fine	

1. Use a rolling pin to flatten out each piece of chicken breast. Next, take three mixing bowls. 2. Combine the mozzarella cheese, coriander, fresh chives, cumin, and mustard in the first one. 3. Whisk the eggs and sweet paprika together in a separate mixing bowl. Combine the salt, pepper, and parmesan cheese in the third dish. 4. Spread the cheese mixture over each piece of chicken. Repeat with the remaining chicken breast pieces, and then roll them up. 5. Each chicken roll should be covered in the whisked egg before being dusted with the parmesan mixture. Lower the rolls onto the Air Fryer cooking basket. Drizzle extra-virgin olive oil over all rolls. 6. Working in batches, air fried for 28 minutes at 175°C. If preferred, top with sour cream and serve warm.
Per Serving: Calories 220; Fat 22.92g; Sodium 797mg; Carbs 4.37g; Fibre 0.9g; Sugar 0.75g; Protein 47.13g

Green Beans and Spinach Salad

Prep time: 10 minutes | Cook time: 20 minutes | Serves:4

200g medium-sized green beans	60g chopped fresh spinach	oil, dried oregano, coconut oil, and chili flakes
	1 tablespoon each of avocado	

1. Combine green beans with avocado oil, chili flakes, and dry oregano. 2. Cook the green beans in the air fryer at 185°C for 20 minutes. Shake them occasionally. 3. After that, thoroughly combine the additional ingredients with the cooked green beans.
Per Serving: Calories 64; Fat 5.15g; Sodium 33mg; Carbs 4.5g; Fibre 2.2g; Sugar 0.73g; Protein 1.42g

Cheese Beef Pizza

Prep time: 10 minutes | Cook time: 15 minutes | Serves:2

200g of beef mince	½ teaspoon of dried oregano	cheese	¼ teaspoon dried coriander
1 tablespoon of marinara sauce	300g of shredded Cheddar	½ teaspoon melted coconut oil	

1. Combine dry oregano and coriander with meat mince. 2. Rub coconut oil on the air fryer basket. 3. From the beef mince, form two flat balls and place them in the air fryer basket. 4. Marinara sauce and Cheddar cheese are added on top. 5. Bake the pizza for 15 minutes at 190°C.
Per Serving: Calories 399; Fat 35.7g; Sodium 129mg; Carbs 1.33g; Fibre 0.3g; Sugar 0.79g; Protein 17.04g

Coconut Omelet with Nutmeg

Prep time: 10 minutes | Cook time: 20 minutes | Serves:4

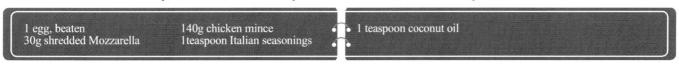

Beaten 6 eggs	25g Parmesan	60g coconut cream
1 teaspoon. powdered nutmeg	½ teaspoon. coconut oil	

1. Grate the Parmesan and combine it with the eggs, coconut cream, coconut oil, and nutmeg. 2. Add the liquid to the omelette in the air fryer basket, and cook it at 180°C for 20 minutes.
Per Serving: Calories 278; Fat 20.7g; Sodium 236mg; Carbs 5.63g; Fibre 0.4g; Sugar 1.1g; Protein 16.8g

Baked Cheese Chicken

Prep time:5 minutes | Cook time: 25 minutes | Serves:4

1 egg, beaten	140g chicken mince	1 teaspoon coconut oil
30g shredded Mozzarella	1teaspoon Italian seasonings	

1. Combine all the ingredients in a mixing dish and stir till just well combined. 2. After that, place it in the air fryer basket and cook for 25 minutes at 185°C .
Per Serving: Calories 1202; Fat 107.2g; Sodium 1994mg; Carbs 49.65g; Fibre 18.1g; Sugar 11.7g; Protein 17.13g

Chicken Frittata with Goat Cheese

Prep time: 10 minutes | Cook time: 10 minutes | Serves:4

360g of crumbled goat cheese	⅓ teaspoon of mustard seeds	⅓ teaspoon of white pepper, ground	Sea salt, fine, to taste
1 teaspoon of rosemary, dry	5 medium-sized beaten eggs	80g green onions, chopped	Nonstick cooking spray
280g of cooked, boneless, and shredded chicken breasts	1 teaspoon crushed red pepper flakes	1 sliced green garlic stalk	

1. Pick choose a baking pan that will fit in your air fryer. 2. Apply your preferred nonstick cooking spray sparingly within the baking dish. Mix everything together except the cheese. Mix thoroughly by stirring. 3. Set your air fryer to cook for 8 minutes at 170°C; check to see if it's finished. Goat cheese crumbles should be sprinkled on top, then eaten right away!
Per Serving: Calories 169; Fat 17,89g; Sodium 426mg; Carbs 1.48g; Fibre 0.3g; Sugar 0.76g; Protein 36.87g

Chicken Rolls Stuffed with Cottage Cheese

Prep time: 10 minutes | Cook time: 22 minutes | Serves:2

240g of cottage cheese	that have been cut in half	1 teaspoon fine sea salt	ground black pepper
2 beaten eggs	2 tablespoons minced fresh coriander	50g of Grated parmesan cheese	3 minced garlic cloves
2 medium-sized chicken breasts		A generous pinch of freshly	

1. First, use a meat tenderizer to flatten the chicken breast. 2. Combine the cottage cheese, garlic, coriander, salt, and black pepper in a medium mixing bowl. 3. Over the first chicken breast, spread a third of the mixture. Continue by using the remaining ingredients. Place toothpicks to hold the chicken together as you roll it around the filling. 4. In a small bowl, whisk the egg right now. Combine the parmesan cheese, salt, and freshly ground black pepper in a separate shallow bowl. 5. Put the chicken breasts in the parmesan cheese after coating them with the whisked egg. 6. Cook for 22 minutes at 185°C in the air fryer frying basket. Serve right away.
Per Serving: Calories 792; Fat 45.71g; Sodium 2091mg; Carbs 7.79g; Fibre 0.1g; Sugar 2.12g; Protein 82.68g

Beans and Onion Stuffed Arepas

Prep time: 10 minutes | Cook time: 20 minutes | Serves: 4

1 tablespoon and 2 teaspoon of olive oil	(any colour)	1½ teaspoons salt, split	
40g red onion and pepper dice	½ teaspoon ground cumin	160g polenta	
	60g of canned black beans	240ml water	

1. Turn the air fryer on at 195°C. 2. Warm 2 teaspoons of olive oil in a small frying pan over medium heat. Add the pepper and onion. Sauté for about 5 minutes, or until somewhat tender. 3. Add the beans, cumin, and ½ teaspoon salt. The frying pan should be taken off the heat and left to cool somewhat. 4. Combine the polenta, water, and final teaspoon of salt in a larger bowl. Mix until a soft dough comes together. 5. Roll the dough into a ball and cut it into four portions of similar size. Each piece should be divided in half, with each half formed into a little disc. Each disc should have 2 teaspoons of filling in the centre. Affirmatively press the edges of the remaining discs together on top. Brush the discs with the final tablespoon of olive oil on both sides. 6. Put the discs in the fryer basket and cook for about 15 minutes, or until crispy. 7. Place the arepas on a dish and give them a moment to cool before serving.
Tips: The red onion and pepper can be prepared alternatively in the air fryer. Combine the onion, pepper, and 2 teaspoons of olive oil in a baking dish. Cook the meal for two to three minutes in the fryer basket. The item should be taken out of the fryer basket and put aside to cool.
To make the meal more satisfying, serve these alongside a fruit smoothie.
Per Serving: Calories 212, Fat 3.18g; Sodium 878mg; Carbs 39.81g; Fibre 3.6g; Sugar 1.34g; Protein 5.59g

Cinnamon Doughnut Bites

Prep time: 10 minutes | Cook time: 6 minutes | Serves:12

1 teaspoon of ground flaxseed	flour	1 teaspoon Baking powder	1 tablespoon melted coconut oil
6 tablespoons of water	½ teaspoon salt	100g of light brown sugar	50g granulated sugar
125g + 2 tablespoons plain	2 teaspoons of cinnamon, split	60ml unsweetened soy milk	

1. Combine the flaxseed and water in a small bowl, mix well. 2. Combine the flour, salt, baking powder, and ½ teaspoon of cinnamon in a big bowl. Add the flaxseed mixture, coconut oil, soy milk, and brown sugar. Mix until a doughy substance develops. The dough needs to be chilled for at least one hour. 3. Lower the air fryer's temperature to 185°C. Spray nonstick cooking spray on the fryer basket. 4. Combine the sugar and the remaining 1½ tablespoons of cinnamon in a small bowl. 5. Make 12 tablespoons of dough with a small cookie scoop. The dough should be rolled into balls and then coated with the cinnamon and sugar mixture. 6. Put the balls in the fryer basket and cook for about 6 minutes, or until puffed and golden brown. 7. Place the doughnut bites on a dish and start serving right away.
Per Serving: Calories 71, Fat 2.17g; Sodium 102mg; Carbs 11.45g; Fibre 1g; Sugar 2.46g; Protein 1.54g

Banana Cinnamon Bread

Prep time: 10 minutes | Cook time: 25 minutes | Serves:8

1 tablespoon Ground flaxseed	½ teaspoon ground cinnamon	60ml of unsweetened almond milk	½ medium-ripe banana, sliced lengthwise
3 tablespoons of water	½ teaspoon. Baking powder	½ teaspoon vanilla extract	2 medium-ripe bananas, mashed
25g almond flour	⅛ teaspoon of salt	60ml Rapeseed oil	
65g plain flour	100g granulated sugar		

1. Set the air fryer temperature to 155°C. Spray nonstick cooking spray in two mini loaf pans. Place aside. 2. Combine the flaxseed and water in a small bowl. Place aside. 3. Combine the all-purpose flour, almond flour, cinnamon, baking powder, and salt in a big bowl. 4. Combine the sugar, almond milk, vanilla extract, rapeseed oil, mashed bananas, and flaxseed mixture in a separate, big bowl. 5. Gently blend the dry ingredients with the wet ones by combining them together. 6. Distribute half of the batter in a pan, then top with a banana slice. With the remaining batter and banana slices, repeat this process. 7. Put the pans in the fryer basket and bake for 22 to 25 minutes, or until a toothpick inserted in the centre comes out clean. 8. Take the pots out of the frying basket. Give the bread at least 10 minutes to cool. Before serving, take the bread out of the pans.
Per Serving: Calories 160, Fat 8.01g; Sodium 46mg; Carbs 21.69g; Fibre 1.6g; Sugar 11.19g; Protein 1.49g

Baked Avocado Egg Boat

Prep time:10 minutes | Cook time: 20 minutes | Serves:2

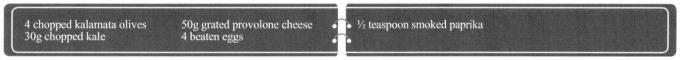

1 pitted and split avocado	2 eggs	25g grated Parmesan	½ teaspoon nutmeg

1. Break the eggs into the avocado hole, then sprinkle the cheese and crushed nutmeg on top. 2. After that, cook the avocado in the air fryer basket for 20 minutes at 190°C.
Per Serving: Calories 346; Fat 25.28g; Sodium 273mg; Carbs 15.54g; Fibre 6.8g; Sugar 1.54g; Protein 16.69g

Cheesy Kale and Egg Mix

Prep time:5 minutes | Cook time: 20 minutes | Serves:4

4 chopped kalamata olives	50g grated provolone cheese	½ teaspoon smoked paprika
30g chopped kale	4 beaten eggs	

1. In a mixing dish, combine all the ingredients. 2. Then put it into the basket of the air fryer. 3. Make the mixture flat, then cook it for 20 minutes at 180°C.
Per Serving: Calories 186; Fat 13.9g; Sodium270 mg; Carbs 1.93g; Fibre 0.3g; Sugar 0.87g; Protein 12.83g

Air Fryer Mozzarella Balls

Prep time:15 minutes | Cook time: 12 minutes | Serves:6

4 tablespoons coconut flour	cheese	2 tablespoons softened coconut oil	¼ teaspoon baking powder
60g shredded mozzarella	1 teaspoon erythritol		1 beaten egg

1. Combine the coconut flour, mozzarella cheese, erythritol, coconut oil, baking powder, and egg in a mixing dish. Knead the dough. 2. Make the balls and then place them in the air fryer. 3. Cook the balls for 12 minutes at 185°C.
Per Serving: Calories 77; Fat 6.16g; Sodium 98 mg; Carbs 1.14g; Fibre 0.3g; Sugar 0.67g; Protein 4.55g

Baked Swiss Chard and Eggs

Prep time:10 minutes | Cook time: 16 minutes | Serves:4

4 beaten eggs	50g chopped Swiss chard	25g shredded Provolone cheese
1 tablespoon coconut cream	½ teaspoon coconut oil	

1. Use coconut oil to grease the air fryer basket. 2. After that, add eggs, Swiss chard, Provolone cheese, and coconut cream. 3. Cook the dish for 16 minutes at 190°C or till the eggs are set.
Per Serving: Calories 174; Fat 13.43g; Sodium 195mg; Carbs 1.95g; Fibre 0.3g; Sugar 0.85g; Protein 11.17g

Pork Lettuce Wraps

Prep time:10 minutes | Cook time: 15 minutes | Serves:2

1. Combine the pork mince with the oregano and jalapeño pepper. 2. Next, preheat the air fryer to 185°C. 3. Add the pork mince mixture and coconut oil. Cook the mixture for 15 minutes. Periodically give it a stir. 4. After that, transfer the pork mince mixture onto the lettuce leaves. Wrap the lettuce leaves and add plain yogurt.
Per Serving: Calories 325; Fat 23.18g; Sodium 77mg; Carbs 1.65g; Fibre 0.7g; Sugar 1.01g; Protein 26.13g

Soft Ham Muffins

Prep time:15 minutes | Cook time: 12 minutes | Serves:4

1. Combine the ham, eggs, coconut cream, dry dill, coconut oil, and chives in a mixing dish. 2. Fill the muffin tins with the mixture, and bake for 12 minutes at 185°C.
Per Serving: Calories 214; Fat 16.8g; Sodium 397mg; Carbs 2.53g; Fibre 0.4g; Sugar 0.65g; Protein 13.49g

Baked Cod and Eggs

Prep time: 5 minutes | Cook time: 20 minutes | Serves:4

1. Finely chop the fish fillet and combine it with salt, chives, eggs, and powdered coriander. 2. Pour the egg mixture into the air fryer basket after brushing it with coconut oil. 3. Bake the fish eggs at 180°C for 20 minutes.
Per Serving: Calories 140; Fat 10.28g; Sodium 394mg; Carbs 2.2g; Fibre 0.3g; Sugar 1.67g; Protein 9.31g

Chicken Cauliflower Casserole

Prep time: 10 minutes | Cook time: 15 minutes | Serves:2

1 chopped jalapeño pepper | 30g shredded Mozzarella | ½ teaspoon coconut oil
230g chicken mince | ½ teaspoon ground cinnamon | 25g chopped cauliflower

1. Combine chicken mince, mozzarella, ground cinnamon, and cauliflower with the jalapeño pepper. 2. Place the mixture inside the air fryer basket after brushing it with coconut oil. 3. Bake the casserole at 190°C for 15 minutes.
Per Serving: Calories 368; Fat 19.16g; Sodium 247mg; Carbs 3.9g; Fibre 1.2g; Sugar 1.63g; Protein 44.77g

Courgette and Chocolate Muffins

Prep time: 10 minutes | Cook time: 36 minutes | Serves: 12

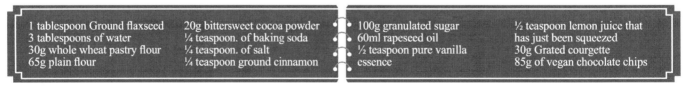

1. Set the air fryer temperature to 130°C. Spray nonstick cooking spray into 12 silicone muffin tins, place aside. 2. Combine the flaxseed and water in a small bowl. 3. Combine the cocoa powder, whole wheat pastry flour, baking soda, salt, cinnamon, and all-purpose flour in a big basin. Add the flaxseed mixture, rapeseed oil, vanilla essence, lemon juice, and sugar. Mix well. Add the courgette and chocolate chips and combine. Fill the muffin tins with the batter. 4. Working in batches, put 6 muffin cups in the fryer basket and bake for 15 to 18 minutes, or until a toothpick inserted in the centre of a muffin comes out clean. 5. Take the muffins out of the cups and let them cool for 10 minutes before serving.
Per Serving: Calories 128, Fat 5.4g; Sodium 86mg; Carbs 19.47g; Fibre 1.5g; Sugar 10.38g; Protein 1.63g

French Toast Casserole with Blueberries

Prep time: 10 minutes | Cook time: 15 minutes | Serves: 2

4 pieces of cubed vegan bread (full grain is advised) 150g Blueberries	Ground flaxseed, 1 tablespoon 3 tablespoons of water 280ml of unsweetened vanilla	almond milk 1 teaspoon Pure vanilla extract 2 tablespoons of maple syrup,	plus more 1 tablespoon orange zest

1. Firstly, preheat the air fryer to 175°C. Apply nonstick cooking spray to a baking pan. 2. Fill the dish with the bread and blueberries, place aside. 3. Combine the flaxseed and water in a small bowl. Mix well. 4. Combine the almond milk, flaxseed mixture, maple syrup, orange zest, and vanilla essence in a medium bowl. Over the bread and blueberries, pour the liquid mixture. To immerse, gently press down on the bread. 5. Put the dish in the fryer basket and bake for 15 minutes, or until the middle is firm and the borders are golden brown. 6. Take the casserole out of the frying basket and let it cool for ten minutes. Before serving, divide the mixture into 2 servings of equal size and add extra maple syrup to the top.
Tip: No blueberries on hand? Use diced plums, peaches, or any seasonal berry.
Per Serving: Calories 491, Fat 8.3g; Sodium 408mg; Carbs 91.8g; Fibre 7.3g; Sugar 62.22g; Protein 14.19g

Breakfast Granola Squares with Raisins

Prep time: 10 minutes | Cook time: 10 minutes | Serves:10

1 tablespoon of chia seeds 2 tablespoons of water 80g rolled oats	130g of crunchy peanut butter 60g pistachios, unsalted 70g of raisins	45g dry coconut flakes without sugar 315g maple syrup	½ teaspoon sea salt

1. Firstly, set the air fryer to 175°C. 2. Combine the chia seeds and water in a small basin. Place aside. 3. In a food processor, combine the other ingredients by pulsing them a few times. The chia seeds should be added and pulsed one or two more times to incorporate. In a 17.5-cm springform pan, firmly and evenly press the mixture into the pan. 4. Put the pan in the fryer basket and cook for 10 minutes or until the sides start to brown. 5. Take the pan out of the fryer basket and let the granola finish cooling in it. 6. Granola should be taken out of the pan and cut into 10 squares.
Tip: Use 2 tablespoons of maple syrup if the peanut butter you use has been sweetened.
Per Serving: Calories 156, Fat 8.86g; Sodium 159mg; Carbs 20.23g; Fibre 3.6g; Sugar 10.79g; Protein 4.62g

Coconut Muesli Bites

Prep time: 20 minutes | Cook time: 3 minutes | Serves:24

90g of dry coconut flakes without sugar 85g of muesli	85g of ground flaxseed 1 tablespoon of chia seeds 55g vegan chocolate chips	½ teaspoon. salt, 130g of nut butter 100g of agave nectar

1. Set the air fryer temperature to 185°C. 2. Fill the baking dish with the coconut. Place the dish in the fryer basket and cook for 2 to 3 minutes, or until the edges are brown. 3. Take the dish out of the fryer basket and spread the coconut out to cool thoroughly on parchment paper. 4. Place the coconut flakes, muesli, flaxseed, chia seeds, chocolate chips, and salt in a sizable bowl. Mix well. Add agave and nut butter. Combine once more. (Add a few more drops of agave if the mixture seems too dry.) 5. Form the mixture into 24 balls using clean hands. Before serving, store the balls in the refrigerator for at least 30 minutes in an airtight container. For up to a week, keep in the refrigerator or freezer.
Tip: For this recipe, make sure to use unsweetened coconut flakes. Varieties with added sugar can burn quickly.
Per Serving: Calories 90, Fat 5.77g; Sodium 75mg; Carbs 7.06g; Fibre 2.4g; Sugar 3.74g; Protein 2.13g

Spicy Chicken Omelet

Prep time: 10 minutes | Cook time: 15 minutes | Serves:2

4 whisked eggs 100g chicken mince 60g chopped spring onions	2 garlic cloves, minced finely ½ teaspoons of salt ½ teaspoon of black pepper,	ground ½ teaspoon of Paprika 1 tablespoon of dried thyme	A dash of hot sauce

1. In a mixing bowl, thoroughly combine all the ingredients. Scrape the egg mixture into two ramekins that can be placed in the oven after being previously oiled with a thin layer of vegetable oil. 2. Set your machine to air-fry for 13 minutes or until the food is thoroughly cooked at 175°C. Serve right away.
Per Serving: Calories 397; Fat 27.99g; Sodium 834mg; Carbs 5.79g; Fibre 1.2g; Sugar 2g; Protein 29.32g

Scones with Sweet Lemon Glaze

Prep time: 10 minutes | Cook time: 12 minutes | Serves:1

125g plain flour	2 tablespoons coconut oil	**For the Glaze**
2 tablespoons Granulated sugar	60ml unsweetened soy milk	1½ teaspoons freshly squeezed
½ teaspoon. baking powder	2 teaspoons of poppy seeds	lemon juice
⅛ teaspoon. of salt	zest of 1 lemon	3 tablespoons powdered sugar

1. Set the air fryer to 160°C. 2. Combine the flour, salt, baking powder, and granulated sugar in a sizable bowl. 3. To equally distribute the coconut oil throughout the dry ingredients and reduce the flour to the size of small peas, cut it into the flour with a pastry cutter. 4. Include the poppy seeds, lemon zest, and soy milk. With clean hands, gently combine the ingredients; do not overmix. In a baking dish, gently press the dough. 5. Put the dish in the fryer basket and bake for 12 minutes, or until the edges are brown. 6. Take the plate out of the basket. Give the scones 10 minutes to cool. Place on a wire rack after being cut into triangles. 7. To make the glaze, combine the powdered sugar and lemon juice in a small dish and whisk until smooth. 8. Pour the glaze on top of the scones. Before serving, let the mixture sit for 15 minutes.
Per Serving: Calories 922, Fat 32.14g; Sodium 356mg; Carbs 147.46g; Fibre 4.8g; Sugar 44.26g; Protein 15.1g

Apricot and Oat Bars

Prep time: 10 minutes | Cook time: 10 minutes | Serves:10

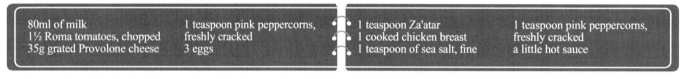

80g rolled oats	85g whole raw almonds	45g dry coconut flakes without	315g of maple syrup
130g of crispy almond butter	270g Apricots, dried	sugar	½ teaspoon. sea salt

1. Firstly, set the air fryer to 175°C. 2. Add the ingredients to a food processor and pulse just long enough to mix everything. In a 17.5-cm springform pan, firmly and evenly press the mixture into the pan. 3. Put the pan in the fryer basket and bake for 10 minutes, or until the edges start to brown. 4. Take the pan out of the fryer basket and let the granola finish cooling in it. 5. Granada should be taken out of the pan and divided into 10 bars.
Tips: To make this dish gluten-free, use gluten-free oats. Granola can also be cut while still hot in the pan, then removed after fully cooling and setting.
Per Serving: Calories 156, Fat 8.86g; Sodium 159mg; Carbs 20.23g; Fibre 3.6g; Sugar 10.79g; Protein 4.62g

Cheesy Chicken and Tomato

Prep time: 10 minutes | Cook time: 20 minutes | Serves:2

80ml of milk	1 teaspoon pink peppercorns,	1 teaspoon Za'atar	1 teaspoon pink peppercorns,
1½ Roma tomatoes, chopped	freshly cracked	1 cooked chicken breast	freshly cracked
35g grated Provolone cheese	3 eggs	1 teaspoon of sea salt, fine	a little hot sauce

1. In a medium-sized mixing bowl, whisk the eggs with the milk, Za'atar, sea salt, and pink peppercorns. 2. Spray the ramekins with cooking oil and then distribute the prepared egg mixture among them. 3. Shred the chicken with a stand mixer or two forks. Then add the cheese, tomato, and shredded chicken to the ramekins. 4. Air-fry it at 185°C for 18 minutes, or until it's done.
Per Serving: Calories 451; Fat 28.56g; Sodium 1575mg; Carbs 10.03g; Fibre 1.5g; Sugar 5.56g; Protein 37.18g

Homemade Everything Bagels

Prep time: 10 minutes | Cook time: 12 minutes | Serves: 4

125g plain flour, plus more	½ teaspoon salt	yogurt without dairy (soy	Seasoning for everything
2 teaspoons baking powder	150g unsweetened	recommended)	bagels

1. Adjust the air fryer's temperature to 160°C. 2. Combine the flour, baking powder, and salt in a big bowl. When a loose dough forms, add the yogurt and stir with a spatula. 3. Extend the dough over a lightly floured surface. The dough should come together after being gently kneaded. 4. Split the dough in half, then cut it into four pieces of equal size. Each piece of dough should be formed into a ball, then gently pressed to flatten. 5. Using a butter knife or a tiny ring mocentreuld, make a hole in the centre of the cake. Apply nonstick frying spray to the dough's surface. Each disc should have 1 to 2 teaspoons of spice on top of it. 6. Put the dough in the fryer basket and bake for 12 minutes, or until puffed and golden brown. 7. Move the bagels to a wire rack so they can cool a little before being served. As desired, slice, toast, and garnish.
Tip: Use vanilla yogurt for a flavour that is a little bit sweeter.
Per Serving: Calories 196, Fat 0.79g; Sodium 1918mg; Carbs 34.44g; Fibre 2.1g; Sugar 1.76g; Protein 8.94g

Vegan Tofu Rancheros

Prep time:10 minutes | Cook time: 5 minutes | Serves:4

500g of firm tofu crumbled	½ teaspoon of salt	1 avocado, cut into slices	suggests this) (optional)
1 teaspoon Dijon mustard	**For Serving:**	fresh coriander, chopped	
1 teaspoon Nutritional yeast	240g Black beans	4 medium corn tortillas	
½ teaspoon ground turmeric	60g of radishes, finely sliced	Hot sauce (Frank's RedHot	

1. Set the air fryer temperature to 200°C. 2. Combine the tofu, mustard, nutritional yeast, turmeric, and salt in a baking dish, mix well. 3. After putting the dish in the fryer basket, heat it for around 5 minutes. 4. Take the food out of the frying basket and give it a quick toss. On the tortillas, distribute the tofu mixture, black beans, radishes, avocado, coriander, and hot sauce (if using). Serve right away.
Tip: Before filling and serving tortillas, air fried them for a few minutes to make them crispier.
Per Serving: Calories 486, Fat 19.84g; Sodium 397mg; Carbs 51.34g; Fibre 15.6g; Sugar 1.63g; Protein 33.23g

Sweet Potato and Mushroom Hash

Prep time: 10 minutes | Cook time: 16 minutes | Serves: 4

Unpeeled 2 large sweet potatoes	into bits	100g Sliced mushrooms
½ small yellow onion, chopped	1 poblano pepper, chopped into big pieces	1 teaspoon salt
		1 tablespoon of olive oil

1. For 3 to 4 minutes in the microwave, soften but do not fully cook the sweet potatoes. Set aside for ten minutes to cool. 2. Adjust the air fryer's temperature to 180°C. 3. Cut the sweet potatoes into big slices after removing the skins. 4. Combine the sweet potatoes, onion, poblano pepper, mushrooms, salt, and olive oil in a medium bowl. Toss gently to coat. 5. After assembling the fryer basket, cook the vegetables for 8 minutes. Wait eight more minutes as you jiggle the basket and pause the machine. 6. Place the hash in a serving bowl and start serving right away.
Tips: For an increase in protein, add black beans or baked tofu. This can be prepared in advance, kept in the refrigerator, and consumed throughout the week.
Per Serving: Calories123, Fat 3.56g; Sodium 615 mg; Carbs 21.5g; Fibre 3.5g; Sugar 7.23g; Protein 2.29g

Walnuts, Mango and Yogurt Parfaits

Prep time: 5 minutes | Cook time: 10 minutes | Serves: 4

80g walnuts	¼ teaspoon ground cinnamon	960g coconut milk yogurt	diced
pinch of salt	1 tablespoon maple syrup	2 large mangoes, peeled and	

1. Adjust the air fryer's temperature to 160°C. 2. Combine the walnuts, salt, cinnamon, and maple syrup in a small basin. Toss well to coat. The walnut mixture should be put in a baking dish. 3. Place the dish in the fryer basket, tossing once halfway through the 10 minutes of toasting. 4. Empty the nuts onto a sheet of parchment paper after removing the dish from the fryer basket. Give them time to totally cool. 5. Alternately layer yoghurt, mango, and nuts in 4 parfait glasses. 5 minutes should pass in the fridge before serving.
Tips: Use any yoghurt you choose that is dairy-free: The most protein-rich food is soy, followed by almond milk and coconut, which are both rich and creamy. The nuts can be prepared up to 5 days ahead of time and kept in an airtight container.
Per Serving: Calories 754, Fat 66.66g; Sodium 135 mg; Carbs 43.79g; Fibre 9g; Sugar 34.34g; Protein 8.92g

Spicy Baked Eggs

Prep time: 10 minutes | Cook time: 25 minutes | Serves:6

6 beaten medium-sized eggs	3 minced garlic cloves	Use hot sauce sparingly	1 teaspoon salt
1 teaspoon Garam masala	280g of shredded leftover chicken	1 teaspoon Turmeric	⅓ teaspoon Smoked paprika
150g of finely chopped spring onions	2 tablespoons Sesame oil	1 teaspoon freshly cracked mixed peppercorns	

1. Warm sesame oil in a sauté pan over a moderate flame; then, sauté the spring onions together with garlic until just fragrant; it takes about 5 minutes. Add the leftover chicken and stir until heated through. 2. Combine all of the ingredients with the eggs in a medium-sized bowl or measuring cup. 3. Then, use a nonstick cooking spray to coat the interior of six oven-safe ramekins. The egg or chicken mixture should be divided among your ramekins. 4. Air-fry approximately 18 minutes at 180°C. Drizzle with hot sauce and serve warm.
Per Serving: Calories 466; Fat 17.38g; Sodium 692mg; Carbs 2.51g; Fibre 0.6g; Sugar 0.61g; Protein 70.64g

Morning Sandwiches with Avocado

Prep time: 5 minutes | Cook time: 8 minutes | Serves:4

4 sliced tiny bagels	4 vegetarian sausages	4 pieces of soy cheese	1 sliced avocado

1. Adjusting the air fryer's temperature to 200°C. 2. Arrange the sausage patties and bagels in the fryer basket, cut sides facing up. It takes about 4 minutes to toast the bagels. 3. Put the machine on hold and take the bagels out. Place aside. 4. Add a slice of cheese on the top of each patty. Restart the oven and cook for a further 4 minutes. 5. Place each patty on top of two bagel halves. Serve each patty right away with slices of avocado on top.
Per Serving: Calories 355, Fat 24.74g; Sodium 535mg; Carbs 19.05g; Fibre 4g; Sugar 0.7g; Protein 15.5g

Leftover Beef and Kale Omelet

Prep time: 10 minutes | Cook time: 20 minutes | Serves:4

Cooking spray that is nonstick 30g of kale, cut into pieces and wilted	1 pepper 6 eggs 225g of leftover meat, coarsely	minced 2 garlic cloves 6 teaspoons sour cream	½ teaspoon of turmeric powder 1 teaspoon of flakes of red pepper Salt and black pepper, to taste

1. Apply cooking spray to the inside of four ramekins. 2. Stir all ingredients thoroughly and distribute the mixture among the prepared ramekins. 3. Check the eggs with a wooden stick after 16 minutes of air-frying at 180°C. 4. If necessary, add a few additional minutes to the air-frying process. Serve right away.
Per Serving: Calories 466; Fat 17.38g; Sodium 692mg; Carbs 2.51g; Fibre 0.6g; Sugar 0.61g; Protein 70.64g

Smoked Salmon and Eggs

Prep time: 10 minutes | Cook time: 25 minutes | Serves:4

⅓ teaspoon of dried Dill weed 30g mozzarella cheese ½ tomatoes	6 eggs, chopped 80ml of milk Pan spray	135g chopped smoked salmon Fine sea salt and freshly cracked black pepper, to taste	⅓ teaspoon of smoked cayenne pepper

1. Your air fryer should be set to 185°C. Whisk the eggs, milk, smoked cayenne pepper, salt, black pepper, and dill weed in a mixing bowl. 2. Distribute the egg or milk mixture among the four ramekins that have been lightly greased with your preferred pan spray. 3. Add the salmon and tomato, and then sprinkle the cheese on top. Last but not least, air fried for 16 minutes.
Per Serving: Calories 255, Fat 18.5g; Sodium 229mg; Carbs 77.15g; Fibre 4.5g; Sugar 3.04g; Protein 17.15g

Breakfast Eggs with Ham and Swiss Chard

Prep time: 10 minutes | Cook time: 20 minutes | Serves:2

2 eggs ¼ teaspoon marjoram, either fresh or dried	2 tablespoons Chili powder ⅓ teaspoon of salt 90g Steamed Swiss chard	¼ teaspoon rosemary, either fresh or dried 4 slices of ham	⅓ teaspoon black pepper, ground, to taste

1. Divide the ham and Swiss chard between two ramekins, and crack an egg into each one. Sprinkle with the seasonings. 2. Cook eggs for 15 minutes at 170°C, or until desired texture is achieved. 3. Serve heated with pickles and hot tomato ketchup.
Per Serving: Calories 1245, Fat 40.59g; Sodium 7049mg; Carbs 3.09g; Fibre 1.3g; Sugar 0.95g; Protein 216.62g

Veggie Sausage Wraps

Prep time: 10 minutes | Cook time: 15 minutes | Serves:2

2 vegetarian sausages 120ml liquid egg replacement	30g of kale, chopped Hot sauce (Frank's RedHot	suggested) 2 large whole wheat flour	tortillas (optional)

1. Heat the air fryer to 175°C. Put the sausage in a baking dish. 2. Place the dish in the fryer basket and cook for 5 minutes. 3. Take the plate out of the basket. Add the egg, greens, and diced sausage to the dish. 4. Place the dish back in the fryer basket and cook the mixture for a further 10 minutes or until it is firm. 5. Take the meal out of the frying basket. Cut the mixture into 8 chunks of the same size. Each tortilla should have 4 pieces, accompanied by hot sauce (if using). Wrap them and serve.
Per Serving: Calories 248, Fat 11.43g; Sodium 556mg; Carbs 21.13g; Fibre 4.3g; Sugar 2.7g; Protein 15.35g

Kale frittata with Onion

Prep time: 5 minutes | Cook time: 18 minutes | Serves:2

300g of chopped kale	240ml of liquid egg	recommended)	¼ teaspoon freshly ground
40g of red onion, finely sliced	replacement (Just egg	½ teaspoon salt	black pepper

1. Set the air fryer temperature to 175°C. Use nonstick cooking spray to coat a baking pan. 2. Add the onion and greens to the pan. Cook the pan for 3 minutes in the fryer basket. 3. Remove the fryer basket from the pan. Salt, pepper, and the egg are added. Gently stir. 4. Add the pan back to the fryer basket and cook for additional 15 minutes, or until the frittata is firm. 5. Place the frittata on a serving plate. Before serving, divide the frittata into two parts of the same size.

Tip: Add a sprinkling of vegan cheese shreds for the final two minutes of cooking, then top with fresh chives to dress this up for brunch visitors.

Per Serving: Calories 69, Fat 0.13g; Sodium 825mg; Carbs 4.79g; Fibre 0.7g; Sugar 3.28g; Protein 12.67g

Spicy Burritos with Black Bean Burgers

Prep time: 10 minutes | Cook time: 10 minutes | Serves: 4

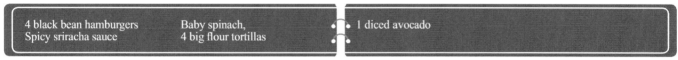

4 black bean hamburgers	Baby spinach,	1 diced avocado
Spicy sriracha sauce	4 big flour tortillas	

1. Set the air fryer temperature to 195°C. 2. After putting the black bean patties in the fryer basket, cook for 4 minutes on each side. 3. Take the hamburgers out of the fryer basket and chop them roughly. Then, evenly distribute the burger, spinach, and avocado on the tortillas after spreading the chili sauce on them. Wrap the filling in the tortillas. 4. Put the burritos in the fryer basket and cook for 2 minutes, or until the tortillas are toasted. 5. Cut the burritos in half after removing them from the fryer basket. For a dinner on the run, wrap them in foil and serve right away.

Per Serving: Calories 267, Fat 14.5g; Sodium 354mg; Carbs 28.3g; Fibre 9.1g; Sugar 1.5g; Protein 12.5g

Pistachio & Coconut Granola

Prep time: 10 minutes | Cook time: 10 minutes | Serves: 2

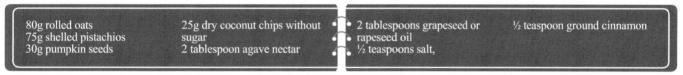

80g rolled oats	25g dry coconut chips without	2 tablespoons grapeseed or	½ teaspoon ground cinnamon
75g shelled pistachios	sugar	rapeseed oil	
30g pumpkin seeds	2 tablespoon agave nectar	½ teaspoons salt,	

1. Adjust the air fryer's temperature to 160°C. 2. The components should be combined in a food processor. Pulse until little clusters have formed. Put the mixture in a baking pan. 3. Put the dish in the fryer basket and cook for 10 minutes, or until it is lightly toasted and golden brown. Every two to three minutes, pause the machine to stir the mixture. 4. Before serving, spread the granola out on a sheet pan that has been lined with parchment paper to cool fully.

Tips: Granola can be kept for up to 5 days in an airtight container. Utilize gluten-free oats to convert this recipe to a gluten-free version.

Per Serving: Calories 558, Fat 42.68g; Sodium 652 mg; Carbs 47.99g; Fibre 12.3g; Sugar 8.3g; Protein 19.13g

Cheesy Frittata with Beef and Egg

Prep time: 10 minutes | Cook time: 27 minutes | Serves:4

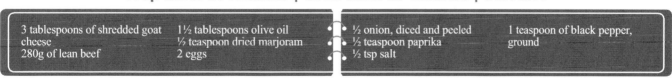

3 tablespoons of shredded goat cheese	1½ tablespoons olive oil	½ onion, diced and peeled	1 teaspoon of black pepper, ground
280g of lean beef	½ teaspoon dried marjoram	½ teaspoon paprika	
	2 eggs	½ tsp salt	

1.To cook, set your air fryer to 175°C. 2. In a frying pan over medium heat, melt the oil. Next, cook the onion until it has softened. Add beef mince and cook until browned; crumble with a fork and set aside, keeping it warm. 3. Whisk the eggs with all the seasonings. 4. Apply pan spray to the inside of a baking dish. Then, add the reserved beef or onion mixture to the baking dish after the beaten egg mixture. 5. Add the goat cheese crumbles on top. 6. Bake for about 27 minutes or until a tester comes out clean and dry when stuck in the centre of the frittata

Per Serving: Calories 676; Fat 35.92g; Sodium 378mg; Carbs 77.15g; Fibre 9.3g; Sugar 51.05g; Protein 17.34g

Chapter 2 Vegetable and Sides Recipes

Vegetarian Indian Kofta

Prep time: 10 minutes | Cook time: 35 minutes | Serves: 4

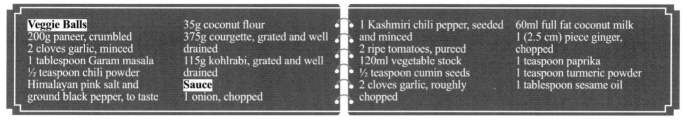

Veggie Balls	35g coconut flour	• 1 Kashmiri chili pepper, seeded	60ml full fat coconut milk
200g paneer, crumbled	375g courgette, grated and well	• and minced	1 (2.5 cm) piece ginger,
2 cloves garlic, minced	drained	• 2 ripe tomatoes, pureed	chopped
1 tablespoon Garam masala	115g kohlrabi, grated and well	• 120ml vegetable stock	1 teaspoon paprika
½ teaspoon chili powder	drained	• ½ teaspoon cumin seeds	1 teaspoon turmeric powder
Himalayan pink salt and	Sauce	• 2 cloves garlic, roughly	1 tablespoon sesame oil
ground black pepper, to taste	1 onion, chopped	• chopped	

1. Set your Air Fryer to 180°C to begin. Courgette, kohlrabi, garlic, Garam masala, paneer, coconut flour, chili powder, salt, and powdered black pepper should all be thoroughly combined. 2. Create little balls out of the vegetable mixture and place them in the frying basket that has been lightly oiled. 3. Cook for 15 minutes at 180°C in the preheated Air Fryer to achieve a well cooked and crispy product. Up till you run out of ingredients, keep repeating the process. 4. Heat the sesame oil in a saucepan over medium heat and add the cumin seeds. Add the ginger, garlic, onions, and chili pepper once the cumin seeds start to turn brown. Cook for two to three minutes. 5. Add the tomatoes, stock, paprika, and turmeric powder; cook, covered, for 4 to 5 minutes while stirring occasionally. 6. The coconut milk is added. Turn off the heat before adding the veggie balls and gently combining.
Per Serving: Calories 281, Fat 12.12g; Sodium 772mg; Carbs 23.5g; Fibre 6.9g; Sugar 12.9g; Protein 19.35g

Tomato Bites with Pecan Sauce

Prep time: 10 minutes | Cook time: 20 minutes | Serves: 4

For the Sauce	½ teaspoon of sea salt, fine	• dry	⅛ teaspoon crushed red pepper
Grated 50g Parmigiano-	80ml extra virgin olive oil	• 200g of thinly sliced Halloumi	flakes
Reggiano cheese	Regarding the Tomato Bites	• cheese	⅛ teaspoon sea salt
4 tablespoons chopped pecans	Cut two large Roma tomatoes	• 1 teaspoon dried basil and 55g	
1 teaspoon of pureed garlic	into thin slices, then pat them	• chopped onions	

1. Set your Air Fryer to 195°C. 2. In your food processor, make the sauce by mixing all ingredients except the extra-virgin olive oil. 3. While the machine is running, slowly and gradually pour in the olive oil; puree until everything is well blended. 4. Next, top each tomato slice with 1 teaspoon of the sauce. Each tomato slice should have a slice of Halloumi cheese on it. Add slices of onion on top. Add basil, red pepper flakes, and sea salt as garnish. 5. Place the assembled bites in the cooking basket of the Air Fryer. Spray with nonstick cooking spray, then bake for about 13 minutes. 6. Place these bites in a pretty serving dish, top with the remaining sauce, and serve warm.
Per Serving: Calories 350, Fat 28.52g; Sodium 1708mg; Carbs 10.67g; Fibre 1.4g; Sugar 5.05g; Protein 14.34g

Green Beans with Toasted Sesame Seeds

Prep time: 10 minutes | Cook time: 12 minutes | Serves: 4

375g green beans, cleaned	¼ teaspoon salt	• freshly cracked	2 tablespoons toasted sesame
1 tablespoon balsamic vinegar	½ teaspoon mixed peppercorns,	• 1 tablespoon butter	seeds, to serve

1. To cook, preheat your Air Fryer to 200°C. 2. With the exception of the sesame seeds, combine the green beans with the ingredients listed above. Set the timer for 10 minutes. 3. Meanwhile, roast the sesame seeds in a small nonstick frying pan while stirring constantly. 4. Serve steamed green beans with toasted sesame seeds on a lovely serving plate.
Per Serving: Calories 71, Fat 5.19g; Sodium 194mg; Carbs 5.45g; Fibre 2.3g; Sugar 1.3g; Protein 1.68g

Broccoli with Tomato Sauce

Prep time: 10 minutes | Cook time: 20 minutes | Serves: 6

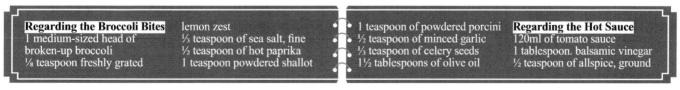

Regarding the Broccoli Bites	lemon zest	• 1 teaspoon of powdered porcini	Regarding the Hot Sauce
1 medium-sized head of	⅓ teaspoon of sea salt, fine	• ½ teaspoon of minced garlic	120ml of tomato sauce
broken-up broccoli	½ teaspoon of hot paprika	• ⅓ teaspoon of celery seeds	1 tablespoon. balsamic vinegar
⅛ teaspoon freshly grated	1 teaspoon powdered shallot	• 1½ tablespoons of olive oil	½ teaspoon of allspice, ground

1. In a mixing dish, combine all the ingredients for the broccoli bites, making sure to completely encircle the broccoli florets. 2. They should be cooked for 13 to 15 minutes at 180°C in the preheated Air Fryer. Combine all the ingredients for the spicy sauce in the meantime. 3. Put your Air Fryer on hold, combine the broccoli and prepared sauce, and cook for an additional three minutes.
Per Serving: Calories 65, Fat 3.6g; Sodium 440 mg; Carbs 6.81g; Fibre 2g; Sugar 3.13g; Protein 1.14g

Cheesy Cauliflower and Broccoli

Prep time: 10 minutes | Cook time: 20 minutes | Serves: 6

455g cauliflower florets	2½ tablespoons sesame oil	pepper	1 tablespoon lemon zest, grated
455g broccoli florets	½ teaspoon smoked cayenne	¾ teaspoon sea salt flakes	50g cheddar cheese, shredded

1. Make the cauliflower and broccoli according to your preferred steaming procedure. After that, thoroughly drain them and add the sesame oil, cayenne, and salt flakes. 2. 16 minutes should be allotted for air-frying at 200°C; be sure to check the vegetables halfway through. 3. Then, add the Colby cheese and lemon zest, toss to combine, and serve right now!
Per Serving: Calories 130, Fat 9.81g; Sodium 405mg; Carbs 6.46g; Fibre 3.6g; Sugar 1.87g; Protein 6.49g

Spinach and Tomato Omelette

Prep time: 10 minutes | Cook time: 15 minutes | Serves: 2

2 tablespoons of olive oil	1 medium tomato	½ teaspoon of coarse salt	20g coarsely chopped fresh
4 eggs, beaten until smooth	1 teaspoon of freshly squeezed	½ teaspoon of black pepper,	basil
125g of fresh spinach	lemon juice	ground	

1. In an Air Fryer baking pan, add the olive oil. To distribute the oil evenly, be careful to tilt the pan. 2. With the exception of the basil leaves, just combine the remaining ingredients and whisk well to blend. 3. Cook for 8 to 12 minutes at 140°C in the air fryer that has been preheated. 4. Fresh basil leaves are a nice garnish. If preferred, top the heated dish with sour cream.
Per Serving: Calories 410, Fat 33.25g; Sodium 846mg; Carbs 7.81g; Fibre 2.6g; Sugar 3.3g; Protein 20.7g

Croquettes of Fried Squash

Prep time: 10 minutes | Cook time: 22 minutes | Serves:4

40g plain flour	⅓ teaspoon of dried sage	⅓ of a grated and peeled	1 teaspoon of sea salt, fine
⅓ teaspoon freshly ground	4 minced garlic cloves	butternut squash	A dash of allspice, ground
black pepper, or as desired	1½ tablespoons of olive oil	2 well-whisked eggs	

1. In a mixing basin, thoroughly combine all the ingredients. 2. Set your Air Fryer's temperature to 175°C, then cook your fritters for 17 minutes or until they are golden brown. 3. Then, serve right immediately.
Per Serving: Calories 190, Fat 10.13g; Sodium 637mg; Carbs 19.39g; Fibre 2.1g; Sugar 2.2g; Protein 6.61g

Herbed Broccoli with Cheese

Prep time: 10 minutes | Cook time: 25 minutes | Serves: 4

35g shredded yellow cheese	finely chopped broccoli	2 teaspoons dried rosemary	To taste, add salt and black
1 large head of stemmed and	2½ tablespoons Rapeseed oil	2 tablespoons dried basil	pepper

1. Lightly salted water in a medium pan should be brought to a boil. The broccoli florets should then be boiled for 3 minutes. 2. After that, thoroughly rinse the broccoli florets and combine them with the rapeseed oil, salt, black pepper, rosemary, and basil. 3. Place the seasoned broccoli in the cooking basket of your Air Fryer, preheat it to 200°C, and set the timer for 17 minutes. Toss the broccoli halfway through the cooking process. 4. Serve hot with grated cheese and take pleasure in!
Per Serving: Calories 131, Fat 12.19g; Sodium 74mg; Carbs 2.87g; Fibre 0.9g; Sugar 1.01g; Protein 3.61g

Garlicky Onion-Stuffed Mushrooms

Prep time: 10 minutes | Cook time: 16 minutes | Serves: 2

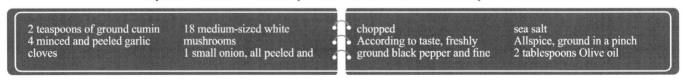

2 teaspoons of ground cumin	18 medium-sized white	chopped	sea salt
4 minced and peeled garlic	mushrooms	According to taste, freshly	Allspice, ground in a pinch
cloves	1 small onion, all peeled and	ground black pepper and fine	2 tablespoons Olive oil

1. To prepare the "shells," firstly, clean the mushrooms and cut off their central stalks. 2. Grab a mixing bowl, and incorporate the remaining ingredients completely. With the prepared mixture, cram the mushrooms. 3. The mushrooms should be heated for 12 minutes to 175°C. Enjoy!
Per Serving: Calories 187, Fat 14.63g; Sodium 1177mg; Carbs 11.82g; Fibre 2.7g; Sugar 4.8g; Protein 6.18g

Cauliflower, Green Beans and Bacon Pie

Prep time: 10 minutes | Cook time: 12 minutes | Serves: 5

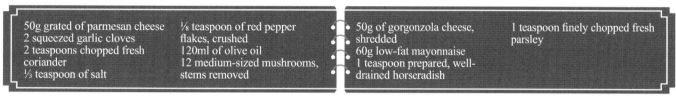

1 onion, chopped	360ml beef bone stock	2 tablespoons olive oil	like consistency
2 garlic cloves, minced	125g green beans, drained	2 peppers, seeded and sliced	120ml milk
80g cooked bacon, diced	Sea salt and freshly ground	200g of cauliflower pulsed in a	1 celery, chopped
2 tablespoons butter, melted	black pepper, to taste	food processor to a fine-crumb-	

1. In a saucepan, heat the olive oil over medium-high heat. Now, sauté the peppers, celery, onion, and garlic for around seven minutes, or until they have softened. 2. Add the stock and the bacon. Cook for another two minutes after bringing to a boil. Green beans, salt, and black pepper should be added at this point. Cook until heated through. 3. Place the mixture in the baking pan that has been lightly oiled. 4. Microwave the cauliflower rice for 5 minutes. 5. The cauliflower, milk, and melted butter should all be combined in a small bowl. Spoon the mixture of vegetables equally over the stirred ingredients. Transferring it to the cooking basket of the Air Fryer, smooth it up with a spatula. 6. Bake for 12 minutes at 200°C in the preheated Air Fryer. Before slicing and serving, place on a wire rack to cool slightly.
Per Serving: Calories 243, Fat 20.15g; Sodium 509mg; Carbs 11.22g; Fibre 3.2g; Sugar 4.4g; Protein 7.64g

Mushrooms with Cheese Stuffing and Horseradish Sauce

Prep time: 10 minutes | Cook time: 15 minutes | Serves: 5

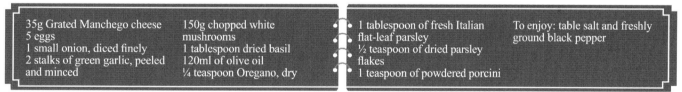

50g grated of parmesan cheese	⅛ teaspoon of red pepper	50g of gorgonzola cheese,	1 teaspoon finely chopped fresh
2 squeezed garlic cloves	flakes, crushed	shredded	parsley
2 teaspoons chopped fresh	120ml of olive oil	60g low-fat mayonnaise	
coriander	12 medium-sized mushrooms,	1 teaspoon prepared, well-	
⅓ teaspoon of salt	stems removed	drained horseradish	

1. Garlic, coriander, salt, red pepper, olive oil, and parmesan cheese should all be thoroughly combined. 2. Add the cheese filling to the mushroom caps. Add grated Gorgonzola on top. 3. Slide the mushrooms into the grill pan of the Air Fryer and turn it on. Grill them for 8 to 12 minutes at 195°C, or until the stuffing is thoroughly heated. 4. Make the horseradish sauce in the meantime by combining the mayonnaise, horseradish, and parsley. Warm fried mushrooms should be served with the horseradish sauce. Enjoy!
Per Serving: Calories 172, Fat 13.26g; Sodium 436mg; Carbs 6.21g; Fibre 0.8g; Sugar 2.08g; Protein 8.45g

Herbed Mushroom Frittata

Prep time: 10 minutes | Cook time:40 minutes | Serves:4

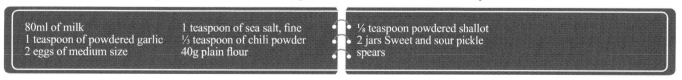

35g Grated Manchego cheese	150g chopped white	1 tablespoon of fresh Italian	To enjoy: table salt and freshly
5 eggs	mushrooms	flat-leaf parsley	ground black pepper
1 small onion, diced finely	1 tablespoon dried basil	½ teaspoon of dried parsley	
2 stalks of green garlic, peeled	120ml of olive oil	flakes	
and minced	¼ teaspoon Oregano, dry	1 teaspoon of powdered porcini	

1.Set your Air Fryer to 175°C to begin. To the baking dish for the Air Fryer, add the oil, mushrooms, onion, and green garlic. This mixture should be baked for 6 minutes, or until soft. 2. In the meantime, crack the eggs into a mixing basin and whisk them vigorously. Remix after adding the seasonings. Remove the baking pan from the oven. 3. In the baking dish with the sautéed mixture, pour the whisked egg mixture. Add some shredded Manchego cheese on top. 4. Your frittata should be baked for about 32 minutes at 160°C or until it has set. Serve hot.
Per Serving: Calories 260, Fat 19.59g; Sodium 377mg; Carbs 6.1g; Fibre 0.9g; Sugar 2.33g; Protein 15.02g

Fried Pickles

Prep time: 10 minutes | Cook time: 20 minutes | Serves:6

80ml of milk	1 teaspoon of sea salt, fine	⅛ teaspoon powdered shallot
1 teaspoon of powdered garlic	⅓ teaspoon of chili powder	2 jars Sweet and sour pickle
2 eggs of medium size	40g plain flour	spears

1. With a kitchen towel, dry the pickle spears. Afterward, get two mixing bowls. 2. In a bowl, combine the egg and milk. All dry ingredients should be combined in another bowl. 3. The pickle spears should first be dipped into the dry mixture, then into the egg or milk mixture, and then back into the dry mixture for a second coating. 4. Air-fried battered pickles for 15 minutes at 195°C. Enjoy!
Per Serving: Calories 58, Fat 1.96g; Sodium 513mg; Carbs 6.76g; Fibre 0.4g; Sugar 0.91g; Protein 3.14g

Sweet Potatoes Glazed in Tamarind

Prep time: 10 minutes | Cook time: 24 minutes | Serves:4

⅓ teaspoon white pepper	5 chopped garnet sweet	1½ tablespoons of fresh lime	1½ teaspoons of allspice,
1 teaspoon melted butter	potatoes, each peeled	juice	ground
½ teaspoon of turmeric powder	A few liquid droplets Stevia	2 teaspoons of tamarind paste	

1. Toss all the ingredients in a mixing dish until the sweet potatoes are thoroughly covered. 2. Fry them for 12 minutes in the air at 170°C. 3. Restart the Air Fryer after pausing it. Cook for a further 10 minutes at a higher temperature of 200°C. Eat warm.
Per Serving: Calories 190, Fat 10.13g; Sodium 637mg; Carbs 19.39g; Fibre 2.1g; Sugar 2.2g; Protein 6.61g

Roasted Cauliflower with Pepper Jack Cheese

Prep time: 10 minutes | Cook time: 25 minutes | Serves: 2

⅓ teaspoon powdered shallot	1½ large cauliflower heads,	½ teaspoon garlic salt	⅓ teaspoon Paprika
1 teaspoon of black pepper,	divided into florets	25g grated Pepper Jack cheese	
ground	¼ teaspoon of cumin powder	1½ tablespoons Vegetable oil	

1. In a big pot of salted water, boil the cauliflower for around five minutes. After that, drain the cauliflower florets. 2. In a bowl, combine the remaining ingredients, including the cauliflower florets. Transfer them to a baking dish. 3. They should be roasted for 16 minutes at 200°C, turning them once. Enjoy!
Per Serving: Calories 199, Fat 15.33g; Sodium 146mg; Carbs 11.6g; Fibre 4.5g; Sugar 3.95g; Protein 7.53g

Spicy Cauliflower Balls

Prep time: 10 minutes | Cook time: 48 minutes | Serves: 6

2 tablespoons Chili powder	marjoram	½ teaspoon of red pepper	370g feta cheese, crumbled
1½ teaspoons salt	270g of floretized cauliflower	flakes, crushed	
1 teaspoon crumbled dried	50g of crumbed tortilla chips	Whisked 3 eggs	

1. Cauliflower florets should be processed in a food processor until they are crushed (it is the size of rice). After that, add the other ingredients with the cauliflower "rice." 2. The cauliflower mixture should now be formed into small balls and chilled for 30 minutes. 3. Set your Air Fryer's temperature to 175°C and a timer for 14 minutes. Cook the balls until they are golden, then serve right immediately.
Per Serving: Calories 220, Fat 15.48g; Sodium 1111mg; Carbs 8.67g; Fibre 1.5g; Sugar 1.33g; Protein 11.89g

Omelet with cheese and mixed greens

Prep time: 10 minutes | Cook time: 17 minutes | Serves: 2

80g of cheese, ricotta	100g of roughly chopped	pepper	½ teaspoon of dried oregano
5 beaten eggs	mixed greens	½ teaspoon of dried basil	
½ cut and seeded red pepper	½ of a sliced, seeded green	½ of chipotle pepper, minced	

1. Apply a thin layer of pan spray into a baking dish. 2. After that, combine all the ingredients in the baking dish and stir well. 3. Bake for 15 minutes at 160°C.
Per Serving: Calories 414, Fat 29.54g; Sodium 336mg; Carbs 7.99g; Fibre 1.4g; Sugar 3.59g; Protein 28.17g

Fried Asparagus with Cheese

Prep time: 10 minutes | Cook time: 15 minutes | Serves: 3

1 bunch of asparagus, trimmed	200g goat cheese, crumbled	pepper, to taste	½ teaspoon salt
½ teaspoon dried dill weed	¼ teaspoon cracked black	1 tablespoon olive oil	

1. The frying basket should be lightly oiled before adding the asparagus spears. Toss the tasparagus in a bowl with the dill, olive oil, salt, and pepper. 2.Cook for 9 minutes at 200°C in the prepared Air Fryer. 3. Serve with goat cheese as a garnish.
Per Serving: Calories 155, Fat 11.3g; Sodium 523mg; Carbs 6.26g; Fibre 3.3g; Sugar 2.95g; Protein 8.77g

Cauliflower Quiche

Prep time: 10 minutes | Cook time: 12 minutes | Serves: 4

Sea salt and ground black pepper, to taste	2 tablespoons peanut oil	particles	2 pepper, chopped
½ teaspoon granulated garlic	215g cauliflower, food-processed into rice-like	4 eggs, beaten	
		70g spring onions, chopped	

1. Use nonstick cooking spray to grease a baking pan. 2. Add the cauliflower rice and the other ingredients to the baking pan. 3. Cook for 12 minutes at 200°C, monitoring to make sure the food is evenly done. Enjoy.
Per Serving: Calories 221, Fat 16.63g; Sodium 123mg; Carbs 7.9g; Fibre 1.9g; Sugar 3.69g; Protein 10.9g

Cream Cheese Stuffed peppers

Prep time: 10 minutes | Cook time: 20 minutes | Serves: 2

2 tablespoons mayonnaise	removed	chopped	160g cream cheese
2 peppers, tops and seeds	1 tablespoon fresh celery stalks,	Salt and pepper, to taste	

1. Place the peppers in the frying basket that has been lightly oiled. Cook for 15 minutes at 200°C in the preheated air fryer, flipping the food over halfway through. 2. Add salt and pepper to taste. 3. Then, combine the cream cheese, mayonnaise, and celery in a mixing dish. Serve the pepper after stuffing it with the cream cheese mixture.
Per Serving: Calories 314, Fat 27.9g; Sodium 560mg; Carbs 9.87g; Fibre 1.3g; Sugar 6.8g; Protein 7.8g

Noodles with Fennel

Prep time: 10 minutes | Cook time: 20 minutes | Serves: 3

Salt and white pepper, to taste	210g noodles, boiled	1 tablespoon soy sauce	2 tablespoons rice wine vinegar
1 clove garlic, finely chopped	1 teaspoon ginger, freshly grated	1 green onion, thinly sliced	2 tablespoons sesame oil
1 fennel bulb, quartered		75g Chinese cabbage, shredded	

1. The first step is to heat your Air Fryer to 185°C. 2. Now, cook the fennel bulb for 15 minutes, shaking the cooking basket once or twice during that time. 3. Allow it to cool completely before combining with the additional ingredients. Serve cold if possible.
Per Serving: Calories 239, Fat 10.4g; Sodium 309mg; Carbs 31.8g; Fibre 3.3g; Sugar 5.91g; Protein 5.17g

Creamy Egg with Swiss Chard

Prep time: 10 minutes | Cook time: 25 minutes | Serves: 2

1 teaspoon of garlic paste	⅓ teaspoon freshly ground black pepper, as desired	1 teaspoon cayenne pepper	40g finely sliced yellow onions
1½ tablespoons of olive oil		10g of shredded Swiss chard	1 teaspoon sea salt
120g of crème fraîche	35g of shredded Swiss cheese	5 eggs	

1. In a mixing bowl, crack the eggs and add the crème fraîche, salt, freshly ground black pepper, and cayenne pepper. 2. Next, drizzle some olive oil into a baking dish and tilt it to distribute it evenly. Place the baking dish with the egg or cream mixture inside. Add the remaining ingredients and well blend. 3. 18 minutes of baking are required at 145°C. Serve right away.
Per Serving: Calories 519, Fat 41.71g; Sodium 1448mg; Carbs 6.2g; Fibre 0.7g; Sugar 2.68g; Protein 28.7g

Herbed Tomatoes with Feta Cheese

Prep time: 10 minutes | Cook time: 20 minutes | Serves: 2

3 medium tomatoes, sliced into four pieces, dried	1 teaspoon dried basil	¼ teaspoon crushed red pepper flakes	½ teaspoon sea salt
	1 teaspoon Oregano, dry		3 Feta cheese slices

1. The tomatoes should be sprayed with cooking oil before being placed in the Air Fryer basket. Season with salt and pepper. Then sprinkle with oregano, basil and red pepper flakes. 2. Cook for about 8 minutes at 175°C, flipping them over halfway through. 3. Add the cheese on top, then simmer for an additional four minutes.
Per Serving: Calories 157, Fat 12.21g; Sodium 1106mg; Carbs 3.74g; Fibre 0.6g; Sugar 2.97g; Protein 8.43g

Cheese Cauliflower Bites

Prep time: 10 minutes | Cook time: 25 minutes | Serves: 4

455g Cauliflower florets	spring onions	pepper	1 teaspoon paprika
2 eggs	1 minced garlic clove	50g of grated parmesan cheese,	
1 tablespoon Olive oil	100g shredded cheddar cheese	to taste	
2 tablespoons finely chopped	sea salt, freshly ground black	¼ of a teaspoon of dried dill	

1. To get the cauliflower al dente, blanch it for 3 to 4 minutes in salted boiling water. Once thoroughly drained, pulse in a food processor. 2. Combine all of the remaining ingredients well before adding. The cauliflower mixture should be formed into bite-sized tots. 3. The Air Fryer basket should be sprayed with cooking spray. 4. Cook for 16 minutes at 190°C in the preheated Air Fryer while shaking the pan halfway through. 5. Serve with your preferred dipping sauce.
Per Serving: Calories 314, Fat 22.7g; Sodium 512mg; Carbs 10.6g; Fibre 2.7g; Sugar 3.38g; Protein 18.4g

Delicious Oyster Mushroom Omelet

Prep time: 10 minutes | Cook time: 42 minutes | Serves: 2

3 sliced thin king oyster mushrooms	35g of grated Swiss cheese	2 teaspoons of melted butter	The right amount of freshly ground black pepper and fine sea salt
1 chopped lemongrass and ½ teaspoon. dried marjoram	2 tablespoons sour cream	½ red onion peeled and cut into small circles	
1½ teaspoons dry rosemary	½ teaspoon of garlic powder	
5 eggs	2 tablespoons crushed red pepper flakes	1 teaspoon of dill herb, dried	

1. In a frying pan over a moderate temperature, melt the butter. After that, sauté the lemongrass, mushrooms, and onion until they are tender and set aside. 2. The Air Fryer should then be preheated to 160°C. The eggs should then be cracked into a mixing basin and thoroughly whisked. After that, whisk well and add in the sour cream. 3. Add the salt, black pepper, red pepper, marjoram, dill, rosemary, and garlic powder at this point. 4. The following step is to apply a thin layer of cooking spray inside an Air Fryer baking dish to oil it. Add the reserved mixture after pouring the egg or seasoning mixture into the baking dish. 5. Add the Swiss cheese on top. 6. 35 minutes should be allotted for cooking; continue cooking until a knife inserted in the centre emerges clean and dry.
Per Serving: Calories 614, Fat 44g; Sodium 417mg; Carbs 21.75g; Fibre 5.8g; Sugar 5.82g; Protein 36.98g

Baked Cheese and Veggies Casserole

Prep time: 10 minutes | Cook time: 50 minutes | Serves: 4

2 medium-sized tomatoes, sliced	100g Monterey cheese, shredded	2 tablespoons olive oil	small florets
1 leek, thinly sliced	3 peppers, thinly sliced	½ teaspoon red pepper flakes, crushed	½ teaspoon freshly ground black pepper
2 garlic cloves, minced	1 serrano pepper, thinly sliced	455g cauliflower, chopped into	Salt, to taste

1. Set your Air Fryer to 175°C to begin. Sprinkle frying oil in a casserole dish. 2. Spread the cauliflower out evenly in the casserole dish and cover with 1 tablespoon of olive oil. Add the salt, black pepper, and red pepper after that. 3. Include 2 peppers and half a leek. Tomatoes and the final 1 tablespoon of olive oil are added. 4. Leeks, minced garlic, and the remaining peppers should be added. Add the cheese on top. 5. Bake the casserole for 32 minutes while it is covered with foil. Bake for a further 16 minutes at 200°C after removing the foil.
Per Serving: Calories 243, Fat 17.24g; Sodium 337mg; Carbs 13.36g; Fibre 3.5g; Sugar 5.2g; Protein 11.5g

Veggies with Yogurt Tahini Sauce

Prep time: 10 minutes | Cook time: 20 minutes | Serves: 4

½ teaspoon white pepper	½ teaspoon mustard seeds	½ teaspoon Aleppo pepper, minced	240g plain yogurt
½ teaspoon dried dill weed	Salt, to taste	2 heaping tablespoons tahini paste	1 tablespoon extra-virgin olive oil
½ teaspoon cayenne pepper	455g button mushrooms	
455g cauliflower florets	2 tablespoons olive oil	
½ teaspoon celery seeds	Yogurt Tahini Sauce:	1 tablespoon lemon juice	

1. Combine olive oil and seasonings with the cauliflower and mushrooms. Heat the air fryer to 195°C. 2. Cook the cauliflower for 10 minutes after adding it to the cooking basket. 3. Turn the heat to 200°C, add the mushrooms, and cook for an additional 6 minutes. 4. Make the sauce by whisking all of the sauce ingredients together while the vegetables are cooking. Warm veggies should be served with the sauce on the side.
Per Serving: Calories 526, Fat 15.94g; Sodium 214mg; Carbs 96.92g; Fibre 16.3g; Sugar 7.99g; Protein 16.7g

Crispy Asparagus Fries

Prep time: 10 minutes | Cook time: 5 minutes | Serves: 4

Sea salt and ground black pepper, to taste	2 eggs 1 teaspoon Dijon mustard	100g Parmesan cheese, grated 120g sour cream	18 asparagus spears, trimmed

1. To begin, warm your air fryer to 200°C. 2. Whisk together the eggs and mustard in a small bowl. Combine the Parmesan cheese, salt, and black pepper in a separate shallow bowl. 3. Before pressing to adhere, dip the asparagus stalks in the egg mixture and then in the parmesan mixture. 4. Work in three batches while cooking for 5 minutes. 5. Sour cream should be served on the side. Enjoy!
Per Serving: Calories 217, Fat 18.75g; Sodium 78mg; Carbs 17.17g; Fibre 3.3g; Sugar 10.07g; Protein 9.56g

Cauliflower and Prawns Casserole

Prep time: 10 minutes | Cook time: 25 minutes | Serves: 4

1 shallot, sliced 455g prawns cleaned and	deveined 2 tablespoons sesame oil	240g tomato paste 215g cauliflower, cut into	florets 2 pepper, sliced

1. Set your Air Fryer to 180°C to begin. Spray cooking spray in the baking pan. 2. Now, place the vegetables and prawns in the baking pan. Then, smear the vegetables with the sesame oil. Over the vegetables, pour the tomato paste. 3. In an Air Fryer that has been heated, cook for 10 minutes. Cook for another 12 minutes while stirring with a big spoon. Serve hot.
Per Serving: Calories 255, Fat 8.85g; Sodium 1044mg; Carbs 18.4g; Fibre 4.3g; Sugar 10.77g; Protein 27.66g

Easy Broccoli with Sesame Seeds

Prep time: 10 minutes | Cook time: 15 minutes | Serves: 3

455g Broccoli florets 2 tablespoons Sesame oil ½ teaspoon powdered shallot	½ teaspoon of powdered porcini 1 teaspoon of powdered garlic	To taste, add sea salt and black pepper ½ teaspoon of cumin powder	¼ teaspoon Paprika 1 tablespoons sesame seeds

1. To begin, set the air fryer to 200°C. 2. Broccoli should be blanched for 3 to 4 minutes, or until al dente, in salted boiling water. Transfer to the basket of the Air Fryer after thoroughly draining. 3. Sesame oil, garlic, shallot, porcini, salt, black pepper, cumin, paprika, and sesame seeds should be added. 4. Cook for 6 minutes, tossing once halfway through.
Per Serving: Calories 160, Fat 13.22g; Sodium 55mg; Carbs 7.75g; Fibre 5.2g; Sugar 1.47g; Protein 6.5g

Spicy Veggie Fritters

Prep time: 10 minutes | Cook time: 12 minutes | Serves: 2

2 tablespoons fresh shallots, minced 1 teaspoon fresh garlic, minced	1 tablespoon peanut oil Sea salt and ground black pepper, to taste	1 teaspoon cayenne pepper 1 courgette, grated and squeezed	180g cauliflower florets, boiled 4 tablespoons Romano cheese, grated

1. All ingredients should be carefully mixed in a basin until everything is nicely distributed. 2. Create patties out of the mixture. The Air Fryer basket should be sprayed with cooking spray. 3. Cook for 6 minutes at 185°C in the air fryer that has been preheated. Cook them for an additional 6 minutes after flipping them. 4. Serve right away and delight in!
Per Serving: Calories 184, Fat 13.6g; Sodium 515mg; Carbs 10.12g; Fibre 2.1g; Sugar 5.3g; Protein 7.08g

Herb Balsamic Vegetables

Prep time: 10 minutes | Cook time: 15 minutes | Serves: 3

½ teaspoon dried thyme ½ teaspoon dried marjoram 225g cauliflower florets	225g button mushrooms, whole 185g pearl onions, whole 1 teaspoon garlic powder	3 tablespoons olive oil Pink Himalayan salt and ground black pepper, to taste	¼ teaspoon smoked paprika 2 tablespoons balsamic vinegar

1. In a sizable mixing bowl, combine all the ingredients. 2. 5 minutes of roasting at 200°C in the air fryer that has been preheated Cook for a further 7 minutes after shaking the basket. 3. Adding additional fresh herbs to the dish is optional.
Per Serving: Calories 391, Fat 14.54g; Sodium 167mg; Carbs 67.09g; Fibre 11.1g; Sugar 6.3g; Protein 9.39g

Herbed Broccoli and Celery Casserole

Prep time: 10 minutes | Cook time: 15 minutes | Serves: 2

2 tablespoons unsalted butter, melted	60ml tomato sauce	1 onion, cut into wedges	225g broccoli florets
120ml chicken stock	1 celery root, peeled and cut into 2.5 cm pieces	1 teaspoon parsley	1 teaspoon thyme
		1 teaspoon rosemary	

1. To begin, preheat your air fryer to 195°C. Fill a casserole dish with all the contents and lightly oil it. Mix thoroughly by stirring. 2. Bake in the preheated Air Fryer for 10 minutes. Cook the vegetables for an additional 5 minutes, gently stirring them with a large spoon. 3. Serve with a few drops of lemon juice in separate bowls.
Per Serving: Calories 281, Fat 12.12g; Sodium 772mg; Carbs 23.5g; Fibre 6.9g; Sugar 12.9g; Protein 19.35g

Fried Yellow Beans with Blue Cheese and Pecans

Prep time: 10 minutes | Cook time: 15 minutes | Serves: 3

4 tablespoons Romano cheese, grated	pepper, to taste	crushed	cleaned
Sea salt and ground black	80g blue cheese, crumbled	2 tablespoons pecans, sliced	2 tablespoons peanut oil
	½ teaspoon red pepper flakes,	375g wax yellow beans,	

1. Combine the Romano cheese, salt, black pepper, red pepper, and peanut oil with the wax beans in a bowl. 2. In the frying basket that has been lightly greased, add the wax beans mixture. 3. Cook for 5 minutes at 200°C in the prepared Air Fryer. Give the basket a couple of shakes. 4. Adding the nuts, heat for a further 3 minutes, or until just lightly toasted. Serve with blue cheese over top and have pleasure!
Per Serving: Calories 253, Fat 21.2g; Sodium 805mg; Carbs 9.28g; Fibre 2.1g; Sugar 3.62g; Protein 8.55g

Cauliflower Croquettes with Cheese and Mustard

Prep time: 10 minutes | Cook time: 30 minutes | Serves: 2

225g cauliflower florets	Black pepper, sea salt, to taste	½ teaspoon powdered shallot	120g of sour cream
2 minced garlic cloves	200g of goat cheese	¼ teaspoon of cumin powder	1 teaspoon Dijon mustard

1. In a saucepan, add the cauliflower florets, bring to a boil, then decrease the heat and cook for 10 minutes, or until soft. 2. Utilizing your blender, mash the cauliflower, add the garlic, cheese, and spices; mix to combine well. 3. The cauliflower mixture should be formed into croquettes. 4. Cook for 16 minutes at 190°C in the preheated Air Fryer while shaking the pan halfway through. 5. Serve with the mustard and sour cream.
Per Serving: Calories 247, Fat 16.6g; Sodium 310mg; Carbs 13.4g; Fibre 2.8g; Sugar 3.7g; Protein 13.06g

Herbed Peppers and Onion with Mayo

Prep time: 10 minutes | Cook time: 20 minutes | Serves: 2

4 sliced and seeded peppers (2.5 cm pieces)	Olive oil, 1 tablespoon	Salt, to taste	80g of mayonnaise
1 sliced onion (2.5 cm pieces)	½ teaspoon of dried rosemary	¼ teaspoon of black pepper, ground	⅓ teaspoon Sriracha
	½ teaspoon of dried basil		

1. Combine the peppers, onions, salt, black pepper, rosemary, basil and olive oil in a bowl. 2. In the cooking basket, arrange the peppers and onion mixture in a uniform layer. Cook for 12 to 14 minutes at 200°C. 3. While waiting, combine the Sriracha and mayonnaise to make the sauce. Serve right away.
Per Serving: Calories 227, Fat 19.55g; Sodium 507mg; Carbs 10.51g; Fibre 2.1g; Sugar 5.12g; Protein 4.29g

Garlicky Cauliflower and Egg Hash

Prep time: 10 minutes | Cook time: 30 minutes | Serves: 2

1 teaspoon fresh garlic, minced	grated	Sea salt and ground black pepper, to taste	½ teaspoon cinnamon
1 tablespoon peanut oil	2 eggs, whisked	¼ teaspoon ground allspice	
300g cauliflower, peeled and	40g spring onions, chopped		

1. Cauliflower should be boiled for 5 to 7 minutes on low heat to reach fork-tenderness. Drain the water, then use a kitchen towel to pat the cauliflower dry. 2. Add the remaining ingredients and mix everything together thoroughly. 3. Cook for 20 minutes at 200°C in the prepared Air Fryer. Give the basket a couple of shakes. With low-carb tomato sauce, serve.
Per Serving: Calories 245, Fat 16.9g; Sodium 152mg; Carbs 12.7g; Fibre 4.1g; Sugar 5.02g; Protein 12.6g

Asparagus and Tomatoes Salad with Boiled Eggs

Prep time: 10 minutes | Cook time: 10 minutes | Serves: 4

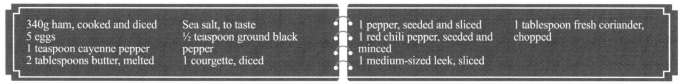

60ml olive oil	60ml balsamic vinegar	½ teaspoon oregano	2 hard-boiled eggs, sliced
455g asparagus, trimmed	2 garlic cloves, minced	Coarse sea salt and ground	
150g cherry tomatoes, halved	2 spring onion stalks, chopped	black pepper, to your liking	

1. Set your Air Fryer to 200°C to begin. One tablespoon of olive oil should be brushed on the frying basket. 2. Add the cherry tomatoes and asparagus to the frying basket. 1 tablespoon of olive oil should be drizzled over your vegetables. 3. Shake the basket midway through the five minutes of cooking. Allow it to cool a little. 4. Add the remaining olive oil, balsamic vinegar, oregano, garlic, spring onions, salt, and black pepper tossing well. 5. After that, top your salad with the hard-boiled eggs and serve.
Per Serving: Calories 266, Fat 18.75g; Sodium 78mg; Carbs 17.17g; Fibre 3.3g; Sugar 10.07g; Protein 9.56g

Courgette Ham Casserole with Eggs

Prep time: 10 minutes | Cook time: 30 minutes | Serves: 4

340g ham, cooked and diced	Sea salt, to taste	1 pepper, seeded and sliced	1 tablespoon fresh coriander,
5 eggs	½ teaspoon ground black	1 red chili pepper, seeded and	chopped
1 teaspoon cayenne pepper	pepper	minced	
2 tablespoons butter, melted	1 courgette, diced	1 medium-sized leek, sliced	

1. The Air Fryer should first be heated to 195°C. Melted butter should be used to grease a baking pan's bottom and sides. 2. Put the ham, leeks, peppers, courgette, and peppers in the baking dish. Bake for 6 minutes in the preheated Air Fryer. 3. On top of the ham and vegetables, crack the eggs and season with cayenne, salt, and black pepper. 20 more minutes of baking is required to thoroughly set the whites. 4. Serve with fresh coriander as a garnish.
Per Serving: Calories 325, Fat 20.9g; Sodium 1268mg; Carbs 7.9g; Fibre 1g; Sugar 2.8g; Protein 26.6g

Crispy Air Fried Vegetables

Prep time: 10 minutes | Cook time: 20 minutes | Serves: 3

½ teaspoon paprika	2 tablespoons olive oil	Salt and ground black pepper,	100g parmesan cheese, grated
1 pepper	7 tablespoons whey protein	to taste	1 onion, cut into rings
1 courgette, cut into slices	isolate	1 tablespoon mirin	1 teaspoon dashi granules
3 asparagus spears	1 teaspoon baking powder	2 eggs	1 tablespoons soda water

1. Whey protein isolate, baking powder, salt, black pepper, paprika, dashi granules, eggs, mirin, and soda water should all be combined in a small basin. 2. Grated parmesan cheese should be placed in another small bowl. 3. After coating them uniformly with tempura batter, roll the vegetables in parmesan cheese. Olive oil should be drizzled over each item. 4. Cook for 10 minutes at 200°C in the preheated Air Fryer while shaking the basket halfway through. As soon as the vegetables are golden and crispy, work in batches.
Per Serving: Calories 336, Fat 24.9g; Sodium 698mg; Carbs 11.15g; Fibre 0.9g; Sugar 3.6g; Protein 18.13g

Real Sicilian peperonata

Prep time: 10 minutes | Cook time: 25 minutes | Serves: 4

80g onion, peeled and sliced	Sea salt and black pepper	4 peppers, seeded and sliced	4 fresh basil leaves
2 garlic cloves, crushed	1 teaspoon cayenne pepper	1 serrano pepper, seeded and	8 Sicilian olives green, pitted
1 large tomato, pureed	4 tablespoons olive oil	sliced	and sliced

1. 1 tablespoon of olive oil should be brushed onto the frying basket's bottom and sides. Garlic, onions, and peppers should be added to the cooking basket. Cook until tender for 5 minutes. 2. Add the remaining tablespoon of olive oil, the tomatoes, salt, black pepper, and cayenne pepper, and cook for 15 minutes at 195°C in the prepared Air Fryer while stirring regularly. 3. Divide among individual bowls, top with basil leaves, and add olives as a garnish.
Per Serving: Calories 168, Fat 14.6g; Sodium 92mg; Carbs 9.51g; Fibre 2g; Sugar 4.83g; Protein 1.93g

Sausage and Mushroom Casserole

Prep time: 10 minutes | Cook time: 20 minutes | Serves: 4

1 teaspoon dried basil	2 Italian peppers, seeded and	Sea salt, to taste	240ml chicken stock
1 teaspoon dried oregano	sliced	2 tablespoons Dijon mustard	
100g mushrooms, sliced	¼ teaspoon black pepper	4 cloves garlic	
1 shallot, sliced	¼ teaspoon cayenne pepper	455g Italian sausage	

1. Put all the ingredients in a baking dish that has been lightly oiled. Ensure that the oil and seasonings are evenly distributed over the sausages and vegetables. 2. Bake for 15 minutes at 195°C in the preheated Air Fryer. 3. Serve heated after dividing into individual bowls.
Per Serving: Calories 412, Fat 25.12g; Sodium 1440mg; Carbs 16.44g; Fibre 4.4g; Sugar 1.86g; Protein 35.2g

Cheesy Aubergine Rolls

Prep time: 10 minutes | Cook time: 45 minutes | Serves: 4

1 tablespoon sea salt	60g mozzarella cheese, grated	455g aubergine, sliced	Sea salt and cracked black
1 egg, whisked	2 tablespoons fresh Italian	50g Romano cheese, preferably	pepper, to taste
100g parmesan, grated	parsley, roughly chopped	freshly grated	

1. Add one tablespoon of salt to the aubergine and let it stand for 30 minutes. Rinse and drain. 2. In a bowl, combine the cheese, salt, and black pepper. Add the whisked egg after that. 3. Slices of aubergine are coated on all sides after being dipped in the batter. Roll them over parmesan. Place in the Air Fryer basket that has been light oiled. 4. Cook for 7 to 9 minutes at 185°C. After flipping each slice over, add the mozzarella. Add 2 more minutes of cooking to get the cheese to melt. 5. Serve with fresh Italian parsley as a garnish.
Per Serving: Calories 207, Fat 10.7g; Sodium 1993mg; Carbs 8.71g; Fibre 3.9g; Sugar 5.05g; Protein 19.41g

Herb Green Beans Salad with Goat Cheese

Prep time: 10 minutes | Cook time: 10 minutes | Serves: 4

1 shallot, thinly sliced	60ml extra-virgin olive oil	leaves	Salt and freshly cracked mixed
1 tablespoon lime juice	1 tablespoon fresh basil leaves,	360g goat cheese, crumbled	pepper, to taste
1 tablespoon champagne	chopped	375g trimmed green beans, cut	½ teaspoon mustard seeds
vinegar	1 tablespoon fresh parsley	into bite-sized pieces	½ teaspoon celery seeds

1. Put the green beans in a lightly greased Air Fryer basket and season with salt and pepper. 2. Cook for five minutes, or until tender, in the preheated Air Fryer at 200°C. 3. Shallots are added, and the mixture is gently stirred. 4. Mix the lime juice, vinegar, olive oil, and spices in a bowl. 5. Add dressing and goat cheese to the green beans salad. Serve refrigerated or at room temperature. Enjoy
Per Serving: Calories 208, Fat 16.39g; Sodium 361mg; Carbs 6.8g; Fibre 2.2g; Sugar 2.29g; Protein 9.59g

Cheesy Egg and Veggie Salad

Prep time: 10 minutes | Cook time: 15 minutes | Serves: 2

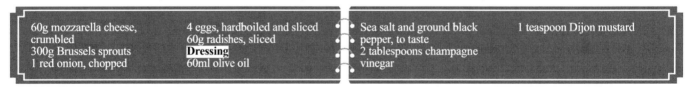

60g mozzarella cheese, crumbled	4 eggs, hardboiled and sliced	Sea salt and ground black	1 teaspoon Dijon mustard
300g Brussels sprouts	60g radishes, sliced	pepper, to taste	
1 red onion, chopped	**Dressing**	2 tablespoons champagne	
	60ml olive oil	vinegar	

1. To begin, preheat your air fryer to 195°C. 2. Add the radishes and Brussels sprouts to the frying basket. Apply cooking spray, then bake for 15 minutes. Give it 15 minutes to reach room temperature. 3. Combine the cheese and red onion with the veggies. 4. The dressing ingredients should be combined thoroughly after being combined. Serve with the hard-boiled eggs on top.
Per Serving: Calories 303, Fat 23.34g; Sodium 233mg; Carbs 8.64g; Fibre 2.4g; Sugar 3.47g; Protein 15.8g

Roasted Vegetable Salad with Kalamata Olives

Prep time: 10 minutes | Cook time: 20 minutes | Serves: 4

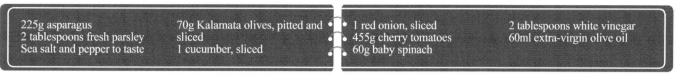

225g asparagus	70g Kalamata olives, pitted and	1 red onion, sliced	2 tablespoons white vinegar
2 tablespoons fresh parsley	sliced	455g cherry tomatoes	60ml extra-virgin olive oil
Sea salt and pepper to taste	1 cucumber, sliced	60g baby spinach	

1. Set your Air Fryer to 200°C to start. 2. In the basket of the Air Fryer that has been lightly greased, add the onion, cherry tomatoes, and asparagus. Bake for 5 to 6 minutes, occasionally tossing the basket. 3. Incorporate into a salad dish. Add the young spinach and cucumber. 4. In a small mixing bowl, combine the vinegar, olive oil, parsley, salt, and black pepper. Add Kalamata olives and dress your salad. 5. After thoroughly combining, serve.
Per Serving: Calories 166, Fat 7.99g; Sodium 255mg; Carbs 23.4g; Fibre 4.7g; Sugar 16.4g; Protein 3.39g

Brussels Sprouts and Pancetta Salad

Prep time: 10 minutes | Cook time: 35 minutes | Serves: 4

300g Brussels sprouts	50g baby rocket	**Lemon Vinaigrette**	2 tablespoons fresh lemon juice
1 tablespoon olive oil	1 shallot, thinly sliced	2 tablespoons extra virgin olive	1 tablespoon honey
Coarse sea salt and ground	100g pancetta, chopped	oil	
black pepper, to taste		1 teaspoon Dijon mustard	

1. Set your Air Fryer at 195°C to begin. 2. Brussels sprouts should be added to the frying basket. Cook for 15 minutes after rubbing with olive oil. Give it 15 minutes to reach room temperature. 3. Combine the baby rocket, shallot, salt, and black pepper with the Brussels sprouts. 4. All dressing components should be combined. Afterward, season your salad, add pancetta as a garnish, and serve it chilled.
Per Serving: Calories 183, Fat 9.95g; Sodium 114mg; Carbs 15.3g; Fibre 3.6g; Sugar 7.91g; Protein 10.76g

Healthy Spinach and Cauliflower Bowl

Prep time: 10 minutes | Cook time: 35 minutes | Serves: 4

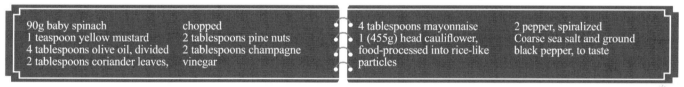

90g baby spinach	chopped	4 tablespoons mayonnaise	2 pepper, spiralized
1 teaspoon yellow mustard	2 tablespoons pine nuts	1 (455g) head cauliflower,	Coarse sea salt and ground
4 tablespoons olive oil, divided	2 tablespoons champagne	food-processed into rice-like	black pepper, to taste
2 tablespoons coriander leaves,	vinegar	particles	

1. Set the Air Fryer to 200°C to begin. 2. Put the peppers and cauliflower florets in the Air Fryer basket that has been lightly greased. Black pepper and salt should be added before cooking. Cook for 12 minutes, tossing once. 3. Add the baby spinach and toss. Add the champagne vinegar, mayonnaise, mustard, and olive oil. Pine nuts and fresh coriander are garnish options.
Per Serving: Calories 206, Fat 18.7g; Sodium 171mg; Carbs 7.93g; Fibre 2.6g; Sugar 3.26g; Protein 3.55g

Cheesy Tomatoes

Prep time: 10 minutes | Cook time: 20 minutes | Serves: 4

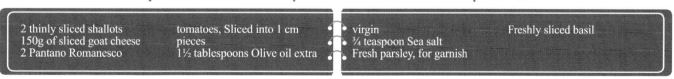

2 thinly sliced shallots	tomatoes, Sliced into 1 cm	virgin	Freshly sliced basil
150g of sliced goat cheese	pieces	¾ teaspoon Sea salt	
2 Pantano Romanesco	1½ tablespoons Olive oil extra	Fresh parsley, for garnish	

1. Set your air fryer to 195°C. 2. Using a paper towel, now dry each tomato slice. Basil leaves should be cut and sprinkled on each slice. 3. Add a slice of goat cheese on top. 4. Slices of shallot are placed on top; then olive oil is drizzled. 5. To the food basket of the air fryer, add the prepared tomato and feta "bits." 6. Cook for approximately 14 minutes in the Air Fryer. Finally, add the seasonings to taste and serve with fresh parsley leaves as a garnish. Enjoy!
Per Serving: Calories 232, Fat 17.52g; Sodium 686mg; Carbs 5.15g; Fibre 1g; Sugar 2.05g; Protein 14.05g

Chapter 3 Poultry Mains Recipes

Spicy Asian Turkey

Prep time: 10 minutes | Cook time: 35 minutes | Serves: 6

1 teaspoon pink Himalayan salt	900g turkey thighs	1 tablespoon Chinese rice vinegar	powder
¼ teaspoon Sichuan pepper	1 tablespoon chili sauce	1 teaspoon Chinese Five-spice	2 tablespoons soy sauce
1 tablespoon sesame oil	1 tablespoon mustard		

1. Turn on the air fryer to 180°C. 2. The turkey thighs should be liberally coated in sesame oil. Season them with spices. 3. Cook for 23 minutes, flipping occasionally. To achieve consistent cooking, make sure to operate in batches. 4. While waiting, mix the remaining ingredients in a prepared wok (or equivalent pan) over medium-high heat. Cook and whisk the sauce until it has almost completely reduced. 5. Add the cooked turkey thighs to the wok and give them a quick toss so the sauce can coat them. 6. 10 minutes should pass before slicing and serving the turkey. Enjoy!

Per Serving: Calories 233, Fat 10.6g; Sodium 2027mg; Carbs 5.52g; Fibre 0.8g; Sugar 3.62g; Protein 27.1g

Chicken Sausage Casserole with Courgette

Prep time: 10 minutes | Cook time: 50 minutes | Serves: 4

50g cheddar cheese, shredded	1 tomato, pureed	1 tablespoon fresh basil leaves,	200g courgette, spiralized
455g smoked chicken sausage, sliced	3 tablespoons Romano cheese, grated	1 tablespoon Italian seasoning mix	

1. The courgette should be salted and left to stand for 30 minutes before being dried with paper towels. 2. After that, coat a baking sheet with cooking spray and add the courgette. Add the Italian seasoning blend, tomato puree, cheese, and chicken sausage. 3. Bake for 11 minutes at 160°C in the prepared Air Fryer. 4. Add some grated Romano cheese on top. Cook for another five minutes, or until the cheese is melted and everything is completely cooked, at 200°C. 5. Add fresh basil leaves as a garnish.

Per Serving: Calories 629, Fat 53.79g; Sodium 515mg; Carbs 4.15g; Fibre 0.9g; Sugar 1.17g; Protein 30.65g

Cheesy Chicken with Peanuts

Prep time: 10 minutes | Cook time: 15 minutes | Serves: 4

1 teaspoon red pepper flakes	Sea salt and ground black pepper, to taste	½ teaspoon garlic powder
2 tablespoons peanuts, roasted and roughly chopped	2 tablespoons peanut oil	675g chicken tenderloins
		50g parmesan cheese, grated

1. Your Air Fryer should first be heated to 180°C. 2. On all sides, coat the chicken tenderloins with peanut oil. 3. Grated parmesan cheese, salt, black pepper, garlic powder, and red pepper flakes should all be completely combined in a mixing dish. Shake off any remaining coating after dredging the chicken in the cheese mixture. 4. The cooking basket should contain chicken tenderloins, cook for 12 to 13 minutes, until the centre is no longer pink. Work in batches; an instant-read thermometer must register a temperature of at least 75°C. 5. Serve with toasted peanuts as a garnish.

Per Serving: Calories 354, Fat 17.91g; Sodium 403mg; Carbs 6.35g; Fibre 0.7g; Sugar 1.46g; Protein 40.7g

Chicken with Hot Sauce

Prep time: 10 minutes | Cook time: 25 minutes | Serves: 8

2 teaspoons fine sea salt	**For the Sauce**	1 tablespoon lime juice	**For Serving**
240ml dill pickle juice	½ teaspoon fine sea salt	⅛ teaspoon garlic powder	Celery sticks
900g chicken drumsticks	80ml hot sauce		120ml Blue Cheese Dressing
	55g unsalted butter, melted		(here) or Ranch Dressing (here)

1. Chicken should be added to the dill pickle liquid in a big shallow dish. Place the chicken in the juice, cover, and refrigerate for two or overnight to marinate. 2. Spray avocado oil on the air fryer basket. Set the air fryer to 200°C for frying. 3. Dry the chicken with paper towels before liberally salting it. Cook in the air fryer for 20 minutes, flipping after 15 minutes, or until the internal temperature reaches 75°C. 4. Make the sauce in the meantime by combining all the ingredients in a large bowl and stirring until thoroughly blended. 5. Take the drumsticks out of the air fryer and put them in the sauce-filled bowl. Use tongs or a slotted spoon to transfer the drumsticks back to the air fryer basket and cook for additional five minutes after thoroughly coating them in the sauce. Serve with any additional blue cheese dressing, celery sticks, and sauce. 6. Extra drumsticks can be kept in the freezer for up to a month or the refrigerator for up to 4 days in an airtight container. Reheat for five minutes in an air fryer that has been warmed to 175°C, then raise the heat to 200°C and continue to cook for three to five minutes more, or until hot and crispy. 7. You can omit the step of marinating the chicken, but it adds a lot of flavour, so it's recommended for busy families.

Per Serving: Calories 295, Fat 22.21g; Sodium 1344mg; Carbs 1.65g; Fibre 0.3g; Sugar 0.88g; Protein 21.1g

Turkey Balls in Lettuce Cups

Prep time: 10 minutes | Cook time: 15 minutes | Serves: 6

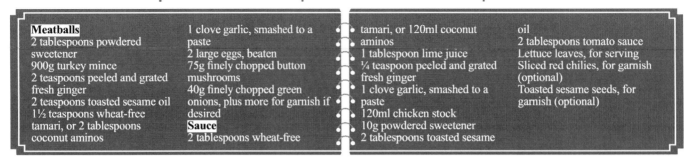

Meatballs	1 clove garlic, smashed to a paste	tamari, or 120ml coconut aminos	oil
2 tablespoons powdered sweetener	2 large eggs, beaten	1 tablespoon lime juice	2 tablespoons tomato sauce
900g turkey mince	75g finely chopped button mushrooms	¼ teaspoon peeled and grated fresh ginger	Lettuce leaves, for serving
2 teaspoons peeled and grated fresh ginger	40g finely chopped green onions, plus more for garnish if desired	1 clove garlic, smashed to a paste	Sliced red chilies, for garnish (optional)
2 teaspoons toasted sesame oil	**Sauce**	120ml chicken stock	Toasted sesame seeds, for garnish (optional)
1½ teaspoons wheat-free tamari, or 2 tablespoons coconut aminos	2 tablespoons wheat-free	10g powdered sweetener	
		2 tablespoons toasted sesame	

1. Set the air fryer temperature to 175°C for frying. 2. In a large basin, combine all the meatball ingredients with your hands to thoroughly incorporate them. Using a pie plate that will fit inside an air fryer, place the mixture into approximately twelve 4 cm meatballs, allowing room between each one. 3. To prepare the sauce, put all of the ingredients in a medium bowl and whisk to incorporate. Over the meatballs, pour the sauce. 4. Place the pan in the air fryer and cook for 15 minutes, rotating the meatballs after 6 minutes, or until the internal temperature reaches 75°C. 5. Place a few lettuce leaves and a few meatballs on a serving plate to serve. If desired, garnish with sesame seeds, green onions, or red chile slices. 6. For up to 4 days in the fridge or a month in the freezer, store leftovers in an airtight container. Reheat for five minutes, or until thoroughly heated, in an air fryer set to 175°C.
Per Serving: Calories 1035, Fat 95.61g; Sodium 306mg; Carbs 8.2g; Fibre 2.7g; Sugar 3.92g; Protein 36.67g

Herbed Spicy Chicken Drumsticks

Prep time: 10 minutes | Cook time: 40 minutes | Serves: 6

6 chicken drumsticks	3 tablespoons olive oil	150g hot sauce	1 teaspoon dried thyme
Sauce	3 tablespoons tamari sauce	½ teaspoon dried oregano	

1. Spray a nonstick cooking spray on the sides and bottom of the cooking basket. 2. Drumsticks of chicken should be cooked for 35 minutes at 195°C, turning them over halfway through. 3. In the meantime, warm the tamari sauce, spicy sauce, olive oil, thyme, and oregano in a frying pan over medium heat; reserve. 4. Chicken drumsticks should be prepared; drizzle sauce over them, toss to thoroughly coat, and serve.
Per Serving: Calories 280, Fat 18.7g; Sodium 401mg; Carbs 2.74g; Fibre 0.7g; Sugar 1.4g; Protein 24.09g

Thai-Style Duck Breasts with Candy Onions

Prep time: 10 minutes | Cook time: 25 minutes | Serves: 4

675g duck breasts, skin removed	½ teaspoon cayenne pepper	1 tablespoon Thai red curry paste	¼ small pack of coriander, chopped
1 teaspoon salt	⅓ teaspoon black pepper	185g candy onions, halved	
	½ teaspoon smoked paprika		

1. Put the duck breasts between two pieces of foil and pound them with a rolling pin until they are 1 inch thick. 2. Set your Air Fryer to 200°C. 3. Salt, cayenne pepper, black pepper, paprika, and red curry paste should all be applied to the duck breasts. Duck breasts should be placed in the cooking basket. 4. Cook for 11 to 12 minutes. Add the candied onions on top, then simmer for an additional 10 to 11 minutes. 5. Enjoy your dish with coriander as a garnish!
Per Serving: Calories 442, Fat 20g; Sodium 713mg; Carbs 26.34g; Fibre 2.5g; Sugar 21.7g; Protein 37.3g

Herbed Chicken with Roma Tomatoes

Prep time: 10 minutes | Cook time: 45 minutes | Serves: 8

2 tablespoons fresh parsley, minced	minced	freshly ground	1.3kg chicken breasts, bone-in
1 teaspoon fresh basil, minced	4 medium-sized Roma tomatoes, halved	½ teaspoon salt	
1 teaspoon fresh rosemary,	½ teaspoon black pepper,	1 teaspoon cayenne pepper	
		2 teaspoons olive oil, melted	

1. Set your Air Fryer to 185°C to begin. One teaspoon of olive oil should be brushed on the frying basket. 2. Sprinkle each of the aforementioned seasonings over the chicken breasts. 3. Cook chicken breasts for 25 minutes, or until they are just starting to brown. Work in groups. 4. Place the tomatoes in the cooking basket and drizzle the last teaspoon of olive oil over them. Use sea salt to season. 5. Cook the tomatoes for 10 minutes at 175°C, shaking the pan halfway through. Add chicken breasts to the dish. Good appetite!
Per Serving: Calories 315, Fat 17.04g; Sodium 256mg; Carbs 2.76g; Fibre 0.9g; Sugar 1.65g; Protein 36.1g

Herbed Bacon Wrapped Chicken Breasts

Prep time: 10 minutes | Cook time: 15 minutes | Serves: 4

1 teaspoon fresh rosemary leaves	½ teaspoon red pepper flakes	Sprigs of fresh rosemary, for garnish (optional)	3 teaspoons fine sea salt
10g roughly chopped fresh chives	4 (100g) boneless, skinless chicken breasts, pounded to ½ cm thick (see Tip)	4 cloves garlic, peeled	1 teaspoon dried rubbed sage
1 teaspoon ground fennel	8 slices bacon	2 tablespoons lemon juice	
		15g fresh parsley leaves	

1. Spray avocado oil on the air fryer basket. Preheat the air fryer to 170°C. 2. In a food processor, blend the parsley, chives, garlic, lemon juice, salt, sage, rosemary, fennel, and red pepper flakes until a paste forms. 3. On a cutting board, arrange the chicken breasts and cover the tops with the paste. Roll each breast up like a jelly roll, short end facing you, to form a log, and fasten it with toothpicks. 4. Each chicken breast log should have two slices of bacon wrapped around it. The bacon is fastened using toothpicks. 5. The chicken breast logs should be placed in the air fryer basket and cooked for 5 minutes before being turned over and cooked for an additional 5 minutes. Cook the bacon for a further 5 minutes at 200°C or until it is crisp. 6. Before serving, take out the toothpicks and, if like, garnish with fresh sprigs of rosemary. 7. For up to 4 days in the fridge or a month in the freezer, store leftovers in an airtight container. Reheat in a preheated 175°C air fryer for 5 minutes, then cook for two minutes at 200°C to crisp the bacon.
Advice: To save time and make this recipe even simpler, I asked my butcher to pound the chicken breasts to the correct thickness.
Per Serving: Calories 511, Fat 35.26g; Sodium 2500mg; Carbs 23.33g; Fibre 0.7g; Sugar 1.01g; Protein 25.72g

Paprika Chicken Legs with Turnip

Prep time: 10 minutes | Cook time: 30 minutes | Serves: 3

½ teaspoon ground black pepper	1 teaspoon butter, melted	455g chicken legs	1 teaspoon paprika
	1 turnip, trimmed and sliced	1 teaspoon Himalayan salt	

1. Spritz the sides and bottom of the cooking basket with a nonstick cooking spray. 2. Season the chicken legs with salt, paprika, and ground black pepper. 3. Cook at 185°C for 10 minutes. Increase the temperature to 195°C. 4. Drizzle turnip slices with melted butter and transfer them to the cooking basket with the chicken. Cook the turnips and chicken for 15 minutes more, flipping them halfway through the cooking time. 5. As for the chicken, an instant-read thermometer should read at least 75°C. 6. Serve and enjoy!
Per Serving: Calories 197, Fat 7.77g; Sodium 934mg; Carbs 1.06g; Fibre 0.5g; Sugar 0.27g; Protein 29.1g

Cheese Turkey Burgers with Bacon

Prep time: 10 minutes | Cook time: 30 minutes | Serves: 4

4 tablespoons tomato ketchup	2 tablespoons vermouth	Sea salt and ground black pepper, to taste	2 tablespoons fish sauce
4 tablespoons mayonnaise	2 strips bacon, sliced	1 teaspoon red pepper flakes	
4 (100g) slices Cheddar cheese	455g turkey mince	2 garlic cloves, minced	
4 lettuce leaves	½ shallot, minced		

1. Set your Air Fryer to 200°C to begin. Vermouth should be brushed on the bacon. Cook for three minutes. 2. Cook the bacon for an additional three minutes after flipping it. 3. The turkey mince, shallots, garlic, fish sauce, salt, black pepper, and red pepper flakes should then be completely combined. Four burger patties made from the meat combination. 4. Bake at 185°C for 10 minutes in the preheated Air Fryer. Cook them for a further 10 minutes on the other side. 5. Serve the turkey burgers immediately with the ketchup, mayonnaise, bacon, cheese, and lettuce.
Per Serving: Calories 683, Fat 57.6g; Sodium 1221mg; Carbs 8.65g; Fibre 1.1g; Sugar 4.95g; Protein 29.7g

Turkey Tenderloins with Pickles

Prep time: 10 minutes | Cook time: 50 minutes | Serves: 4

½ teaspoon xanthan gum	1 teaspoon Italian seasoning mix	mustard	4 pickles, sliced
4 tablespoons tomato ketchup	240ml turkey stock	1 tablespoon olive oil	
4 tablespoons mayonnaise	1 tablespoon Dijon-style	Sea salt and ground black pepper, to taste	
455g turkey tenderloins			

1. Olive oil and mustard are rubbed into the turkey tenderloins. Add Italian spice blend, black pepper, and salt to taste. 2. Cook the turkey tenderloins for 30 minutes at 175°C, turning them over halfway. Before slicing, allow them to rest for 5 to 7 minutes. 3. The drippings from the roasted turkey should be placed in a saucepan to make the gravy. Bring to a boil after adding the turkey stock. 4. Add the xanthan gum and blend by whisking. Allow to simmer for 5 to 10 more minutes or until it begins to thicken. As it cools, gravy will get even thicker. 5. Serve turkey tenderloins with pickles, mayonnaise, tomato ketchup, and gravy. Dispense and savor!
Per Serving: Calories 701, Fat 61.1g; Sodium 502mg; Carbs 4.81g; Fibre 1.2g; Sugar 2.16g; Protein 31.3g

Delicious Chicken Pockets

Prep time: 15 minutes | Cook time: 25 minutes | Serves: 4

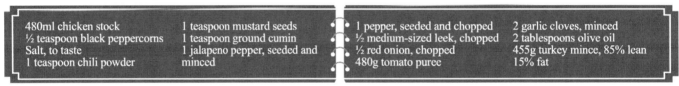

230g unsalted butter, softened (or butter-flavoured coconut oil for dairy-free)
2 tablespoons lemon juice
2 tablespoons plus 1 teaspoon

chopped fresh parsley leaves, divided, plus more for garnish
2 tablespoons chopped fresh tarragon leaves
3 cloves garlic, minced

1 teaspoon fine sea salt, divided
4 (100g) boneless, skinless chicken breasts
2 large eggs
150g parmesan, grated

1 teaspoon ground black pepper
Sprig of fresh parsley, for garnish
Lemon slices, for serving

1. Spray avocado oil on the air fryer basket. Set the air fryer to 175°C for frying. 2. Butter, lemon juice, 2 teaspoons of parsley, 2 tablespoons of tarragon, ¼ teaspoon of salt, and 2 tablespoons of garlic should all be combined in a medium-sized bowl. Cover and put in the refrigerator to solidify for 7 minutes. 3. One of the chicken breasts should be placed on a chopping board while the butter mixture chills. Make a 2.5 cm-wide incision at the top of the breast with a sharp knife held parallel to a cutting board. Leave a 2.5 cm border on the sides and bottom and carefully cut a huge pocket into the breast. Repeat on the remaining three breasts. 4. Each chicken breast should have a quarter of the butter mixture stuffed within it. Use toothpicks to close the openings. 5. In a small dish that is shallow, beat the eggs. Add the remaining 1 teaspoon of parsley, the remaining ¾ teaspoon of salt, and the pepper to the parmesan in another shallow dish. 6. One at a time, dredge the chicken breasts in the mixture of parmesan and flour after dipping them in the egg and shaking off any excess. To create a beautiful crust, massage the parmesan with your hands onto each breast. Dip it once more in the egg and pork grit for a thicker coating. As soon as you're done, spritz each chicken breast with avocado oil and put it in the basket of the air fryer. 7. Cook the chicken in the air fryer for 15 minutes, then flip the breasts over and cook for additional 10 minutes, or until the chicken is 75°C inside and the crust is golden brown. 8. Serve with lemon slices on the side and garnished with chopped fresh parsley and a sprig of parsley. 9. Store leftovers in an airtight container in the refrigerator for up to 4 days or in the freezer for up to a month. Reheat for five minutes, or until thoroughly heated, in an air fryer set to 175°C.
Per Serving: Calories 633, Fat 45.25g; Sodium 1068mg; Carbs 3.66g; Fibre 0.4g; Sugar 0.58g; Protein 45.27g

Traditional Spicy Turkey with Leek

Prep time: 10 minutes | Cook time: 40 minutes | Serves: 4

480ml chicken stock
½ teaspoon black peppercorns
Salt, to taste
1 teaspoon chili powder

1 teaspoon mustard seeds
1 teaspoon ground cumin
1 jalapeno pepper, seeded and minced

1 pepper, seeded and chopped
½ medium-sized leek, chopped
½ red onion, chopped
480g tomato puree

2 garlic cloves, minced
2 tablespoons olive oil
455g turkey mince, 85% lean 15% fat

1. Set your Air Fryer to 185°C to begin. 2. In a baking pan, combine the leeks, onion, garlic, and peppers. Drizzle the olive oil evenly over the top. Cook for 4 to 6 minutes. 3. Add the turkey mince. Cook for a further 6 minutes, or until the meat no longer pink. 4. The baking pan should now contain the tomato puree, 240ml chicken stock, salt, black peppercorns, chili powder, mustard seeds, and cumin. Stirring every 7 to 10 minutes, the cooking time is 24 minutes.
Per Serving: Calories 765, Fat 70.79g; Sodium 467mg; Carbs 16.89g; Fibre 3.5g; Sugar 7.89g; Protein 121.7g

Crispy Chicken Drumsticks with Chives

Prep time: 10 minutes | Cook time: 30 minutes | Serves: 3

1 heaping tablespoon fresh chives, chopped
1 teaspoon garlic paste

½ teaspoon ground white pepper
1 teaspoon seasoning salt

1 whole egg + 1 egg white
6 chicken drumsticks
1 teaspoon rosemary

35g almond meal

1. Set your Air Fryer to 200°C to begin. 2. In a small bowl, combine the rosemary, garlic paste, salt, white pepper, and almond meal. 3. The eggs should be beaten till foamy in another basin. 4. The chicken should be coated with flour mixture once more after being dipped in beaten eggs and flour mixture. 5. Cook the chicken drumsticks for 22 minutes. Serve hot with chives as a garnish.
Per Serving: Calories 464, Fat 11.41g; Sodium 1107mg; Carbs 0.78g; Fibre 0.2g; Sugar 0.11g; Protein 86.3g

Dijon-glazed chicken sausage

Prep time: 10 minutes | Cook time: 20 minutes | Serves: 4

1 tablespoon balsamic vinegar
4 chicken sausages

60g mayonnaise
2 tablespoons Dijon mustard

½ teaspoon dried rosemary

1. Place the sausages in the Air Fryer after arranging them on the grill pan. 2. The sausages should be grilled for around 13 minutes at 175°C. Halfway through cooking, turn them. 3. In the interim, make the sauce by whisking the remaining ingredients together. 4. Serve cooled Dijon sauce beside the warm sausages. Enjoy!
Per Serving: Calories 129, Fat 10.18g; Sodium 454mg; Carbs 4.4g; Fibre 1.3g; Sugar 0.8g; Protein 6.46g

Cheese Chicken Breasts in Wine Sauce

Prep time: 10 minutes | Cook time: 35 minutes | Serves: 6

1 teaspoon freshly cracked black pepper	35g Parmigiano-Reggiano cheese, freshly grated	breasts, cut into small pieces	minced
2 tablespoons olive oil	3 cloves garlic, minced	80ml cooking wine (such as Sauvignon Blanc)	1 teaspoon fresh rosemary leaves, minced
1 teaspoon seasoned salt	3 boneless and skinless chicken	1 teaspoon fresh sage leaves,	

1. In a sauté pan, warm the oil over a moderate temperature. The garlic should then be sautéed until just fragrant. 2. After that, turn off the heat and add the cooking wine. Once the seasonings have been added, mix everything together thoroughly. Put this mixture in a baking dish that has been lightly greased. 3. Add the chicken breast pieces and roast for 32 minutes at 160°C in the preheated Air Fryer. 4. After serving the chicken on separate dishes, top with grated cheese.
Per Serving: Calories 231, Fat 9.64g; Sodium 549mg; Carbs 1.81g; Fibre 0.2g; Sugar 0.16g; Protein 32.39g

Peppercorns Chicken Breasts

Prep time: 10 minutes | Cook time: 40 minutes | Serves: 4

¾ teaspoon fine sea salt	chopped	stock	1 teaspoon cumin powder
1½ tablespoons Worcester sauce	1 pepper, deveined and chopped	2 chicken breasts, cut into halves	1½ teaspoons sesame oil
75g of spring onions, chopped	1 tablespoon tamari sauce	¼ teaspoon mixed peppercorns, freshly cracked	
1 Serrano pepper, deveined and	480ml of roasted vegetable		

1. Deep-fry the chicken breasts in the vegetable stock for 10 minutes, then turn down the heat and simmer for an additional 10 minutes. 2. After that, let the chicken cool somewhat and shred it with two forks or a stand mixer. 3. Toss the shredded chicken with the salt, cracked peppercorns, cumin, sesame oil and the Worcester sauce; air-fry them at 195°C for 18 minutes; check for doneness. 4. The remaining ingredients are prepared in the meantime over a medium flame in a nonstick frying pan. 5. The onions and peppers should be cooked until soft and aromatic. 6. After turning off the heat, add the chicken shreds and stir everything together. Serve immediately.
Per Serving: Calories 1229, Fat 124.5g; Sodium 613mg; Carbs 4.88g; Fibre 1.1g; Sugar 1.39g; Protein 31.79g

Crispy Chicken with Lemon Butter Sauce

Prep time: 10 minutes | Cook time: 10 minutes | Serves: 2

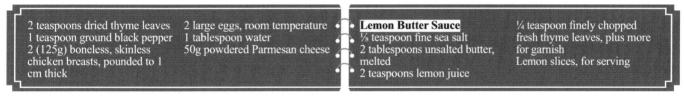

2 teaspoons dried thyme leaves	2 large eggs, room temperature	**Lemon Butter Sauce**	¼ teaspoon finely chopped fresh thyme leaves, plus more for garnish
1 teaspoon ground black pepper	1 tablespoon water	⅛ teaspoon fine sea salt	
2 (125g) boneless, skinless chicken breasts, pounded to 1 cm thick	50g powdered Parmesan cheese	2 tablespoons unsalted butter, melted	Lemon slices, for serving
		2 teaspoons lemon juice	

1. Spray avocado oil on the air fryer basket. the air fryer to 200°C before using. 2. In a small bowl, beat the eggs. Add the water, and whisk thoroughly. 3. Mix the Parmesan, thyme, and pepper thoroughly in a different shallow dish. 4. Chicken breasts should be coated on both sides with the Parmesan mixture after being dipped in the eggs one at a time and letting any excess drop off. Place the breaded chicken in the air fryer basket as soon as you're done. 5. The chicken should be cooked thoroughly and the internal temperature should reach 75°C. After 5 minutes in the air fryer, the chicken should be flipped and cooked for an additional 5 minutes. 6. Make the lemon butter sauce while the chicken cooks by combining all the ingredients in a small dish and stirring until smooth. 7. Place the chicken on a plate and top it with the sauce. Serve with lemon slices and fresh thyme that has been chopped. 8. For up to four days, keep leftovers in the refrigerator in an airtight container. Reheat for five minutes, or until well heated, in an air fryer set to 200°C.
Per Serving: Calories 547, Fat 32.19g; Sodium 1353mg; Carbs 7.24g; Fibre 0.6g; Sugar 0.86g; Protein 55.39g

Paprika Turkey with Tarragon

Prep time: 10 minutes | Cook time: 40 minutes | Serves: 6

1 tablespoon fresh tarragon leaves, chopped	2 tablespoons olive oil	2 tablespoons dry white wine	to taste
	900g turkey tenderloins	Salt and ground black pepper,	1 teaspoon smoked paprika

1. Olive oil should be brushed on the turkey tenderloins. Add paprika, black pepper, and salt for seasoning. 2. Add the white wine and tarragon after that. 3. Cook the turkey tenderloins for 30 minutes at 175°C, turning them over halfway. Before cutting and serving, give them a five to nine-minute rest. Enjoy
Per Serving: Calories 788, Fat 71.8g; Sodium 68mg; Carbs 4.18g; Fibre 0.3g; Sugar 0.43g; Protein 29.34g

Chicken and Ham Meatballs with Dijon Sauce

Prep time: 10 minutes | Cook time: 15 minutes | Serves: 4

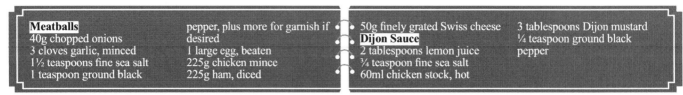

Meatballs	pepper, plus more for garnish if	50g finely grated Swiss cheese	3 tablespoons Dijon mustard
40g chopped onions	desired	**Dijon Sauce**	¼ teaspoon ground black
3 cloves garlic, minced	1 large egg, beaten	2 tablespoons lemon juice	pepper
1½ teaspoons fine sea salt	225g chicken mince	¾ teaspoon fine sea salt	
1 teaspoon ground black	225g ham, diced	60ml chicken stock, hot	

1. Spray avocado oil on the air fryer basket. the air fryer to 200°C before using. 2. With your hands, thoroughly combine all the meatball ingredients in a large basin. Make twelve 5 cm balls out of the beef mixture. Leave room between the meatballs when you place them in the air fryer basket, and cook for 15 minutes, or until the meatballs are thoroughly cooked and the internal temperature reaches 75°C. 3. Make the sauce in the meantime by combining all the ingredients in a small bowl and stirring until thoroughly blended. 4. The meatballs should be arranged on top of the sauce in a serving bowl. If preferred, garnish with fresh thyme leaves and pounded black pepper. 5. Meatballs can be kept in the freezer or refrigerator for up to a month when sealed in an airtight container. Reheat for four minutes, or until well heated, in an air fryer set to 175°C.
Per Serving: Calories 247, Fat 12.6g; Sodium 2487mg; Carbs 5.93g; Fibre 0.9g; Sugar 0.81g; Protein 27.76g

Piri Piri Chicken Wings

Prep time: 10 minutes | Cook time: 90 minutes | Serves: 6

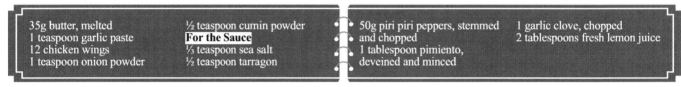

35g butter, melted	½ teaspoon cumin powder	50g piri piri peppers, stemmed	1 garlic clove, chopped
1 teaspoon garlic paste	**For the Sauce**	and chopped	2 tablespoons fresh lemon juice
12 chicken wings	⅓ teaspoon sea salt	1 tablespoon pimiento,	
1 teaspoon onion powder	½ teaspoon tarragon	deveined and minced	

1. Use a steamer basket over a saucepan of boiling water to steam the chicken wings; then turn down the heat. 2. The wings should now be steam-cooked for ten minutes over a moderate heat. Butter, onion powder, cumin powder, and garlic paste should be mixed with the wings. 3.The chicken wings should be allowed to reach room temperature. After that, chill them for 45 to 50 minutes. 4. Make care to rotate them halfway through roasting in the preheated Air Fryer at 165°C for 25 to 30 minutes. 5. Prepare the sauce by combining all of the sauce's components in a food processor while the chicken wings are cooking. Add the prepared Piri Piri Sauce to the wings before serving.
Per Serving: Calories 132, Fat 7.88g; Sodium 223mg; Carbs 1.9g; Fibre 0.3g; Sugar 0.65g; Protein 13.16g

Pepperoni Chicken Pizza

Prep time: 10 minutes | Cook time: 20 minutes | Serves: 4

16 slices pepperoni	shredded	4 small-sized chicken breasts,
Salt and pepper, to savor	1½ tablespoons dried oregano	boneless and skinless
60g mozzarella cheese,	1½ tablespoons olive oil	60ml pizza sauce

1. Apply a rolling pin to the chicken breast and gently flatten it. 2. Divide the ingredients among four chicken fillets. Roll the chicken fillets with the stuffing and seal them using a small skewer or two toothpicks. 3. Roast in the Air Fryer grill pan that has been warmed to 185°C for or 13 to 15 minutes.
Per Serving: Calories 662, Fat 40.91g; Sodium 522mg; Carbs 3.16g; Fibre 0.7g; Sugar 1.5g; Protein 66.76g

Simple Turkey Breast for Thanksgiving

Prep time: 5 minutes | Cook time: 30 minutes | Serves: 4

1 teaspoon ground black pepper	1½ teaspoons fine sea salt	1 teaspoon chopped fresh	1 (900g) turkey breast
1 teaspoon chopped fresh	3 tablespoons ghee or unsalted	tarragon	
rosemary leaves	butter, melted	1 teaspoon chopped fresh	
1 teaspoon chopped fresh sage	3 tablespoons Dijon mustard	thyme leaves	

1. Spray avocado oil on the air fryer. the air fryer to 200°C before using. 2. Stir the herbs, salt, and pepper together thoroughly in a small bowl. Season the turkey breast liberally with the spice all over. 3. Stir the ghee and Dijon together in a separate little bowl. The turkey breast should be covered in the ghee mixture on all sides. 4. The turkey breast should be cooked for 30 minutes, or until it reaches an internal temperature of 75°C in the air fryer basket. After moving the breast to a cutting board, give it 10 minutes to rest before slicing it into 2.5 cm-thick pieces. 5. For up to 4 days in the fridge or a month in the freezer, store leftovers in an airtight container. Reheat for four minutes, or until thoroughly warmed, in an air fryer set to 175°C.
Per Serving: Calories 177, Fat 11.37g; Sodium 1048mg; Carbs 1.45g; Fibre 0.8g; Sugar 0.12g; Protein 16.91g

Chicken with Herb Sauce

Prep time: 10 minutes | Cook time: 20 minutes | Serves: 4

½ teaspoon whole grain mustard	½ teaspoon smoked paprika	Salt and freshly cracked black pepper, to taste	120ml white wine
1½ tablespoons mayonnaise	455g chicken thighs, boneless, skinless, and cut into pieces	2 heaping tablespoons fresh rosemary, minced	120g full-fat sour cream
3 cloves garlic, minced	1½ tablespoons olive oil		1 teaspoon ground cinnamon

1. First, combine the chicken thighs with the white wine and olive oil in a mixing bowl and swirl to coat. 2. Then add the garlic, smoked paprika, cinnamon powder, salt, and black pepper; cover and chill for one to three hours. 3. Set the Air Fryer to 190°C to cook. The chicken thighs should be roasted for 18 minutes, flipping once halfway through. 4. Sour cream, whole grain mustard, mayonnaise, and rosemary are combined to form the sauce. Enjoy the chicken together with the mustard or rosemary sauce!
Per Serving: Calories 349, Fat 25.8g; Sodium 180mg; Carbs 8.16g; Fibre 0.9g; Sugar 1.12g; Protein 20.61g

Cheese Chicken Burgers

Prep time: 10 minutes | Cook time: 25 minutes | Serves: 4

1 palmful dried basil	2 teaspoons dried marjoram	⅓ teaspoon red pepper flakes, crushed	⅓ teaspoon porcini powder
2 teaspoons dried parsley flakes	⅓ teaspoon ancho chili powder	1 teaspoon freshly cracked black pepper	1 teaspoon sea salt flakes
½ teaspoon onion powder	**Toppings**		455g chicken mince
35g parmesan cheese, grated	2 teaspoons cumin powder		

1. Grease the frying basket for an Air Fryer generously with vegetable oil. 2. Combine the chicken flesh and all of the ingredients in a mixing bowl. Grate some parmesan cheese over the four patties after shaping. 3. Working in batches, cook the chicken burgers in the preheated Air Fryer for 15 minutes at 175°C, flipping them once. 4. Serve with your preferred toppings.
Per Serving: Calories 349, Fat 25.8g; Sodium 180mg; Carbs 8.16g; Fibre 0.9g; Sugar 1.12g; Protein 20.61g

Chicken Breasts in White Wine Sauce

Prep time: 10 minutes | Cook time: 30 minutes | Serves: 4

3 medium-sized boneless chicken breasts, cut into small pieces	½ teaspoon grated fresh ginger	1½ tablespoons sesame oil	120ml dry white wine
	80ml coconut milk	3 green garlic stalks, finely chopped	⅓ teaspoon freshly cracked black pepper
	½ teaspoon sea salt flakes		

1. In a deep sauté pan over medium heat, warm the sesame oil. The green garlic should then be sautéed until slightly aromatic. 2. White wine and coconut milk are added after the pan has been taken off the heat. Add the fresh ginger, sea salt, and freshly cracked black pepper next. Put a baking dish with this mixture in it. 3. Add the chicken bits and stir. 4. Cook for 28 minutes at 170°C in the air fryer that has been preheated. Eat warm after serving on individual plates.
Per Serving: Calories 349, Fat 25.8g; Sodium 180mg; Carbs 8.16g; Fibre 0.9g; Sugar 1.12g; Protein 20.61g

Chicken Strips with Butter Sauce

Prep time: 5 minutes | Cook time: 10 minutes | Serves: 4

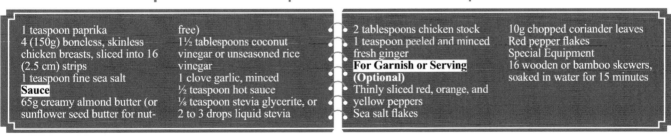

1 teaspoon paprika	free)	2 tablespoons chicken stock	10g chopped coriander leaves
4 (150g) boneless, skinless chicken breasts, sliced into 16 (2.5 cm) strips	1½ tablespoons coconut vinegar or unseasoned rice vinegar	1 teaspoon peeled and minced fresh ginger	Red pepper flakes
		For Garnish or Serving (Optional)	Special Equipment
1 teaspoon fine sea salt	1 clove garlic, minced		16 wooden or bamboo skewers, soaked in water for 15 minutes
Sauce	½ teaspoon hot sauce	Thinly sliced red, orange, and yellow peppers	
65g creamy almond butter (or sunflower seed butter for nut-	⅛ teaspoon stevia glycerite, or 2 to 3 drops liquid stevia	Sea salt flakes	

1. Spray avocado oil on the air fryer basket. Set the air fryer to 200°C for frying. 2. The skewers should be threaded with chicken strips. Salt and paprika should be used to season everything. The chicken skewers should be placed in the air fryer basket and fried for 5 minutes, turned over, and cooked for an additional 5 minutes, or until the internal temperature of the chicken reaches 75°C. 3. Make the sauce in a medium bowl while the chicken skewers cook by stirring the ingredients together until thoroughly blended. To your pleasure, taste and adjust the sweetness and heat. 4. If preferred, serve the chicken with sliced peppers and garnish with coriander, red pepper flakes, and salt flakes. Sauce should be served separately. 5. For up to 4 days in the refrigerator or a month in the freezer, store leftovers in an airtight container. Reheat for three minutes on each side, or until well heated, in an air fryer set to 175°C.
Per Serving: Calories 280, Fat 13.56g; Sodium 1166mg; Carbs 3.73g; Fibre 1.2g; Sugar 1.07g; Protein 34.81g

Cheese Chicken Veggie Frittata

Prep time: 10 minutes | Cook time: 25 minutes | Serves: 4

1 teaspoon sea salt	375g leftover vegetables	280g cooked chicken, shredded	½ red onion, thinly sliced
⅓ teaspoon red pepper flakes, crushed	½ teaspoon dried marjoram	or chopped	3 eggs, whisked
	40g mozzarella cheese, grated	3 cloves garlic, finely minced	

1. Use a large spatula to easily combine the ingredients listed above, cheese excluded. 2. Scrape the mixture into a baking dish that has already been buttered. 3. Set your Air Fryer for 22 minutes of cooking at 185°C. until everything is bubbling, air fry. 4. Serve hot with shredded cheese on top.
Per Serving: Calories 1334, Fat 142.42g; Sodium 782mg; Carbs 1.84g; Fibre 0.1g; Sugar 0.74g; Protein 21.08g

Minty Turkey Meatballs

Prep time: 10 minutes | Cook time: 15 minutes | Serves: 6

1 teaspoon onion powder	1½ teaspoons garlic paste	455g turkey mince	25g grated Pecorino Romano
55g melted butter	1 teaspoon crushed red pepper	1 tablespoon fresh mint leaves,	
¾ teaspoon fine sea salt	flakes	finely chopped	

1. All of the aforementioned ingredients should be put into a mixing bowl and blended thoroughly. 2. Make meatballs the size of golf balls using an ice cream scoop. 3. Working in batches, air fry the meatballs for about 7 minutes at 195°C, stirring them to achieve equal cooking. 4. Serve with a straightforward tomato sauce and fresh basil leaves as a garnish.
Per Serving: Calories 440, Fat 41.6g; Sodium 402mg; Carbs 0.65g; Fibre 0.1g; Sugar 0.08g; Protein 14.94g

Easy Turkey Patties with Chive Mayo

Prep time: 10 minutes | Cook time: 20 minutes | Serves: 6

For the Turkey Sliders	20g pickled jalapeno, chopped	pepper, to savor	1 teaspoon salt
1-2 cloves garlic, minced	1 tablespoon oyster sauce	**For the Chive Mayo**	
1 tablespoon chopped fresh coriander	2 tablespoons chopped spring onions	1 tablespoon chives 240g mayonnaise	
375g turkey mince	Sea salt and ground black	Zest of 1 lime	

1. Combine all of the ingredients for the turkey patties in a mixing bowl. 2. Shape the ingredients into 6 slider patties of the same size. Then, air-fry them for 15 minutes at 185°C. 3. While waiting, combine the remaining ingredients for the chive mayonnaise. Serve hot.
Per Serving: Calories 726, Fat 67.01g; Sodium 834mg; Carbs 3.54g; Fibre 0.8g; Sugar 1.07g; Protein 25.96g

Thai - Style Turkey Drumsticks

Prep time: 10 minutes | Cook time: 25 minutes | Serves: 2

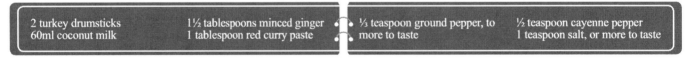

2 turkey drumsticks	1½ tablespoons minced ginger	⅓ teaspoon ground pepper, to	½ teaspoon cayenne pepper
60ml coconut milk	1 tablespoon red curry paste	more to taste	1 teaspoon salt, or more to taste

1. First, put the turkey drumsticks and all the other ingredients in the refrigerator and let them marinate for the entire night. 2. Make sure to rotate the turkey drumsticks over halfway through the 23-minute cooking time at 195°C. 3. Serve with the salad on the side.
Per Serving: Calories 263, Fat 12.25g; Sodium 2307mg; Carbs 3.3g; Fibre 0.3g; Sugar 2.07g; Protein 32.91g

Chicken Sausage and Egg Cups

Prep time: 10 minutes | Cook time: 20 minutes | Serves: 6

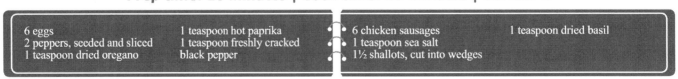

6 eggs	1 teaspoon hot paprika	6 chicken sausages	1 teaspoon dried basil
2 peppers, seeded and sliced	1 teaspoon freshly cracked	1 teaspoon sea salt	
1 teaspoon dried oregano	black pepper	1½ shallots, cut into wedges	

1. Divide the pepper, shallot, and chicken sausage among the six ramekins. Cooking at 155°C for 12 minutes. 2. Crack one egg into each ramekin at this time. Add salt, cracked black pepper, fiery paprika, basil, and oregano to the eggs. 3. Cook at 210°C for a further five minutes.
Per Serving: Calories 212, Fat 14.8g; Sodium 743mg; Carbs 5.95g; Fibre 1.4g; Sugar 1.49g; Protein 14.67g

Tangy Turkey Drumsticks

Prep time: 10 minutes | Cook time: 45 minutes | Serves: 6

80ml tamari sauce	2 sprigs rosemary, chopped	3 turkey drumsticks	blend
80ml pear or apple cider vinegar	1½ tablespoons olive oil	1½ tablespoons yellow mustard	A pinch of salt and pepper, to taste
	½ lemon, juiced	1½ tablespoons herb seasoning	

1. Place each ingredient in a mixing bowl. Allow it to marinade all night. 2. To cook, set your air fryer to 180°C. 3. Drumsticks from a turkey are roasted for 28 minutes at 180°C after being salted and peppered. One drumstick is cooked at a time. 4. After 14 minutes, stop the machine and turn the turkey drumstick.
Per Serving: Calories 169, Fat 9.14g; Sodium 863mg; Carbs 4.31g; Fibre 0.8g; Sugar 2.24g; Protein 16.32g

Cheese Chicken Nuggets

Prep time: 10 minutes | Cook time: 20 minutes | Serves: 6

½ teaspoon dried thyme	455g chicken breast mince	⅓ teaspoon ground black pepper, to taste	2 teaspoon sage, ground
2 tablespoons melted butter	1 teaspoon hot paprika	1 teaspoon salt	⅓ teaspoon powdered ginger
3 eggs, beaten	50g parmesan cheese, grated		

1. Combine chicken mince, seasonings, and an egg thoroughly in a mixing bowl. The melted butter should then be added and thoroughly combined. 2. The remaining eggs are whisked in a small basin. 3. Create chicken nugget shapes out of the mixture; next, cover them in the beaten eggs; and finally, roll them in the grated parmesan cheese. 4. Cook for 8 minutes at 210°C in the prepared Air Fryer.
Per Serving: Calories 399, Fat 27.09g; Sodium 1001mg; Carbs 3.24g; Fibre 0.4g; Sugar 0.57g; Protein 34.14g

Buttery and Spicy Chicken

Prep time: 10 minutes | Cook time: 13 minutes | Serves: 4

2 tablespoons melted butter	sauce	4 chicken drumsticks, rinsed and halved	1 tablespoon cider vinegar
½ teaspoon smoked paprika	1 teaspoon finely grated orange zest	1 teaspoon sea salt flakes	½ teaspoon mixed peppercorns, freshly cracked
½ tablespoon Worcestershire			

1. Dry the chicken drumsticks first by patting them. Put the melted butter on all sides of them. Combine the other ingredients and toss in the chicken drumsticks. 2. Place them in the Air Fryer cooking basket and roast at 175°C or approximately 13 minutes.
Per Serving: Calories 264, Fat 17.76g; Sodium 786mg; Carbs 0.96g; Fibre 0.1g; Sugar 0.38g; Protein 23.62g

Chicken in General Tso's Sauce

Prep time: 10 minutes | Cook time: 20 minutes | Serves: 4

455g boneless, skinless chicken breasts or thighs, cut into 2.5 cm cubes	40g thinly sliced green onions, plus more for garnish if desired	120ml chicken stock	Sautéed broccoli rabe
Fine sea salt and ground black pepper	1 tablespoon plus 1¼ teaspoons wheat-free tamari, or 60ml coconut aminos	10g powdered sweetener	**For Garnish (Optional)**
General Tso's Sauce	3 small dried red chilies, chopped	1½ teaspoons grated fresh ginger	Sesame seeds
60ml coconut vinegar or unseasoned rice vinegar	1 clove garlic, minced	1 teaspoon toasted sesame oil	Diced red chiles
		¼ teaspoon guar gum (optional)	Red pepper flakes
		For Serving (Optional)	
		Fried Cauliflower Rice (here)	

1. Set the air fryer to 200°C for frying. 2. Salt and pepper the chicken very lightly on all sides (the sauce will add seasoning). Cook the chicken for 5 minutes in an air fryer-compatible pie pan with the chicken spread out in a single layer. 3. Make the sauce while the chicken cooks by combining all of the ingredients (excluding the guar gum) in a small bowl and stirring until thoroughly blended. If using, sift in the guar gum and whisk to thoroughly mix. 4. Pour the sauce over the chicken and simmer for an additional 12 to 15 minutes, stirring every five minutes, or until the sauce is bubbling and thick and the internal temperature of the chicken reaches 75°C. 5. Removing the chicken and cooking the sauce for a further 5 to 10 minutes in the air fryer will make it even thicker and tastier. 6. Place the chicken in a large bowl. If preferred, top with diced red chiles, sliced green onions, red pepper flakes, and sesame seeds and serve over fried cauliflower rice and sautéed broccoli rabe. 7. For up to four days, keep leftovers in the refrigerator in an airtight container. Reheat for five minutes, or until well heated, in an air fryer set to 190°C. Guar gum is a good thickening for store-bought soup, but you probably won't need it if you're using homemade chicken stock. Much sauce is produced by this recipe. If you have any leftovers, try pouring it over some fried cauliflower rice.
Per Serving: Calories 424, Fat 24.23g; Sodium 513mg; Carbs 33.65g; Fibre 4.7g; Sugar 11.27g; Protein 19.75g

Cheese Chicken with Salsa

Prep time: 10 minutes | Cook time: 23 minutes | Serves: 4

2 large eggs	100g parmesan	chicken breasts or thighs,	cheese (omit for dairy-free)
1 tablespoon water	1 teaspoon ground cumin	pounded to ½ cm thick	Sprig of fresh coriander, for
Fine sea salt and ground black	1 teaspoon smoked paprika	230g salsa	garnish (optional)
pepper	4 (125g) boneless, skinless	100g shredded Monterey Jack	

1. Spray avocado oil on the air fryer basket. Set the air fryer to 200°C for frying. 2. In a small baking dish, crack the eggs, add the water, a bit of salt, and some pepper. Whisk to incorporate. Stir the parmesan, cumin, and paprika together thoroughly in a different shallow baking dish. 3. Salt and pepper the chicken breasts well on both sides. One chicken breast should be dipped in the eggs, let any excess drip off, and then should be coated on both sides with the parmesan mixture. Place the breast in the air fryer basket after spraying it with avocado oil. With the remaining 3 chicken breasts, repeat the process. 4. Cook the chicken in the air fryer for 20 minutes, flipping halfway through, or until the breading is golden brown and the internal temperature reaches 75°C. 5. Each chicken breast should have ¼ of salsa and 25g of cheese on it. Back in the air fryer, cook the breasts for an additional three minutes to melt the cheese. If preferred, garnish with coriander before serving. 6. For up to four days, keep leftovers in the refrigerator in an airtight container. Reheat for five minutes, or until thoroughly heated, in an air fryer set to 200°C.
Tip: You can use chicken breasts or thighs, but the coating adheres better to chicken breasts because of the extra fat in thighs, which makes the coating slide off the meat.
Per Serving: Calories 588, Fat 32.68g; Sodium 1308mg; Carbs 31.5g; Fibre 1.6g; Sugar 3.42g; Protein 42.57g

Tasty Lime Chicken Thighs

Prep time: 10 minutes | Cook time: 23 minutes | Serves: 4

Juice of ½ lime	2 tablespoons chopped fresh	1½ teaspoons chicken	on
1 tablespoon reduced-sodium	coriander	seasoning	
soy sauce	1 tablespoon olive oil	8 bone-in chicken thighs, skin	

1. Combine the olive oil, lime juice, soy sauce, and chicken spice in a gallon-size resealable bag. Chicken thighs should be added, the bag should be sealed, and the chicken should be properly covered. Place in the refrigerator for at least two hours, ideally overnight. 2. Set the air fryer to 200°C for frying. 3. Place the chicken in the air fryer basket in a single layer after removing it from the marinade (and discarding the marinade). Air fried the chicken for 20 to 25 minutes, flipping it halfway through cooking, or until a thermometer inserted into the thickest section reads 75°C. 4. Before serving, place the chicken on a serving plate and garnish with the coriander.
Per Serving: Calories 896, Fat 68.2g; Sodium 377mg; Carbs 2.47g; Fibre 0.1g; Sugar 0.87g; Protein 64.15g

Simple Turkey Kabobs

Prep time: 10 minutes | Cook time: 10 minutes | Serves: 8

100g parmesan cheese, grated	2 small eggs, beaten	30g chopped fresh parsley	1 heaping teaspoon fresh
360ml of water	1 teaspoon ground ginger	2 tablespoons almond meal	rosemary, finely chopped
350g turkey mince	2½ tablespoons vegetable oil	¾ teaspoon salt	½ teaspoon ground allspice

1. In a bowl, combine the ingredients listed above. With your hands, knead the mixture. 2. After that, scoop out little amounts and form them into balls gently. 3. Your Air Fryer should now be preheated to 195°C. In the air fryer basket, air fried for eight to ten minutes. Serve with skewers on a serving tray and serve with your preferred dipping sauce.
Per Serving: Calories 347, Fat 30.9g; Sodium 484mg; Carbs 2.62g; Fibre 0.4g; Sugar 0.13g; Protein 14.5g

Turkey Breasts with Yogurt Mustard Sauce

Prep time: 10 minutes | Cook time: 73 minutes | Serves: 4

1 teaspoon fine sea salt	900g of turkey breasts,	2 cloves garlic, smashed	1½ tablespoons mayonnaise
Freshly cracked mixed	quartered	½ teaspoon hot paprika	360g Greek yogurt
peppercorns, to savor	½ teaspoon cumin powder	**For the Mustard Sauce**	
Fresh juice of 1 lemon	2 tablespoons melted butter	½ tablespoon yellow mustard	

1. Take a medium-sized mixing bowl and add the melted butter and garlic; massage this mixture all over the turkey. 2. Add the paprika, salt, peppercorns, cumin powder, and lemon juice last. Place for at least 55 minutes in the refrigerator. 3. To cook, set your Air Fryer to 190°C for 18 minutes. Turning halfway through the cooking time, cook the turkey in batches. 4. Make the mustard sauce in the interim by combining all of the sauce's components. Serve the mustard sauce and heated turkey.
Per Serving: Calories 439, Fat 23.71g; Sodium 831mg; Carbs 2.28g; Fibre 0.3g; Sugar 0.77g; Protein 51.43g

Cheese Olive Stuffed Chicken Pockets

Prep time: 10 minutes | Cook time: 23 minutes | Serves: 4

1 teaspoon minced fresh rosemary or ½ teaspoon ground dried rosemary 50g almond meal	60ml balsamic vinegar 4 of small boneless, skinless chicken breast halves (about 675g)	Salt and freshly ground black pepper 100g goat cheese 6 pitted Kalamata olives,	coarsely chopped Zest of ½ lemon 6 tablespoons unsalted butter

1. Set the temperature of air fryer to 180°C. 2. Cut a broad pocket into the thickest portion of each chicken breast half with a boning knife, being careful not to cut all the way through. Use equal amounts of salt and freshly ground black pepper to season the chicken on both sides. 3. Combine the cheese, olives, lemon zest, and rosemary in a small bowl. Put the cheese mixture inside the pockets, then fasten them with toothpicks. 4. After dredging the chicken in the almond meal and brushing off the extra, place it in a shallow basin. Spray some olive oil on lightly. 5. Place the chicken breasts in the air fryer basket in a single layer, working in batches if required. Air fried the chicken for 20 to 25 minutes, flipping it halfway through cooking, or until a thermometer inserted into the thickest section reads 75°C. 6. Make the sauce while the chicken bakes. Balsamic vinegar should be simmered for about 5 minutes or until it becomes thick and syrupy in a small pan over medium heat. Until the chicken is finished, set aside. 7. When it's time to serve, reheat the sauce over medium heat and add the butter, 1 tablespoon at a time, whisking until it melts and is smooth. Use salt and pepper to taste to season. 8. Drizzle the sauce over the chicken breasts before serving.
Per Serving: Calories 327, Fat 26.07g; Sodium 321mg; Carbs 9.1g; Fibre 0.3g; Sugar 3.18g; Protein 14.17g

Fried Chicken with Cheese and Pesto

Prep time: 10 minutes | Cook time: 23 minutes | Serves: 4

120g shredded mozzarella cheese Finely chopped fresh basil, for garnish (optional) Grape tomatoes, halved, for	serving (optional) 2 large eggs 4 (125g) boneless, skinless chicken breasts or thighs, pounded to ½ cm thick (see	Note; see Tip, here) 230g pesto 1 tablespoon water Fine sea salt and ground black pepper	100g powdered Parmesan cheese 2 teaspoons Italian seasoning

1. Spray avocado oil on the air fryer basket. Set the air fryer to 200°C for frying. 2. In a small baking dish, crack the eggs, add the water, a bit of salt, and some pepper. Whisk to incorporate. Combine the Parmesan and Italian seasoning thoroughly in a different shallow baking dish. 3. Salt and pepper the chicken breasts well on both sides. One chicken breast should be dipped in the eggs, let any excess drop off, and then should be coated on both sides with the Parmesan mixture. Place the breast in the air fryer basket after spraying it with avocado oil. With the remaining 3 chicken breasts, repeat the process. 4. Cook the chicken in the air fryer for 20 minutes, flipping halfway through, or until the breading is golden brown and the internal temperature reaches 75°C. 5. Add 60g of pesto to each chicken breast before adding mozzarella on top. Back in the air fryer, cook the breasts for an additional three minutes to melt the cheese. If preferred, serve with halved grape tomatoes on the side and garnish with basil. 6. For up to four days, keep leftovers in the refrigerator in an airtight container. Reheat for five minutes, or until thoroughly heated, in an air fryer set to 200°C.
Tip: You can use chicken breasts or thighs, but the coating adheres better to chicken breasts because of the extra fat in thighs, which makes the coating slide off the meat.
Per Serving: Calories 740, Fat 48.61g; Sodium 2025mg; Carbs 9.38g; Fibre 1.5g; Sugar 1.91g; Protein 66.47g

Chicken Cauliflower Pizza

Prep time: 10 minutes | Cook time: 23 minutes | Serves: 2

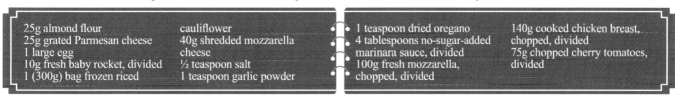

25g almond flour 25g grated Parmesan cheese 1 large egg 10g fresh baby rocket, divided 1 (300g) bag frozen riced	cauliflower 40g shredded mozzarella cheese ½ teaspoon salt 1 teaspoon garlic powder	1 teaspoon dried oregano 4 tablespoons no-sugar-added marinara sauce, divided 100g fresh mozzarella, chopped, divided	140g cooked chicken breast, chopped, divided 75g chopped cherry tomatoes, divided

1. Set the air fryer to 200°C for frying. To fit the air fryer basket, cut 4 pieces of parchment paper. Olive oil should be brushed on, then put aside. 2. The cauliflower should be microwaved in a sizable glass bowl as directed on the package. To remove extra moisture, lay the cauliflower on a clean towel, pull up the sides, and squeeze firmly over a sink. Add the shredded mozzarella, almond flour, Parmesan, egg, salt, garlic powder, and oregano to the bowl with the cauliflower once more. Stir everything together completely. 3. Make two equal parts of the dough. On the prepared parchment paper, place one piece of dough and gently press into a thin, flat disc that is 18 to 20 cm in diameter. Until the crust starts to brown, air fry for 15 minutes. Allow to cool for five minutes. 4. Place the parchment paper on a baking sheet with the crust still on it. Over the crust, lay a second piece of parchment paper. Carefully pull the crust off the baking sheet, flip it over, and re-place it in the air fryer basket while holding the edges of the two sheets together. The fresh parchment paper is now positioned at the bottom. After 15 minutes, take the top piece of paper off and continue to air fry the crust until the top starts to brown. From the air fryer, take out the basket. 5. Top the crust with 2 tablespoons of marinara sauce, half of the fresh mozzarella, chicken, cherry tomatoes, and rocket. Continue to air fry for an additional 5 to 10 minutes, or until the cheese is melted and starting to colour. Before serving, take the pizza out of the oven and let it rest for ten minutes. Make a second pizza by repeating the process with the remaining ingredients.
Per Serving: Calories 888, Fat 9.59g; Sodium 2747mg; Carbs 91.35g; Fibre 43.9g; Sugar 42.3g; Protein 129.7g

Lemony Chicken Legs

Prep time: 10 minutes | Cook time: 23 minutes | Serves: 2

¼ teaspoon freshly ground black pepper 1 tablespoon olive oil	1½ teaspoons lemon-pepper seasoning ½ teaspoon paprika	8 bone-in chicken thighs, skin on ½ teaspoon garlic powder	Juice of ½ lemon

1. Set temperature of the air fryer to 180°C. 2. In a big bowl, put the chicken and sprinkle with the olive oil. Add freshly ground black pepper, paprika, garlic powder, and lemon-pepper spice on top. Spin until completely coated. 3. Place the chicken in the air fryer's basket in a single layer, working in batches if required. Air fried the chicken for 20 to 25 minutes, turning it over halfway through cooking, or until a thermometer put into the thickest portion reads 75°C. 4. Place the lemon juice on top of the chicken after transferring it to a serving plate.
Per Serving: Calories 890, Fat 67.5g; Sodium 391mg; Carbs 2.57g; Fibre 0.3g; Sugar 0.31g; Protein 63.9g

Bacon Wrapped Chicken Pockets

Prep time: 10 minutes | Cook time: 20 minutes | Serves: 4

8 slices thin-cut bacon 4 (125g) boneless, skinless	chicken breasts, pounded to ½ cm thick	Sprig of fresh coriander, for garnish (optional)	2 (130g) packages Boursin cheese

1. Spray avocado oil on the air fryer basket. Set the air fryer to 200°C for frying. 2. One of the chicken breasts should be placed on a cutting board. Make a 2.5 cm-wide incision at the top of the breast with a sharp knife held parallel to a cutting board. Leave a 2.5 cm border on the sides and bottom and carefully cut a huge pocket into the breast. Continue with the remaining 3 chicken breasts. 3. Cut a 1.5 cm hole in the corner of a sizable resealable plastic bag. Put the Boursin cheese in the bag, divide it evenly among the chicken breasts, and then pipe the cheese into their pockets. 4. Each chicken breast is wrapped with two pieces of bacon, and the ends are fastened with toothpicks. Place the bacon-wrapped chicken in the air fryer basket and cook for 18 to 20 minutes, rotating the chicken after 10 minutes, or until the bacon is crisp and the internal temperature of the chicken reaches 75°C. If preferred, garnish the dish with a sprig of coriander before serving. 5. Keep leftovers in the refrigerator in an airtight container for up to four days. Reheat for five minutes, or until thoroughly heated, in an air fryer set to 200°C.
Advice: You can substitute cream cheese for Boursin cheese if you can't locate any and add 2 tablespoons of finely chopped fresh chives.
Per Serving: Calories 841, Fat 60.74g; Sodium 1314mg; Carbs 25.83g; Fibre 0g; Sugar 0.8g; Protein 47.52g

Parmesan Crusted Chicken Drumsticks

Prep time: 10 minutes | Cook time: 6 minutes | Serves: 4

150g crushed parmesan 1 teaspoon salt	8 chicken drumsticks, skin on 240ml buttermilk	2–3 sprigs fresh thyme 1 tablespoon lemon juice

1. Combine the buttermilk, thyme, lemon juice, and salt. Refrigerate for two hours after adding the drumsticks and giving the bag a final massage to ensure that the chicken is well-coated. 2. Heat the air fryer to 180°C. 3. Parmesan should be in a separate resealable bag. Remove the chicken from the buttermilk mixture, one or two drumsticks at a time, and place it in the bag with the parmesan. Seal the bag and give it a gentle shake to coat the chicken (discard the marinade). 4. Place the drumsticks in the air fryer basket, making sure they don't touch, working in batches if required. Air fry the chicken for 20 minutes, turning it over halfway through cooking, or until the skin is browned and a thermometer inserted into the thickest part reads 75°C.
Per Serving: Calories 446, Fat 24.57g; Sodium 974mg; Carbs 3.83g; Fibre 0.2g; Sugar 3.03g; Protein 49.19g

Spiced Chicken Thighs

Prep time: 10 minutes | Cook time: 23 minutes | Serves:6

1 teaspoon dried thyme ½ teaspoon ground cinnamon ½ teaspoon ground nutmeg	900g boneless chicken thighs, skin on 2 tablespoons vegetable oil	2 teaspoons ground coriander 1 teaspoon ground allspice 1 teaspoon cayenne pepper	1 teaspoon ground ginger 1 teaspoon salt

1. Coriander, allspice, cayenne, ginger, salt, thyme, cinnamon, and nutmeg should all be combined in a small basin. Stir everything together completely. 2. Put the chicken in a 23 x 33 cm baking dish and blot dry with paper towels. Give the chicken a thorough coating of the spice mixture on both sides. For at least two hours and ideally overnight, cover and chill the dish. 3. Preheat the air fryer to 180°C. 4. The chicken should be placed in the air fryer basket in a single layer and lightly coated with vegetable oil. If required, prepare the chicken in batches. Air fried the chicken for 15 to 20 minutes, flipping it halfway through cooking, or until a thermometer inserted into the thickest section reads 75°C.
Per Serving: Calories 379, Fat 29.8g; Sodium 511mg; Carbs 1.29g; Fibre 0.4g; Sugar 0.05g; Protein 25.09g

Cheesy Chicken Ham Casserole

Prep time: 10 minutes | Cook time: 25 minutes | Serves:4

55g unsalted butter, softened	2 tablespoons white wine	280g shredded cooked chicken	cheese
100g cream cheese, softened	vinegar	115g ham, chopped	
1½ teaspoons Dijon mustard	60ml water	100g sliced Swiss or Provolone	

1. Set the air fryer's temperature to 195°C. An 20 cm round pan or other 6-cup casserole dish that will fit in the air fryer should be lightly oiled with olive oil and set aside. 2. Use an electric mixer to thoroughly blend the butter, cream cheese, vinegar, and Dijon mustard in a big bowl. Add the water gradually while the machine is running at a low speed, then beat until smooth. Place aside. 3. Arrange an even layer of chicken in the bottom of the prepared pan, followed by the ham. Spread the butter and cream cheese mixture on top of the ham, followed by the cheese slices on the top layer. Air fry for 20 to 25 minutes until warmed through and the cheese has browned.
Per Serving: Calories 539, Fat 47.18g; Sodium 798mg; Carbs 2g; Fibre 0.1g; Sugar 1.17g; Protein 25.99g

Turkey Mushroom Meatloaf

Prep time: 15 minutes | Cook time: 50 minutes | Serves:4

200g sliced mushrooms	675g 85% lean turkey mince	25g almond meal	black pepper
1 small onion, coarsely	2 eggs, lightly beaten	2 tablespoons milk	1 Roma tomato, thinly sliced
chopped	1 tablespoon dried oregano	1 teaspoon salt	
2 cloves garlic	1 tablespoon tomato paste	½ teaspoon freshly ground	

1. Set the air fryer to 175°C for frying. Set aside an 20 cm round pan that has been lightly coated with olive oil. 2. The mushrooms, onion, and garlic should be combined in a food processor with a metal blade. To finely chop, pulse many times. Add the veggies to a sizable mixing basin. 3. Add the oregano, salt, black pepper, tomato paste, milk, eggs, almond meal, and turkey. Gently blend all ingredients together. Place the ingredients in the pan that has been prepared and form it into a loaf. On top, arrange the tomato slices. 4. The meatloaf should be cooked in the air fryer for 50 minutes, or until it is beautifully browned and a thermometer put into the thickest section reads 75°C. Before slicing, remove from the air fryer and let rest for about 10 minutes.
Per Serving: Calories 344, Fat 18.9g; Sodium 866mg; Carbs 6.31g; Fibre 1.2g; Sugar 3.63g; Protein 38.14g

Easy Turkey Meatballs

Prep time: 10 minutes | Cook time: 10 minutes | Serves: 4

1 egg, lightly beaten	black pepper	2 cloves garlic, coarsely	675g 85% lean turkey mince
50g grated Parmesan cheese	1 red pepper, seeded and	chopped	1 teaspoon salt
½ teaspoon freshly ground	coarsely chopped	10g chopped fresh parsley	

1. Set the air fryer to 200°C for frying. 2. Pepper, garlic, and parsley are combined in a food processor with a metal blade. To finely chop, pulse many times. Add the veggies to a sizable mixing basin. 3. Add the Parmesan, salt, black pepper, egg and turkey. Gently blend all ingredients together. Make meatballs measuring 3 cm out of the mixture. 4. The meatballs should be placed in the air fryer basket in a single layer and lightly sprayed with olive oil spray. If required, work in batches. Air fried the meatballs for 7 to 10 minutes, shaking the basket halfway through cooking, or until lightly browned and a thermometer inserted into the centre of a meatball reads 75°C.
Per Serving: Calories 345, Fat 19.8g; Sodium 1006mg; Carbs 4.14g; Fibre 0.4g; Sugar 1.04g; Protein 37.75g

Yogurt-Marinated Chicken

Prep time: 10 minutes | Cook time: 20 minutes | Serves:6

2 cloves garlic, minced	1 lemon, cut into 6 wedges	2 tablespoons chopped fresh	½ teaspoon ground cayenne
1 teaspoon ground cumin	½ sweet onion, sliced	coriander	½ teaspoon ground turmeric
1 teaspoon salt	900g boneless chicken thighs,	1 tablespoon grated fresh	½ teaspoon garam masala
60g plain Greek yogurt	skin on	ginger	

1. Yogurt, garlic, ginger, cayenne, turmeric, garam masala, cumin, and salt should be mixed in a small bowl. Stir everything together completely. 2. Put the yogurt mixture in a large bag that can be sealed. To ensure that the chicken is covered uniformly, add the chicken, close the bag, and massage the bag. Keep cold for one hour (or up to 8 hours). 3. Set the temperature of the air fryer to 180°C. 4. Place the chicken in the air fryer basket in a single layer after removing it from the marinade (and discarding the marinade). Air fried the chicken for 15 to 20 minutes, flipping it halfway through cooking, or until a thermometer inserted into the thickest section reads 75°C. 5. Put the chicken on a dish for serving. Serve with lemon wedges, chopped onion, and coriander on top.
Per Serving: Calories 467, Fat 41.51g; Sodium 301 mg; Carbs 4.51g; Fibre 0.6g; Sugar 1.18g; Protein 18.12g

Parmesan Chicken with Marinara Sauce

Prep time: 10 minutes | Cook time: 20 minutes | Serves:4

1 tablespoon olive oil	4 slices mozzarella cheese	Salt and freshly ground black	50g grated Parmesan cheese
240ml no-sugar-added marinara	2 large skinless chicken breasts	pepper	2 teaspoons Italian seasoning
sauce	(about 570g)	50g almond meal	1 egg, lightly beaten

1. Set the temperature of the air fryer to 180°C. 2. To get four thinner chicken breasts, cut the chicken breasts in half horizontally. Place the chicken between two sheets of parchment paper, working with one piece at a time, and pound with a rolling pin or meat mallet to flatten to an equal thickness. Add salt and freshly ground black pepper to both sides. 3. Almond meal, Parmesan, and Italian seasoning should all be blended thoroughly in a big shallow basin. Put the egg in a different big shallow bowl. 4. To make an even coating, press the almond meal mixture firmly into the chicken after dipping it in the egg and almond mixture. 5. Place the chicken breasts in the air fryer basket in a single layer and lightly brush both sides with vegetable oil, working in batches if required. Air fried the chicken for 15 minutes, or until a thermometer put into the thickest section reads 75°C, pausing halfway during the cooking time to flip the chicken. 6. Sprinkle mozzarella cheese on top of each piece of chicken after adding the marinara sauce. To melt the cheese, air fried for a further 3 to 5 minutes.
Per Serving: Calories 487, Fat 31.6g; Sodium 430mg; Carbs 7.31g; Fibre 0.2g; Sugar 2.27g; Protein 41.87g

Chicken Cobb Salad

Prep time: 10 minutes | Cook time: 23 minutes | Serves: 4

8 slices reduced-sodium bacon	sliced	chopped	⅛ teaspoon ground cumin
240g chopped romaine lettuce	8 chicken breast tenders (about	1 clove garlic	Salt and freshly ground black
150g cherry tomatoes, halved	675g)	120g plain Greek yogurt	pepper
¼ red onion, thinly sliced	**Avocado-Lime Dressing**	60ml milk	½ avocado
2 hard-boiled eggs, peeled and	3 spring onions, coarsely	2 tablespoons fresh coriander	Juice of ½ lime

1. Set the air fryer to 200°C for frying. 2. Each piece of chicken should have a piece of bacon wrapped around it, fastened with a toothpick. Place the bacon-wrapped chicken in the air fryer basket in a single layer, working in batches if necessary. A thermometer inserted into the thickest piece of chicken should read 75°C. After 8 minutes of air frying, once the bacon has been browned. Slice into bite-sized pieces after allowing to cool for a few minutes. 3. To prepare the dressing, put the yoghurt, milk, avocado, lime juice, spring onions, garlic, coriander, and cumin in a food processor or blender. until smooth, puree. Add salt and freshly ground pepper to taste. 4. To assemble the salad, put the lettuce, tomatoes, and onion in a large bowl. Over the veggies, drizzle the dressing and gently toss to incorporate. Just before serving, arrange the chicken and eggs on top.
Per Serving: Calories 879, Fat 53.11g; Sodium 420mg; Carbs 19.21g; Fibre 8.2g; Sugar 7.69g; Protein 80.84g

Chicken Lettuce Tacos

Prep time: 10 minutes | Cook time: 6 minutes | Serves: 4

¼ teaspoon fine sea salt	2 tablespoons lime juice	2 tablespoons wheat-free tamari	**For Garnish (Optional)**
455g chicken mince	65g creamy peanut butter, room	or coconut aminos	Coriander leaves
2 cloves garlic, minced	temperature	1½ teaspoons hot sauce	Shredded purple cabbage
40g diced onions (about 1	2 tablespoons chicken stock,	**For Serving**	Sliced green onions
small onion)	plus more if needed	2 small heads butter lettuce,	
Sauce	2 tablespoons grated fresh	leaves separated	
5 drops liquid stevia (optional)	ginger	Lime slices (optional)	

1. Set the air fryer to 175°C for frying. 2. In a dish that will fit in your air fryer or a 15 cm pie pan, combine the chicken mince, onions, garlic, and salt. Use a spatula to chop up the chicken. Put the chicken in the air fryer and cook for 5 minutes, or until it is thoroughly cooked and browned. Once more, crush the chicken into tiny pieces. 3. Make the sauce by combining the stock, ginger, tamari, spicy sauce, lime juice, peanut butter, and stevia (if using) in a medium-sized bowl. Add a tablespoon or two more of stock if the sauce is too thick. If desired, taste and add more hot sauce. 4. Chicken and sauce should be combined in a pan. Cook for a further minute, stirring frequently, until well cooked. 5. Place a few lettuce leaves on a serving platter before assembling the tacos. Each lettuce leaf should contain a few teaspoons of the chicken mixture. If preferred, add some coriander, purple cabbage, and sliced green onions as garnish. Serve the leftover sauce separately. If desired, garnish with lime slices. 6. You can keep leftover meat mixture in the fridge in an airtight container for up to 4 days; sauce, lettuce, and garnishes should be kept separate. In an air fryer set to 175°C, reheat the beef mixture for three minutes, or until well heated.
Per Serving: Calories 442, Fat 28.67g; Sodium 404 mg; Carbs 19.2g; Fibre 6.2g; Sugar 9.66g; Protein 30.79g

Spinach Stuffed Chicken

Prep time: 10 minutes | Cook time: 23 minutes | Serves: 4

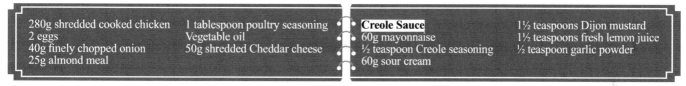

2 tablespoons grated Parmesan cheese	pepper	4 small boneless, skinless chicken breast halves (about	80g ricotta cheese
3 cloves garlic, minced	3 tablespoons pine nuts	675g)	
Salt and freshly ground black	20g frozen spinach, thawed and squeezed dry	8 slices bacon	

1. In a small pan, put the pine nuts and then place the pan in the air fryer basket, air-fried for 2 to 3 minutes at 200°C. Continue heating up the air fryer while removing the pine nuts to a mixing basin. 2. Combine the spinach, ricotta, Parmesan, and garlic in a big bowl. Salt and pepper to taste, then whisk everything together completely. 3. Use a sharp knife to slice into the chicken breasts, opening them up like a book while being careful not to cut through completely. Salt and pepper the chicken as desired. 4. Give each piece of chicken the same amount of the spinach mixture to stuff, then fold the top of the chicken breast back over the stuffing. Each chicken breast is encased in two slices of bacon. 5. When the bacon is crisp and a thermometer put into the thickest portion of the chicken reads 75°C, air fried the chicken for 18 to 20 minutes, working in batches if necessary.
Per Serving: Calories 630, Fat 49.18g; Sodium 594mg; Carbs 13.4g; Fibre 0.9g; Sugar 1.15g; Protein 34.03g

Cheddar Chicken Croquettes with Creole Sauce

Prep time: 10 minutes | Cook time: 40 minutes | Serves:4

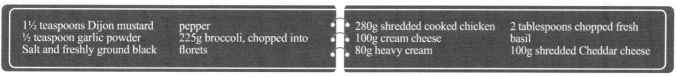

280g shredded cooked chicken	1 tablespoon poultry seasoning	**Creole Sauce**	1½ teaspoons Dijon mustard
2 eggs	Vegetable oil	60g mayonnaise	1½ teaspoons fresh lemon juice
40g finely chopped onion	50g shredded Cheddar cheese	½ teaspoon Creole seasoning	½ teaspoon garlic powder
25g almond meal		60g sour cream	

1. Combine the chicken, Cheddar, eggs, onion, almond meal, and poultry spice in a sizable bowl. Gently stir until everything is mixed. 30 minutes of refrigeration under cover. 2. In the meantime, prepare the ingredients for the Creole sauce in a small bowl by whisking together the mayonnaise, sour cream, Dijon mustard, lemon juice, garlic powder, and Creole spice. Refrigerate with a cover until ready to serve. 3. Set the air fryer to 200°C for frying. Make 8 equal pieces of the chicken mixture into patties. 4. Place the patties in the air fryer basket in a single layer and lightly brush both sides with vegetable oil, working in batches if required. Air fry the patties for 10 minutes, or until they are just lightly browned and the cheese has melted, pausing midway during the cooking process to flip the patties. With the Creole sauce, serve.
Per Serving: Calories 467, Fat 41.51g; Sodium 301mg; Carbs 4.51g; Fibre 0.6g; Sugar 1.18g; Protein 18.12g

Chicken and Broccoli Casserole

Prep time: 10 minutes | Cook time: 25 minutes | Serves:4

1½ teaspoons Dijon mustard	pepper	280g shredded cooked chicken	2 tablespoons chopped fresh basil
½ teaspoon garlic powder	225g broccoli, chopped into florets	100g cream cheese	
Salt and freshly ground black		80g heavy cream	100g shredded Cheddar cheese

1. Turn the air fryer to 200°C before using. Apply a thin layer of olive oil to a 6-cup casserole dish that will fit in an air fryer, such as 20 cm round pan, and put it aside. 2. In a large glass bowl, combine the broccoli with 1 tablespoon of water, and then cover with a microwave-safe plate. Broccoli should be brilliant green but still firm when microwaved on high for 2 to 3 minutes. If required, drain and add to another big dish with the chicken shreds. 3. Cream cheese and cream are combined in the same glass bowl that was used to microwave the broccoli. Stir until smooth after 30 seconds to 1 minute on high in the microwave. Add the garlic powder, mustard, and season with salt and freshly ground black pepper to taste. Smooth out the sauce with a whisk. 4. Add the basil after drizzling the heated sauce over the chicken and broccoli mixture. Gently fold the ingredients with a silicone spatula until well blended. 5. Add the cheese on top after adding the chicken mixture to the casserole dish that has been prepared. For 20 to 25 minutes in the air fryer, the cheese should be browned and well warmed.
Per Serving: Calories 676, Fat 65.17g; Sodium 312mg; Carbs 6.31g; Fibre 1.7g; Sugar 4.25g; Protein 18.19g

Chapter 4 Beef, Pork, and Lamb Recipes

Traditional Smoked Pork Chops

Prep time: 5 minutes | Cook time: 20 minutes | Serves: 6

1 teaspoon onion powder	½ teaspoon cayenne pepper	6 pork chops	Ground black pepper, to savor
½ teaspoon garlic powder	35g almond meal	Hickory-smoked salt, to savor	

1. Simply combine the ingredients mentioned above in a zip-top plastic bag and shake to coat evenly. 2. Transfer the chops to the Air Fryer cooking basket after spraying them with a pan spray (rapeseed spray works great in this situation). 3. At 190°C, roast them for 20 minutes. Serve alongside fried veggies
Per Serving: Calories 158, Fat 17.4g; Sodium 87mg; Carbs 0.85g; Fibre 0.2g; Sugar 0.05g; Protein 40.37g

Classic Air Fryer Schnitzel

Prep time: 5 minutes | Cook time: 15 minutes | Serves: 2

½ teaspoon mustard	pepper	parsley	½ teaspoon fennel seed
⅓ tablespoon cider vinegar	1 teaspoon garlic salt	50g parmesan	2 pork schnitzel, halved
⅓ teaspoon ground black	½ heaping tablespoon of fresh	2 eggs, beaten	

1. In your food processor, blend the vinegar, black pepper, garlic salt, mustard, fennel seeds, fresh parsley, and parmesan until they are consistent in texture. 2. Pour the combined ingredients into a small bowl. To another small bowl, add the beaten egg. 3. Before dredging them in the herb mixture, coat the pork schnitzel with the beaten egg. 4. Cook for approximately 14 minutes in the preheated Air Fryer at 180°C.
Per Serving: Calories 249, Fat 14.17g; Sodium 146mg; Carbs 2.36g; Fibre 0.4g; Sugar 0.7g; Protein 25.08g

Tangy Pork Bolognese

Prep time: 5 minutes | Cook time: 15 minutes | Serves: 4

⅓ teaspoon freshly cracked black pepper	80g tomato paste	⅓ teaspoon cayenne pepper	½ tablespoon extra-virgin olive oil
½ teaspoon grated fresh ginger	3 cloves garlic, minced	675g pork mince	
1 teaspoon salt	½ medium-sized white onion, peeled and chopped	⅓ tablespoon fresh coriander, chopped	

1. Set your Air Fryer to 200°C to start. 2. Next, thoroughly blend everything together until it forms a homogenous mixture. 3. Cook the beef mixture for 14 minutes after transferring it to the Air Fryer baking dish. Enjoy the dish with courgette noodles.
Per Serving: Calories 540, Fat 36.24g; Sodium 734mg; Carbs 6.44g; Fibre 1.3g; Sugar 3.28g; Protein 44.99g

Pork Bacon with Mixed Greens

Prep time: 5 minutes | Cook time: 10 minutes | Serves: 2

2 shallots, peeled and diced	175g mixed greens	8 thick slices pork bacon	Nonstick cooking spray

1. Set the air fryer to 175°C to get started. 2. Now include the bacon and shallot in the cooking basket of the Air Fryer, and set the timer for 2 minutes. Use a nonstick frying spray to spritz. 3. After stopping the Air Fryer, add the mixed greens, stir well, and fry for a further five minutes. Serve hot.
Per Serving: Calories 259, Fat 16.42g; Sodium 1002mg; Carbs 9.87g; Fibre 4.6g; Sugar 2.73g; Protein 18.5g

Sausage Meatballs with Marinara Sauce

Prep time: 5 minutes | Cook time: 20 minutes | Serves: 4

½ jar marinara sauce	50g parmesan cheese, preferably freshly grated	½ teaspoon fine sea salt	¾ teaspoon paprika
1 shallot, finely chopped		¼ teaspoon ground black	
455g pork sausage meat	2 garlic cloves, finely minced	pepper, or more to taste	

1. In a sizable bowl, combine everything listed above except the marinara sauce and stir until well combined. 2. Shape into meatballs. Air-fry them at 180°C for 10 minutes; pause the Air Fryer, shake them up and cook for additional 6 minutes or until the balls are no longer pink in the middle. 3. Over a medium burner, warm the marinara sauce in the meantime. Serve marinara sauce beside the pork sausage meatballs.
Per Serving: Calories 229, Fat 7.23g; Sodium 639mg; Carbs 3.28g; Fibre 0.4g; Sugar 0.46g; Protein 35.82g

Pork Casserole with Peppers and Cheese

Prep time: 10 minutes | Cook time: 40 minutes | Serves: 4

480ml water	½ teaspoon mustard seeds	1 red pepper	1 teaspoon oregano
1 tablespoon chicken bouillon granules	2 tablespoons fresh coriander, chopped	2 tablespoons olive oil	1 tablespoon fish sauce
2 tablespoons sherry wine	Salt and ground black pepper,	1 large-sized shallot, chopped	100g grated cheese blend
2 ripe tomatoes, pureed	to taste	455g pork mince	
1 teaspoon dried marjoram	2 chili peppers	2 garlic cloves, minced	
		½ teaspoon celery seeds	

1. The peppers should be roasted in the preheated Air Fryer for 10 minutes at 200°C, turning them over halfway through. 2. After 10 minutes of steaming, remove the skin and throw away the seeds and stems. Peppers should be cut in half. 3. Heat the olive oil in a baking pan at 195°C for 2 minutes; add the shallots and cook for 4 minutes. Add the pork mince and garlic; cook for a further 4 to 5 minutes. 4. Add the tomatoes, marjoram, celery, mustard, oregano, fish sauce, coriander, salt, and pepper after that. Sliced peppers should be layered in the baking dish. 5. Sherry wine, chicken bouillon granules, and water should be combined. Fill the baking pan with the mixture. 6. Cook for 10 minutes at 200°C in the preheated Air Fryer. Cheese should melt after an extra 5 minutes of baking after being topped with it. Serve right away.
Per Serving: Calories 544, Fat 38.98g; Sodium 562mg; Carbs 9.95g; Fibre 1.8g; Sugar 5.06g; Protein 38.06g

Spiced Roast Pork

Prep time: 10 minutes | Cook time: 55 minutes | Serves: 6

1 teaspoon red pepper flakes, crushed	crushed	¾ teaspoon sea salt flakes	1 teaspoon porcini powder
2 dried sprigs of thyme,	675g boneless pork loin roast, washed	1 teaspoon mustard seeds	1 teaspoon shallot powder
		1 teaspoon garlic powder	2 tablespoons lime juice

1. To start, use a tiny knife to score the meat, being careful not to go too far. 2. Place all of the seasonings in a small mixing bowl and stir to thoroughly incorporate. 3. To spread the spice mixture uniformly, massage it into the pork meat. Add the lime juice drizzle. 4. Then, set your Air Fryer to 180°C to begin cooking. Roast the pork for 25 to 30 minutes after placing it in the Air Fryer basket. Pause the machine, check for doneness and cook for 25 minutes more.
Per Serving: Calories 156, Fat 4.74g; Sodium 347mg; Carbs 1.28g; Fibre 0.2g; Sugar 0.19g; Protein 25.64g

Pork Shoulder with Coriander-Garlic Sauce

Prep time: 5 minutes | Cook time: 35 minutes | Serves: 4

Salt and ground black pepper, to taste	preferably freshly squeezed	meal	10g fresh coriander leaves
1 tablespoon olive oil	1 egg white, well whisked	**For the Coriander-Garlic Sauce**	½ tablespoon salt
1 tablespoon coconut aminos	455g pork shoulder, cut into pieces of 5 cm long	10g fresh parsley leaves	1 teaspoon lemon juice
1 teaspoon lemon juice,	1 teaspoon golden flaxseed	80ml extra-virgin olive oil	
		3 garlic cloves, peeled	

1. Pork strips, flaxseed meal, egg white, salt, pepper, olive oil, coconut aminos, and lemon juice should all be combined. Refrigerate for 30 to 45 minutes with a cover on. 2. After that, put nonstick cooking spray on the pork strips. 3. To cook, set your Air Fryer to 195°C. Press the power button to start the air fryer. After 15 minutes, stop it, shake the basket, and continue cooking for another 15 minutes. 4. In the interim, finely mince the garlic in a food processor. The parsley, coriander, salt, and lemon juice should now be pureed. Olive oil should be carefully added while the machine is running. 5. Enjoy the pork with the thoroughly chilled sauce!
Per Serving: Calories 422, Fat 31.56g; Sodium 1114mg; Carbs 2.79g; Fibre 0.7g; Sugar 0.88g; Protein 30.13g

Pork Ribs with Red Wine Sauce

Prep time: 10 minutes | Cook time: 15 minutes | Serves: 4

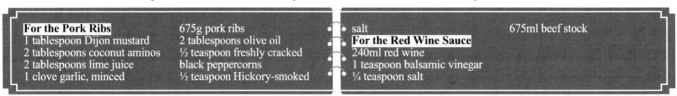

For the Pork Ribs	675g pork ribs	salt	675ml beef stock
1 tablespoon Dijon mustard	2 tablespoons olive oil	**For the Red Wine Sauce**	
2 tablespoons coconut aminos	½ teaspoon freshly cracked	240ml red wine	
2 tablespoons lime juice	black peppercorns	1 teaspoon balsamic vinegar	
1 clove garlic, minced	½ teaspoon Hickory-smoked	¼ teaspoon salt	

1. Place all ingredients for the pork ribs in a large-sized mixing dish. Cover and marinate in your refrigerator overnight or at least 3 hours. 2. The pork ribs should be air-fried for 10 minutes at 160°C. 3. Make the sauce in the interim. In a deep frying pan over a moderate flame, add some beef stock and boil it down to about half its original volume. 4. Turn up the heat to high and then add the other ingredients. Allow it to simmer for an additional 10 minutes, or until the sauce has reduced by half. 5. Red wine sauce should be used with the pork ribs.
Per Serving: Calories 390, Fat 19.36g; Sodium 817mg; Carbs 3.38g; Fibre 0.3g; Sugar 1.71g; Protein 47.89g

Homemade Sloppy Joes

Prep time: 5 minutes | Cook time: 45 minutes | Serves: 4

1 pepper, chopped	blend	**Keto Buns**	protein isolate
455g pork mince	2 garlic cloves, minced	1 egg	80g mozzarella cheese, shredded
1 ripe medium-sized tomato, pureed	Dash ground allspice	45g coconut flour	50g almond flour
1 tablespoon poultry seasoning	1 tablespoon olive oil	80g ricotta cheese, crumbled	1 teaspoon baking soda
	1 shallot, chopped	1½ tablespoons plain whey	

1. Set your Air Fryer to 200°C to begin. For a short while, let the olive oil warm up. 2. The shallots should be sautéed once hot until just tender. Add the pepper and garlic; sauté for an additional 4 minutes, or until fragrant. 3. With a fork, crumble the pork mince as it cooks for an additional 5 minutes. The spices and tomato puree are added next. Cook for a further 10 minutes at 185°C. Reserve. 4. To make the keto buns, microwave the cheese for 1 minute 30 seconds, stirring twice. In the bowl of a food processor, add the cheese and pulse until smooth. Add the egg after mixing once more. 5. Blend one more after including the flour, baking soda, and plain whey protein isolate. Scrape the batter onto the middle of a cling film that has been lightly greasing. 6. Cut the dough into four pieces, shape it into a disc, and place it on a baking sheet lined with parchment paper to cool in the freezer (make sure to grease your hands). Bake at 200°C in the preheated oven for about 14 minutes. 7. Place the keto buns in the cooking basket after spooning the meat mixture into them. Cook for another 7 minutes to fully reheat.
Per Serving: Calories 587, Fat 39.89g; Sodium 240mg; Carbs 15.57g; Fibre 1.2g; Sugar 6.66g; Protein 40.07g

Greek Pork Sirloin with Tzatziki Sauce

Prep time: 5 minutes | Cook time: 55 minutes | Serves: 4

Greek Pork	2 cloves garlic, finely chopped	**Tzatziki**	240g full-fat Greek yogurt
1 teaspoon fennel seeds	900g pork sirloin roast	1 teaspoon balsamic vinegar	1 garlic clove, minced
1 teaspoon Ancho chili powder	Salt and black pepper, to taste	1 teaspoon minced fresh dill	1 tablespoon extra-virgin olive oil
1 teaspoon turmeric powder	½ teaspoon celery seeds	A pinch of salt	
½ teaspoon ground ginger	1 teaspoon smoked paprika	½ cucumber, finely chopped and squeezed	
2 tablespoons olive oil	½ teaspoon mustard seeds		

1. Combine all the ingredients for the Greek pork in a sizable bowl. Till the meat is thoroughly covered, toss. 2. Cook for 30 minutes at 180°C in the prepared Air Fryer before turning it over and cooking for an additional 20 minutes. 3. While waiting, combine all the ingredients for the tzatziki. Until you are ready to use, place in the refrigerator. 4. Tzatziki should be served on the side with the chilled pork sirloin roast. Enjoy!
Per Serving: Calories 600, Fat 32.25g; Sodium 355mg; Carbs 8.35g; Fibre 1.5g; Sugar 4.66g; Protein 66.24g

Roasted Pork Loin in Italian Style

Prep time: 5 minutes | Cook time: 50 minutes | Serves: 3

1 teaspoon sea salt	60ml red wine	455g pork top loin
½ teaspoon black pepper, freshly cracked	2 tablespoons mustard	1 tablespoon Italian herb seasoning blend
	2 garlic cloves, minced	

1. Combine the salt, black pepper, red wine, mustard, and garlic in a ceramic bowl. After adding, give the top loin of pork at least 30 minutes to marinate. 2. Spray a nonstick cooking spray on the sides and bottom of the cooking basket. 3. Put the top piece of pork in the basket and season with the Italian herb seasoning mix. 4. Ten minutes of cooking the pork tenderloin at 185°C. Cook for an additional 5 to 6 minutes after flipping halfway through and spraying with cooking oil. Serve right away.
Per Serving: Calories 213, Fat 5.54g; Sodium 1172mg; Carbs 3.46g; Fibre 1g; Sugar 0.64g; Protein 34.68g

Meatballs with Cheese

Prep time: 5 minutes | Cook time: 15 minutes | Serves: 4

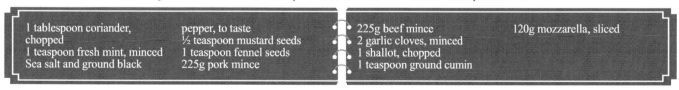

1 tablespoon coriander, chopped	pepper, to taste	225g beef mince	120g mozzarella, sliced
1 teaspoon fresh mint, minced	½ teaspoon mustard seeds	2 garlic cloves, minced	
Sea salt and ground black	1 teaspoon fennel seeds	1 shallot, chopped	
	225g pork mince	1 teaspoon ground cumin	

1. Combine all the ingredients excluding the mozzarella in a mixing bowl. 2. Create balls out of the mixture and place them in a frying basket that has been lightly oiled. 3. The meatballs should be cooked in the preheated Air Fryer for 10 minutes at 195°C. About halfway through the cooking process, check the meatballs. 4. Add some sliced mozzarella on top and bake for three more minutes. Place everything on a lovely serving plate to serve.
Per Serving: Calories 343, Fat 18.39g; Sodium 289mg; Carbs 3.54g; Fibre 1.1g; Sugar 1.23g; Protein 39.24g

Easy Roast Steak

Prep time: 5 minutes | Cook time: 15 minutes | Serves: 4

1 teaspoon salt	⅓ teaspoon celery seed	pepper, or to taste
2 teaspoons cayenne pepper	4- steaks	1½ tablespoons extra-virgin
120ml herb vinegar	¼ teaspoon ground black	olive oil

1. In a mixing bowl, combine all the ingredients. Marinate the steaks in the refrigerator for about 3 hours with the dish covered. 2. Finally, cook minute steaks at 180°C for 13 minutes. 3. Served heated with your choose salad and chips.
Per Serving: Calories 283, Fat 15.13g; Sodium 1138mg; Carbs 1.02g; Fibre 0.3g; Sugar 0.22g; Protein 34.97g

Paprika Pork Sirloin with Spice Salsa Sauce

Prep time: 5 minutes | Cook time: 55 minutes | Serves: 3

1 tablespoon smoked paprika	675g pork sirloin	black pepper, to taste
2 teaspoons peanut oil	Coarse sea salt and ground	70g prepared salsa sauce

1. Set your Air Fryer to 180°C to begin. 2. Drizzle the oil all over the pork sirloin. Add paprika, black pepper, and salt to taste. 3. Cook in the preheated Air Fryer for 50 minutes. 4. With two forks, shred the roast after removing it from the Air Fryer. Add the salsa sauce and stir. Enjoy!
Per Serving: Calories 301, Fat 7.24g; Sodium 269mg; Carbs 4.1g; Fibre 1.4g; Sugar 1.85g; Protein 52.85g

Simple Crusted Beef Steak

Prep time: 10 minutes | Cook time: 10 minutes | Serves: 4

2 eggs	2 teaspoons caraway seeds	1 tablespoon melted butter	Fine sea salt and cayenne
35g almond flour	4 beef steaks	2 teaspoons garlic powder	pepper, to taste

1. Garlic powder, caraway seeds, salt, and cayenne pepper should all be liberally sprinkled on steaks. 2. Melted butter and almond flour should be completely combined in a mixing bowl. Be sure to thoroughly whisk the eggs in a separate basin. 3. Beef steaks should first be covered with beaten egg before being covered in the buttered flour mixture. 4. The steaks should be cooked for 10 minutes at 180°C in the cooking basket of the Air Fryer.
Per Serving: Calories 430, Fat 20.77g; Sodium 211mg; Carbs 3.25g; Fibre 0.7g; Sugar 0.95g; Protein 54.46g

Mexican Cheese Steak

Prep time: 10 minutes | Cook time: 15 minutes | Serves: 6

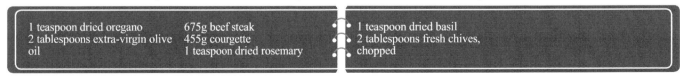

80g feta cheese	3 eggs, whisked	pepper, to taste
100g parmesan cheese	1½ tablespoons olive oil	2 tablespoons Mexican spice
6 minute steaks	Fine sea salt and ground black	blend

1. Start by seasoning the steaks with salt, pepper, and a Mexican spice combination. 2. The oil, feta cheese, and parmesan cheese should all be properly combined in a mixing bowl. The eggs must be beaten in a different mixing bowl. 3. Minute steaks should first be dipped in the egg and then the cheese mixture. 4. Work in batches while air-frying for 15 minutes at 175°C.
Per Serving: Calories 255, Fat 17.72g; Sodium 222mg; Carbs 4.38g; Fibre 0.1g; Sugar 0.74g; Protein 19.4g

Herbed Beef Steak with Courgette

Prep time: 10 minutes | Cook time: 12 minutes | Serves: 4

1 teaspoon dried oregano	675g beef steak	1 teaspoon dried basil
2 tablespoons extra-virgin olive oil	455g courgette	2 tablespoons fresh chives, chopped
	1 teaspoon dried rosemary	

1. Set your Air Fryer to 200°C to begin. 2. Combine the seasonings, oil, and courgette with the meat. After transferring, cook for 6 minutes in the cooking basket. 3. Flip and cook it for a further 6 minutes. Fresh chives should be added as a garnish before serving. Enjoy!
Per Serving: Calories 291, Fat 12.87g; Sodium 162mg; Carbs 3.88g; Fibre 1.5g; Sugar 0.04g; Protein 39.16g

Japanese-Style Flank Steak

Prep time: 5 minutes | Cook time: 15 minutes | Serves: 4

1 tablespoon olive oil 570g flank steak	2 garlic cloves, pressed 1½ tablespoons sake	1 tablespoon brown miso paste

1. Put all the ingredients in a sealable food bag, shake to coat fully, and then chill for at least a half-hour. 2. Then, cover the steak completely on all sides with a nonstick cooking spray. Put the steak on the baking pan for the Air Fryer. 3. To cook, set your Air Fryer to 200°C. 12 minutes of roasting, flipping twice. Serve right away.
Per Serving: Calories 242, Fat 10.73g; Sodium 234mg; Carbs 1.89g; Fibre 0.3g; Sugar 0.28g; Protein 31g

Tasty Keto Cheeseburgers

Prep time: 5 minutes | Cook time: 15 minutes | Serves: 4

675g beef mince 1 sachet onion soup mix	Salt and freshly ground black pepper, to taste	1 teaspoon paprika 4 slices Monterey Jack cheese

1. Combine the ground chuck, onion soup mix, salt, black pepper, and paprika in a mixing bowl well. 2. Set your Air Fryer to cook at 195°C after that. Make 4 patties out of the mixture. Give them a 10-minute air-fry. 3. The next step is to top the warm burgers with slices of cheese. Air fry for an additional minute. 4. Serve with your choice of pickled salad and mustard.
Per Serving: Calories 365, Fat 21.59g; Sodium 466mg; Carbs 2.09g; Fibre 0.4g; Sugar 0.31g; Protein 40.56g

Teriyaki Steak with Broccoli

Prep time: 10 minutes | Cook time: 55 minutes | Serves: 4

2 red peppers, sliced Fine sea salt and ground black	pepper, to taste 225g rump steak	½ head broccoli, broken into florets	80ml keto teriyaki marinade 1½ teaspoons sesame oil

1. In a mixing bowl, combine the teriyaki marinade and the rump roast; whisk to combine. Give it around 40 minutes to marinate. 2. Then roast for 13 minutes at 200°C in the preheated Air Fryer. Stir halfway through the cooking process. 3. In the meantime, sauté the broccoli and sliced capsicum in the hot sesame oil until the broccoli is soft. Then, season to taste with salt and pepper. 4. Put the cooked rump steak on a serving plate and top with sautéed broccoli to serve.
Per Serving: Calories 248, Fat 11.92g; Sodium 461mg; Carbs 19.16g; Fibre 1.2g; Sugar 15.8g; Protein 16.7g

Roasted New York Strip with Mustard Butter Sauce

Prep time: 5 minutes | Cook time: 15 minutes | Serves: 4

Sea salt and freshly cracked black pepper, to taste	900g New York Strip 1 teaspoon cayenne pepper	1 teaspoon whole-grain mustard	55g butter, softened 1 tablespoon peanut oil

1. Season the steak with cayenne pepper, salt, and black pepper after rubbing it with peanut oil. 2. Cook for 7 minutes in the prepared Air Fryer at 200°C, then flip it over and cook for another 7 minutes. 3. Whip the butter and whole-grain mustard together to make the mustard butter. 4. Serve the roasted New York Strip with mustard butter dollops on the side.
Per Serving: Calories 389, Fat 21.15g; Sodium 194mg; Carbs 1.81g; Fibre 0.3g; Sugar 0.63g; Protein 48.6g

Roast Beef with Jalapeño Peppers

Prep time: 5 minutes | Cook time: 45 minutes | Serves: 8

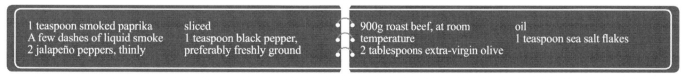

1 teaspoon smoked paprika A few dashes of liquid smoke 2 jalapeño peppers, thinly	sliced 1 teaspoon black pepper, preferably freshly ground	900g roast beef, at room temperature 2 tablespoons extra-virgin olive	oil 1 teaspoon sea salt flakes

1. The Air Fryer should first be heated to 165°C. 2. After that, use kitchen towels to pat the roast dry. Rub with liquid smoke, extra virgin olive oil, and all other ingredients. 3. In the preheated Air Fryer, cook for 30 minutes; pause the appliance and flip the roast; roast for an additional 15 minutes. 4. Serve with sliced jalapenos on top after using a meat thermometer to determine whether the dish is done.
Per Serving: Calories 227, Fat 11.17g; Sodium 412mg; Carbs 1.45g; Fibre 0.4g; Sugar 0.61g; Protein 30.54g

Thai-Style Lime Meatballs

Prep time: 10 minutes | Cook time: 15 minutes | Serves:4

½ lime, rind and juice 455g beef mince	1 teaspoon Thai seasoning blend	2 teaspoons lemongrass, finely chopped	1 tablespoon sesame oil 1 teaspoon red Thai curry paste

1. In a mixing bowl, thoroughly combine all the ingredients. 2. 24 meatballs should be formed, then placed in the cooking basket of the air fryer. Cook at 195°C for 10 minutes; pause the machine and cook for a further 5 minutes, or until cooked through. 3. Serve with the dipping sauce on the side.
Per Serving: Calories 279, Fat 16.08g; Sodium 123mg; Carbs 1.23g; Fibre 0.4g; Sugar 0.2g; Protein 30.35g

Sherry-Braised Ribs with Grape Tomatoes

Prep time: 5 minutes | Cook time: 35 minutes | Serves: 2

1 rack ribs, cut in half to fit the Air Fryer 60ml sherry wine	2 tablespoons coconut aminos 1 tablespoon Dijon mustard Sea salt and ground black	pepper, to taste 150g grape tomatoes 1 teaspoon dried rosemary	

1. Combine the mustard, sherry wine, coconut aminos, salt, and black pepper with the pork ribs. 2. Add the ribs to the frying basket that has been lightly oiled. Cook for 25 minutes at 185°C in the preheated Air Fryer. 3. Cook for an additional 5 minutes after flipping the ribs over and adding the tomatoes and rosemary. Serve right away.
Per Serving: Calories 667, Fat 46.13g; Sodium 216mg; Carbs 17.2g; Fibre 1.5g; Sugar 13.6g; Protein 44.85g

French Style Pork Chops

Prep time: 5 minutes | Cook time: 12 minutes | Serves: 4

2 tablespoons coconut aminos 455g pork loin centre rib chops, bone-in	1 teaspoon Herbes de Provence 1 tablespoon Dijon mustard 2 tablespoons French wine	Celtic salt and ground black pepper, to taste 2 tablespoons rice vinegar	

1. Combine the vinegar, wine, and coconut aminos thoroughly. Add the pork and let it marinate for 1 hour in the refrigerator. 2. Add salt, black pepper, and Herbes de Provence to the pork chops. Apply mustard liberally to the pork chops. 3. Cook for 12 minutes at 200°C in the preheated Air Fryer. If desired, serve warm with mashed potatoes.
Per Serving: Calories 221, Fat 9.65g; Sodium 117mg; Carbs 1.72g; Fibre 0.4g; Sugar 0.91g; Protein 29.71g

Authentic Pork Kebabs

Prep time: 10 minutes | Cook time: 15 minutes | Serves: 3

1 teaspoon mustard 1 teaspoon coriander Salt and ground black pepper, to taste	6 tablespoons parmesan cheese, grated 455g lean pork mince 1 onion, chopped	1 garlic clove, smashed 1 teaspoon coriander seed, ground ½ teaspoon cumin powder	1 Thai bird chili, deveined and finely chopped

1. Utilizing your hands, combine all components. Knead everything together thoroughly. 2. Wrap flat skewers in the meat mixture (sausage shapes). 3. Cook for 11 to 12 minutes at 185°C, flipping them over one or twice. Work in groups. Serve!
Per Serving: Calories 252, Fat 11.28g; Sodium 1914mg; Carbs 9.47g; Fibre 1.3g; Sugar 4.53g; Protein 29.65g

Breakfast Sausage, Bacon and Egg Cups

Prep time: 5 minutes | Cook time: 20 minutes | Serves: 5

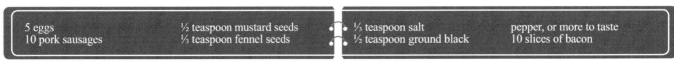

5 eggs 10 pork sausages	½ teaspoon mustard seeds ⅓ teaspoon fennel seeds	⅓ teaspoon salt ½ teaspoon ground black	pepper, or more to taste 10 slices of bacon

1. Divide the sausages and bacon among five ramekins; crack an egg into each ramekin. Sprinkle with seasonings. 2. Cook for 18 minutes at 175°C, or until desired doneness. 3. Serve warm with spicier tomato ketchup and Dijon mustard.
Per Serving: Calories 525, Fat 46.45g; Sodium 1.018g; Carbs 3.14g; Fibre 0.2g; Sugar 1.1g; Protein 22.39g

Romano Cheese Crusted Beef Schnitzel

Prep time: 10 minutes | Cook time: 13 minutes | Serves: 2

1 teaspoon paprika	1 tablespoon ghee, melted	2 beef schnitzel	½ teaspoon ground black
½ teaspoon coarse sea salt	1 egg, beaten	50g Romano cheese, grated	pepper

1. Your Air Fryer should first be heated to 180°C. 2. Whisk the egg with the salt, pepper, and paprika in a small bowl. 3. In another shallow bowl, thoroughly mash the Romano cheese with the ghee. The schnitzel should be pounded with a meat mallet to ½ cm thickness. 4. The schnitzel should be first dipped in the egg mixture before being coated completely on all sides with the Romano cheese mixture. 5. In an Air Fryer that has been heated, cook for 13 minutes.
Per Serving: Calories 282, Fat 22.36g; Sodium 901mg; Carbs 1.84g; Fibre 0.6g; Sugar 0.62g; Protein 18.68g

Pork Sausage with Eggs and Peppers

Prep time: 5 minutes | Cook time: 24 minutes | Serves: 6

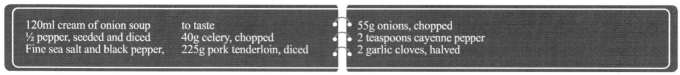

1 green pepper, seeded and thinly sliced	minced	sliced	6 pork sausages
6 medium-sized eggs	½ teaspoon sea salt	1 teaspoon tarragon	
1 Habanero pepper, seeded and	2 teaspoons fennel seeds	½ teaspoon freshly cracked	
	1 red pepper, seeded and thinly	black pepper	

1. Put all of the peppers and the sausages in the cooking basket for the Air Fryer. Cook for 9 minutes at 170°C. 2. Divide the eggs among 6 ramekins; sprinkle each egg with the seasonings. 3. Cook at 200°C for a further 11 minutes. Serve warm.
Per Serving: Calories 166, Fat 12.51g; Sodium 517mg; Carbs 3.64g; Fibre 0.7g; Sugar 1.33g; Protein 9.52g

Air Fryer Pork Tenderloin with Vegetables

Prep time: 5 minutes | Cook time: 20 minutes | Serves: 2

120ml cream of onion soup	to taste	55g onions, chopped
½ pepper, seeded and diced	40g celery, chopped	2 teaspoons cayenne pepper
Fine sea salt and black pepper,	225g pork tenderloin, diced	2 garlic cloves, halved

1. Set your air fryer at 195°C to start. 2. Add all ingredients to a baking dish that has already been lightly coated with rapeseed oil; bake for about five minutes. 3. Give the mixture a little stir, then heat for a further 12 minutes.
Per Serving: Calories 223, Fat 5.75g; Sodium 314mg; Carbs 10.64g; Fibre 1.9g; Sugar 2.97g; Protein 31.77g

Pork with Green Olives & Padrón Peppers

Prep time: 5 minutes | Cook time: 30 minutes | Serves: 4

1 teaspoon Celtic salt	1 tablespoon olive oil	drained	200g Padrón peppers
1 teaspoon paprika	1 heaped tablespoon capers,	8 green olives, pitted and halved	900g pork loin, sliced

1. Drizzle olive oil all over the Padrón peppers and cooked in an air fryer that has been warmed to 200°C for 10 minutes, occasionally flipping the peppers to ensure even cooking. 2. Then raise the heat to 180°C. 3. Salt and paprika are used to season the pork loin. Capers are added, and they are cooked for 16 minutes while being turned over halfway through. 4. Serve with the saved Padrón peppers and olives.
Per Serving: Calories 536, Fat 29.49g; Sodium 845mg; Carbs 5.99g; Fibre 1.3g; Sugar 2.99g; Protein 59.41g

Pork Sausage with Sauerkraut

Prep time: 5 minutes | Cook time: 30 minutes | Serves: 4

455g sauerkraut	4 pork sausages, smoked	2 bay leaves	2 garlic cloves, minced
1 teaspoon cayenne pepper	½ teaspoon black peppercorns	2 tablespoons rapeseed oil	

1. Set your Air Fryer to 180°C to begin. 2. The sausages should be placed in the cooking basket after being forked with holes made in them. Cook for 14 minutes while occasionally shaking the basket. Place aside. 3. Now, heat the rapeseed oil in a baking pan at 195°C. Add the garlic and cook for 1 minute. Add the bay leaves, cayenne pepper, peppercorns, and sauerkraut right away. 4. Allow it to cook for 15 minutes, stirring every five minutes. 5. Serve in individual bowls with warm sausages on the side!
Per Serving: Calories 149, Fat 10.41g; Sodium 766mg; Carbs 6.14g; Fibre 3.6g; Sugar 2.06g; Protein 8.57g

Shoulder Steak with Veggies and Herbs

Prep time: 5 minutes | Cook time:30 minutes | Serves: 4

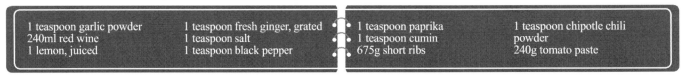

1 tablespoon red wine vinegar	pepper	225g Brussels sprouts, cleaned	455g beef chuck shoulder steak
1 teaspoon fine sea salt	1 teaspoon smoked paprika	and halved	2 tablespoons vegetable oil
1 teaspoon dried sage	1 teaspoon onion powder	½ teaspoon fennel seeds	
½ teaspoon ground black	½ teaspoon garlic powder	1 teaspoon dried basil	

1. The beef should first be marinated in a mixture of vegetable oil, wine vinegar, salt, black pepper, paprika, onion powder, and garlic powder. Let the meat marinate for at least three hours after applying the marinade. 2. Cook for 10 minutes at 200°C. Stop the machine and add the cooked Brussels sprouts. Then, add the basil, sage, and fennel seeds. 3. Press the power button, turn the temperature to 195°C, and cook for an additional 5 minutes. Restart the appliance, stir, and cook for an additional 10 minutes. 4. Next, take the meat out of the cooking basket and, if necessary and to your taste, simmer the vegetables for an additional few minutes. Serve with the mayo sauce of your choice.
Per Serving: Calories 252, Fat 13.38g; Sodium 663mg; Carbs 6.72g; Fibre 2.8g; Sugar 1.38g; Protein 26.23g

Spicy Short Ribs with Wine Sauce

Prep time: 5 minutes | Cook time: 15 minutes | Serves:4

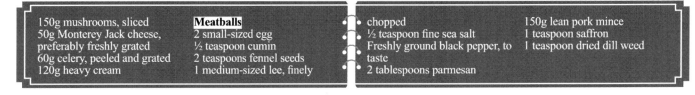

1 teaspoon garlic powder	1 teaspoon fresh ginger, grated	1 teaspoon paprika	1 teaspoon chipotle chili
240ml red wine	1 teaspoon salt	1 teaspoon cumin	powder
1 lemon, juiced	1 teaspoon black pepper	675g short ribs	240g tomato paste

1. The beef ribs, wine, lemon juice, ginger, salt, black pepper, paprika, and chipotle chili powder should all be combined in a ceramic bowl. In the refrigerator, cover it and let it marinade for three hours. 2. Short ribs are added to the Air Fryer basket once the marinade has been discarded. Cook for 10 minutes at 195°C in the prepared Air fryer, flipping them halfway through. 3. While waiting, preheat the pan over medium heat, add the reserved marinade, and whisk in the tomato paste, cumin, and garlic powder. Cook just until the sauce starts to slightly thicken. 4. Serve the sauce over the still-warm ribs right away.
Per Serving: Calories 327, Fat 10.34g; Sodium 1047mg; Carbs 42.73g; Fibre 6g; Sugar 21.9g; Protein 19.17g

Cheese Mushroom and Meatball Casserole

Prep time: 10 minutes | Cook time: 35 minutes | Serves: 4

150g mushrooms, sliced	**Meatballs**	chopped	150g lean pork mince
50g Monterey Jack cheese,	2 small-sized egg	½ teaspoon fine sea salt	1 teaspoon saffron
preferably freshly grated	½ teaspoon cumin	Freshly ground black pepper, to	1 teaspoon dried dill weed
60g celery, peeled and grated	2 teaspoons fennel seeds	taste	
120g heavy cream	1 medium-sized lee, finely	2 tablespoons parmesan	

1. Start by bringing the Air Fryer's temperature to 200°C. 2. Combine the meatball ingredients in a bowl. Create little meatballs out of the mixture. 3. Toss the celery and mushrooms with the cream in a baking dish for the Air Fryer, and cook for 23 minutes. 4. Stop the machine and sprinkle the celery or mushroom mixture with the reserved meatballs in a single layer. 5. Add the grated Monterey Jack cheese on top and bake for an additional 9 minutes. Serve hot.
Per Serving: Calories 340, Fat 20.58g; Sodium 224mg; Carbs 2.21g; Fibre 0.7g; Sugar 0.79g; Protein 36.23g

Pork Stuffed Peppers with Cheese

Prep time: 5 minutes | Cook time: 30 minutes | Serves: 3

½ teaspoon sea salt	2 ripe tomatoes, pureed	1 tablespoon olive oil	3 peppers, stems and seeds
½ teaspoon black pepper	75g Monterey Jack cheese,	3 spring onions, chopped	removed
1 tablespoon fish sauce	grated	1 teaspoon fresh garlic, minced	150g lean pork mince

1. Boil the peppers in salted water for 4 minutes. 2. Olive oil should be heated over medium heat in a nonstick frying pan. Then, cook the garlic and spring onions in a frying pan until aromatic and soft. 3. Stir in the pork mince and continue sautéing until the pork has browned; drain off the excess fat. 4. Add the salt, black pepper, fish sauce, and 1 pureed tomato; give it a good stir. 5. Divide the filling among the peppers. 6. In a baking dish that has been lightly coated with cooking oil, arrange the peppers. Surround the peppers with the remaining tomato puree. 7. Bake for 13 minutes at 195°C in the prepared Air Fryer. Add cheese shavings, then bake for an additional six minutes. 8. Enjoy warm servings!
Per Serving: Calories 425, Fat 25.94g; Sodium 1101mg; Carbs 9.59g; Fibre 2.2g; Sugar 5.17g; Protein 38.3g

Celery and Shallot Steak

Prep time: 10 minutes | Cook time:13 minutes | Serves: 6

75g tomatoes, crushed	2 sprigs fresh rosemary, chopped	1 teaspoon ground black pepper, or to taste	wedges
2 sprigs fresh thyme, chopped	120g celery, sliced	6 lean steaks, cut into strips	½ teaspoon cayenne pepper
1 teaspoon salt	4 tablespoons dry white wine	3 shallots, peeled and cut into	
80ml cream of shallot soup			

1. Add all the ingredients to an Air Fryer baking pan, cook for 13 minutes at 200°C. 2. Work in batches and pause the machine a few times to shake the food.
Per Serving: Calories 344, Fat 8.79g; Sodium 992mg; Carbs 52.1g; Fibre 3.5g; Sugar 11.38g; Protein 14.46g

Grilled Short Loin Steak with Mayo

Prep time: 10 minutes | Cook time:15 minutes | Serves: 4

1 tablespoon fresh rosemary, finely chopped	sauce	675g short loin steak	1 teaspoon smoked paprika
2 tablespoons Worcestershire	Sea salt, to taste	½ teaspoon ground black pepper	1 teaspoon garlic, minced
	240g mayonnaise		

1. Mix the salt, pepper, paprika, garlic, rosemary, Worcestershire sauce, and mayonnaise and combine well. 2. Apply the mayonnaise mixture on the steak now and brush it on both sides. Lower the steak onto the grill pan. 3. Grill for 8 minutes at 200°C in the prepared Air Fryer. Grill the steaks for an additional 7 minutes on the other side. 4. Use a meat thermometer to check the doneness. Enjoy warm servings!
Per Serving: Calories 682 Fat 56.9g; Sodium 735mg; Carbs 4.36g; Fibre 1g; Sugar 1.43g; Protein 36.07g

BBQ Skirt Steak with Herb

Prep time: 10 minutes | Cook time:12 minutes | Serves 5

1 tablespoon coconut aminos	Sea salt, to taste	¼ teaspoon black pepper, freshly cracked	2 tablespoons tomato paste
60ml rice vinegar	½ teaspoon dried dill	900g skirt steak	1 tablespoon olive oil
1 tablespoon fish sauce	½ teaspoon dried rosemary		

1. Put all the ingredients in a sizable ceramic dish, and refrigerate for three hours to let the flavours blend. 2. Apply cooking spray to the Air Fryer's bottom and sides. 3.Place the steak in the frying basket but keep the marinade aside. Turning over a couple of times, basting with the reserved marinade, cook the skirt steak in the preheated Air Fryer at 200°C for 12 minutes.
Per Serving: Calories 401 Fat 21.18g; Sodium 1108mg; Carbs 1.79g; Fibre 0.4g; Sugar 1.04g; Protein 51.03g

Herbed Cheese Fillet Mignon

Prep time: 10 minutes | Cook time: 13 minutes | Serves:4

1 small-sized egg, well-whisked	½ teaspoon cayenne pepper	Sea salt and ground black pepper, to your liking	1 teaspoon dried thyme
50g parmesan cheese, grated	1 teaspoon dried basil	1 teaspoon dried rosemary	1 tablespoon sesame oil
	455g filet mignon		

1. Basil, rosemary, thyme, cayenne pepper, salt, and black pepper are used to season the fillet mignon. Brush with sesame oil. 2. In a small plate, place the egg. The parmesan cheese should now be added on another plate. 3. Lay the fillet mignon into the parmesan cheese after coating it with the egg. Set your Air Fryer to 180°C to cook. 4. Cook until golden, about 10 to 13 minutes. Enjoy! Serve with a variety of salad greens.
Per Serving: Calories 253, Fat 13.15g; Sodium 315mg; Carbs 3.21g; Fibre 0.3g; Sugar 0.64g; Protein 30.75g

Herbed Beef Steaks with Chives

Prep time: 10 minutes | Cook time: 20 minutes | Serves: 4

2 tablespoons soy sauce	3 tablespoons dry white wine	½ teaspoon dried basil	1 teaspoon sea salt, or more to taste
3 heaping tablespoons fresh chives	4 small-sized beef steaks	½ teaspoon dried rosemary	
2 tablespoons olive oil	2 teaspoons smoked cayenne pepper	1 teaspoon freshly ground pepper	

1. Firstly, coat the steaks with the cayenne pepper, black pepper, salt, basil, and rosemary. 2. Drizzle the steaks with olive oil, white wine, and soy sauce. 3. Finally, roast in an Air Fryer basket for 20 minutes at 170°C. 4. Serve garnished with fresh chives. Bon appétit!
Per Serving: Calories 445, Fat 21.3g; Sodium 838mg; Carbs 9.68g; Fibre 0.7g; Sugar 1.7g; Protein 50.66g

Creamy and Balsamic Sirloin Steak

Prep time: 5 minutes | Cook time:20 minutes | Serves: 4

240ml beef stock	Sea salt flakes and	2½ tablespoons tomato paste	1 tablespoon brown mustard
45g leek, chopped	1 tablespoon butter	570g beef sirloin steak, cut into	
2 cloves garlic, crushed	crushed red pepper, to taste	small-sized strips	
1 teaspoon cayenne pepper	240g sour cream	60ml balsamic vinegar	

1. In a mixing bowl, combine the mustard, balsamic vinegar, and beef. Cover and refrigerate for approximately an hour to let the flavours blend. 2. Place the steak inside a baking dish that has been butter-lined. 3. Add the leeks, garlic, and stock. Cook for 8 minutes at 195°C. Stop the machine and stir in the cayenne, salt, red pepper, sour cream, and tomato paste. Continue cooking for an additional 7 minutes.
Per Serving: Calories 447, Fat 27.59g; Sodium 401mg; Carbs 15.17g; Fibre 1.7g; Sugar 6.11g; Protein 33.37g

Turkey, Pork and Veggie Meatloaf

Prep time: 5 minutes | Cook time: 30 minutes | Serves: 6

3 tablespoons fresh panko	2 gloves garlic, minced	2 sprigs rosemary, leaves only,	375g spicy pork mince sausage
Salt and freshly ground pepper,	1 tablespoon Worcestershire	crushed	Non-stick cooking spray
to your liking	sauce	10g minced fresh parsley	1 shallot, finely chopped
80g tomato paste	115g turkey mince	1 egg, lightly whisked	1 rib celery, finely chopped

1. Cooking spray should be used to coat a cast-iron frying pan. The shallots, celery, and garlic should then be sautéed until just soft and aromatic. 2. The sautéed mixture should now include Worcestershire sauce and both types of meat. Remove from the heat. Add the salt, pepper, egg, fresh panko, rosemary, and parsley; stir to thoroughly blend. 3. Shape the mixture into a loaf and transfer to the baking pan. Tomato paste should be applied to the prepared meatloaf. 4. 25 minutes of air-frying at 200°C or until well warmed.
Per Serving: Calories 318, Fat 25.64g; Sodium 539mg; Carbs 5.62g; Fibre 1.1g; Sugar 3.17g; Protein 16.54g

Ribeye Steak with Garlic Mayo

Prep time: 10 minutes | Cook time: 15 minutes | Serves: 3

3 tablespoons mayonnaise	½ teaspoon dried dill	675g ribeye, bone-in	1 teaspoon ground coriander
Salt, to taste	½ teaspoon cayenne pepper	1 tablespoon butter, room	
½ teaspoon crushed black	½ teaspoon garlic powder	temperature	
pepper	1 teaspoon garlic, minced	½ teaspoon onion powder	

1. Set your Air Fryer to 200°C to begin. 2. The ribeye should be thoroughly dried before being covered in softened butter. Add the seasonings, then move to the cooking basket. 3. Cook for 15 minutes in the preheated Air Fryer, turning them over halfway through. 4. Meanwhile, simply combine the mayonnaise and garlic, then store in the fridge until ready to serve.
Per Serving: Calories 392, Fat 19.31g; Sodium 297mg; Carbs 2.26g; Fibre 0.6g; Sugar 0.21g; Protein 52.6g

Pork and Mushroom Cheeseburgers

Prep time: 10 minutes | Cook time: 20 minutes | Serves: 4

1 tablespoon rapeseed oil	455g pork mince	Salt and black pepper, to taste	½ teaspoon dried dill
1 onion, chopped	225g brown mushrooms,	1 teaspoon cayenne pepper	4 slices Cheddar cheese
2 garlic cloves, minced	chopped	½ teaspoon dried rosemary	

1. To begin, warm your air fryer to 185°C. 2. Combine the oil, onions, garlic, pork mince, mushrooms, salt, black pepper, cayenne pepper, rosemary, and dill in a mixing bowl until well-combined. 3. Patties made from the meat mixture should be four. 4. Frying spray should be applied to the cooking basket's base. The meatballs should be cooked for 20 minutes at 185°C in the prepared Air Fryer, turning them over halfway through. 5. Add cheese to the heated burgers before serving. Enjoy!
Per Serving: Calories 593, Fat 29.67g; Sodium 367mg; Carbs 49.59g; Fibre 7.4g; Sugar 4.76g; Protein 38.05g

Lemony Pork Skewers

Prep time: 5 minutes | Cook time: 25 minutes | Serves: 4

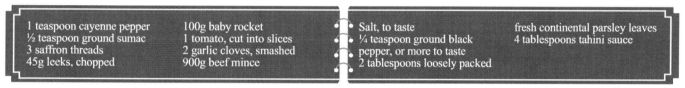

Sea salt and freshly ground black pepper, to taste	oil	1 teaspoon ground cumin	into bite-sized pieces
2 garlic cloves, minced	1 teaspoon oregano	60ml dry red wine	2 teaspoons sweet Spanish paprika
2 tablespoons extra virgin olive	½ teaspoon ground turmeric	1 lemon, ½ juiced ½ wedges	
	½ teaspoon ground coriander	900g centre cut loin chop, cut	

1. In a sizable ceramic dish, combine all the ingredients except for the lemon wedges. Put it in the refrigerator and let it marinade for two hours. 2. Throw away the marinade. The pork slices should now be skewered and placed in the frying basket. 3. Cook for 15 to 17 minutes at 180°C in the preheated Air Fryer, shaking the basket every 5 minutes. Work in groups. 4. Serve right away with lemon slices as a garnish.
Per Serving: Calories 330, Fat 11.74g; Sodium 195mg; Carbs 2.64g; Fibre 0.7g; Sugar 0.47g; Protein 50.36g

Beef Kebab with Baby Rocket

Prep time: 5 minutes | Cook time: 30 minutes | Serves:4

1 teaspoon cayenne pepper	100g baby rocket	Salt, to taste	fresh continental parsley leaves
½ teaspoon ground sumac	1 tomato, cut into slices	¼ teaspoon ground black	4 tablespoons tahini sauce
3 saffron threads	2 garlic cloves, smashed	pepper, or more to taste	
45g leeks, chopped	900g beef mince	2 tablespoons loosely packed	

1. Mix the minced leeks, minced garlic, beef mince, and spices in a bowl; then, using your hands, combine the ingredients thoroughly. 2. Now form a pointed-ended sausage by piling the beef mixture around a wooden skewer. 3. Cook for 25 minutes at 180°C in the preheated air fryer. 4. Serve your kebab with baby rocket, tomato, and tahini sauce. Enjoy!
Per Serving: Calories 363, Fat 17.79g; Sodium 271mg; Carbs 5.5g; Fibre 1.4g; Sugar 1.9g; Protein 46.12g

Crispy Pork Chops

Prep time: 50 minutes | Cook time: 18 minutes | Serves: 4

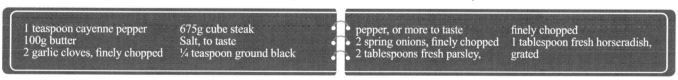

½ tablespoon soy sauce	4 large-sized pork chops	pepper, to taste	1½ tablespoons olive oil
2 tablespoons Worcestershire sauce	2 teaspoons mustard powder	1 teaspoon red pepper flakes, crushed	3 eggs, well-beaten
½ teaspoon dried rosemary	2 teaspoons fennel seeds	½ teaspoon dried thyme	100g Romano cheese, grated
	Salt and freshly cracked black		

1. Put the pork chops in a resealable plastic bag with the olive oil, soy sauce, Worcestershire sauce, herbs and seasonings. Refrigerate the pork chops for 50 minutes to marinate. 2. The pork chops should then be dipped into the beaten eggs and covered on both sides with Romano cheese. Indent the pork chops deeply with the breading. 3. Cook for 18 minutes with one flip at 210°C in the air fryer.
Per Serving: Calories 616, Fat 40.29g; Sodium 504mg; Carbs 4.96g; Fibre 0.8g; Sugar 2.52g; Protein 55.65g

Traditional Cube Steak with Butter Sauce

Prep time: 5 minutes | Cook time: 15 minutes | Serves: 4

1 teaspoon cayenne pepper	675g cube steak	pepper, or more to taste	finely chopped
100g butter	Salt, to taste	2 spring onions, finely chopped	1 tablespoon fresh horseradish, grated
2 garlic cloves, finely chopped	¼ teaspoon ground black	2 tablespoons fresh parsley,	

1. The cube steak should be dried off and seasoned with salt and black pepper. Spray cooking oil on the Air Fryer basket. Fill the basket with the meat. 2. Cook for 14 minutes at 200°C in the preheated air fryer. 3. In the meantime, gently heat the butter in a frying pan. When the sauce has slightly thickened and decreased, add the other ingredients and continue to cook. 4. Serve the Cowboy sauce on top of the warm cube steaks right away.
Per Serving: Calories 753 Fat 46.88g; Sodium 414 mg; Carbs 1.46g; Fibre 0.4g; Sugar 0.4g; Protein 77.7g

Creamy Beef with Sage and Green Onion

Prep time: 5 minutes | Cook time:15 minutes | Serves: 2

80g sour cream	3 cloves garlic, smashed	2 tablespoons fresh sage,	⅓ teaspoon black pepper, or to
80g green onion, chopped	455g beef flank steak, trimmed	minced	taste
1 tablespoon mayonnaise	and cubed	½ teaspoon salt	

1. In a baking dish that will fit in your air fryer, place beef cubes on the bottom and season the meat with salt and pepper. 2. Add the garlic and green onions and air fry for 7 minutes at 195°C. 3. Add the cream, mayonnaise, and sage after the beef begins to get soft, and air-fry for a further 8 minutes.
Per Serving: Calories 406, Fat 18.12g; Sodium 795mg; Carbs 6.96g; Fibre 1.4g; Sugar 0.92g; Protein 51.1g

Parmesan Beef Schnitzel

Prep time: 5 minutes | Cook time:10 minutes | Serves: 2

35g coconut flour	or more to taste	2 beef schnitzels	1 teaspoon cayenne pepper, or
25g parmesan cheese	Wedges of 1 fresh lemon, to	1 teaspoon fine sea salt	more to taste
⅓ freshly ground black pepper,	serve	2 medium-sized eggs	1½ tablespoons rapeseed oil

1. Season beef schnitzel with salt, cayenne pepper, and ground black pepper. 2. Mix the coconut flour, parmesan cheese, and oil in a bowl. Whisk the eggs in another bowl until they are light and foamy. 3. Beef schnitzels should first be covered with whisked eggs before being covered in the parmesan mixture. 4. 10 minutes of air-frying at 180°C. Enjoy when warm and garnished with lemon wedges!
Per Serving: Calories 383 Fat 25.3g; Sodium 1586mg; Carbs 5.59g; Fibre 0.7g; Sugar 1.65g; Protein 34.15g

Chili Beef Sausage Meatballs

Prep time: 10 minutes | Cook time:20 minutes | Serves: 4

2 tablespoons flaxseed meal	1 tablespoon poblano pepper,	pepper, to taste	½ teaspoon parsley flakes
3 cloves garlic, finely minced	chopped	½ tablespoon fresh chopped sage	2 teaspoons onion flakes
1 teaspoon Mexican oregano	Fine sea salt and ground black	160g green onion, finely minced	455g chili sausage, crumbled

1. In a bowl, combine all the ingredients and stir until the batter is evenly distributed. 2. Make bite-sized balls, then place them in a baking dish. 3. Cook for 18 minutes at 175°C in the prepared Air Fryer. Enjoy your food on wooden sticks!
Per Serving: Calories 368 Fat 18.55g; Sodium 3258mg; Carbs 62.55g; Fibre 41.08g; Sugar 10.33g; Protein 17.18g

Beef Burrito

Prep time: 5 minutes | Cook time:20 minutes | Serves: 4

1 teaspoon piri piri powder	1 head romaine lettuce,	1 teaspoon Mexican oregano	½ teaspoon onion powder
455g rump steak	separated into leaves	Salt and ground black pepper,	½ teaspoon cayenne pepper
100g grated cheese blend	1 teaspoon garlic powder	to taste	

1. Combine the Mexican oregano, garlic powder, onion powder, cayenne pepper, piri piri powder, salt, and black pepper with the rump steak. 2. Cook for 10 minutes at 200°C in the preheated Air Fryer. Cut into tiny strips going against the grain. Cook for another two minutes after adding the cheese mixture. 3. Fill the romaine lettuce leaves with the beef mixture, fold them up like a burrito, and then serve.
Per Serving: Calories 365 Fat 20.03g; Sodium 571mg; Carbs 7.81g; Fibre 3.7g; Sugar 2.85g; Protein 40.51g

Flank Steak with Wine Marinade

Prep time: 5 minutes | Cook time:12 minutes | Serves: 4

1 teaspoon thyme	675g flank steak	½ teaspoon ground black	crushed
2 tablespoons soy sauce	120ml red wine	pepper	½ teaspoon dried basil
Salt, to taste	60ml apple cider vinegar	½ teaspoon red pepper flakes,	

1. Add all ingredients to a large ceramic bowl. Cover and let it marinate for 3 hours in your refrigerator. 2. Transfer the flank steak to the Air Fryer basket that is previously greased with nonstick cooking oil. 3. Cook in the preheated Air Fryer at 200°C for 12 minutes, flipping over halfway through the cooking time. Bon appétit!
Per Serving: Calories 266 Fat 9.97g; Sodium 311mg; Carbs 2.94g; Fibre 0.3g; Sugar 2g; Protein 37.24g

Chapter 5 Fish and Seafood Recipes

Spicy Bacon Wrapped Scallops

Prep time: 15 minutes | Cook time:7 minutes | Serves: 4

| 455g scallops | 1 teaspoon chili powder | 100g bacon, sliced | 1 teaspoon avocado oil |

1. Wrap the scallops in bacon, then top with chili powder and avocado oil. 2. Place the scallops in the air fryer and cook for 7 minutes at 200°C.
Per Serving: Calories 178, Fat 10.15g; Sodium 879mg; Carbs 5.73g; Fibre 1g; Sugar 0.05g; Protein 16.79g

Easy Almond Catfish

Prep time: 10 minutes | Cook time: 12 minutes | Serves: 4

| 1 teaspoon avocado oil | 1 teaspoon salt | 2 eggs, beaten |
| 900g catfish fillet | 50g almond flour | |

1. Sprinkle the catfish fillet with salt and dip in the eggs. 2. Then coat the fish in the almond flour and put in the air fryer basket. Sprinkle the fish with avocado oil. 3. Cook the fish for 6 minutes per side at 195°C.
Per Serving: Calories 291, Fat 12.42g; Sodium 730mg; Carbs 0.54g; Fibre 0g; Sugar 0.33g; Protein 41.67g

Lemony Salmon

Prep time: 10 minutes | Cook time: 20 minutes | Serves: 4

| 1 teaspoon lemon zest, grated | 455g salmon fillets, boneless | 1 teaspoon avocado oil | 2 tablespoons lemon juice |

1. Combine avocado oil, lemon juice, and lemon zest. 2. Next, carefully rub the lemon mixture into the salmon fillets before placing them in the air fryer. 3. Cook the salmon for 10 minutes at 180°C on each side.
Per Serving: Calories 185, Fat 9.28g; Sodium 491mg; Carbs 0.61g; Fibre 0g; Sugar 0.22g; Protein 23.43g

Simple Fried Prawns

Prep time: 10 minutes | Cook time: 5 minutes | Serves: 3

| 1 teaspoon avocado oil | 455g prawns, peeled | 1 teaspoon onion powder | ½ teaspoon salt |

1. Season the prawns with salt, onion powder, and avocado oil. 2. Place the prawns in the air fryer and cook for five minutes at 200°C.
Per Serving: Calories 167, Fat 3.56g; Sodium 1704mg; Carbs 0.63g; Fibre 0.1g; Sugar 0.05g; Protein 30.96g

Bacon Wrapped Halibut

Prep time: 15 minutes | Cook time: 10 minutes | Serves: 2

| 1 teaspoon ground black pepper | 2 150g halibut steaks | 1 teaspoon avocado oil | 100g bacon, sliced |

1. Season the halibut steaks with freshly ground black pepper and avocado oil. 2. After that, wrap the fish in bacon pieces and air fry it. 3. Cook the fish for five minutes on each side at 200°C.
Per Serving: Calories 556, Fat 39.61g; Sodium 515mg; Carbs 2.86g; Fibre 0.9g; Sugar 0.57g; Protein 45.9g

Tangy Balsamic Tilapia

Prep time: 5 minutes | Cook time: 15 minutes | Serves: 4

| 1 teaspoon avocado oil | 4 tilapia fillets, boneless | 2 tablespoons balsamic vinegar | 1 teaspoon dried basil |

1. Drizzle balsamic vinegar, avocado oil, and dried basil over the tilapia fillets. 2. After that, place the fillets in the air fryer basket and cook for 15 minutes at 185°C.
Per Serving: Calories 129, Fat 3.1g; Sodium 62mg; Carbs 1.47g; Fibre 0.1g; Sugar 1.2g; Protein 23.37g

Easy Rosemary Salmon

Prep time: 10 minutes | Cook time: 9 minutes | Serves:3

| 2 tablespoons olive oil | 455g salmon | 1 teaspoon dried rosemary | ½ teaspoon salt |

1. Drizzle salt, olive oil, and dried rosemary over the salmon. 2. Place the salmon in the air fryer and cook for 9 minutes at 200°C.
Per Serving: Calories 311, Fat 19.85g; Sodium 1043mg; Carbs 0.05g; Fibre 0g; Sugar 0g; Protein 31.2g

Roasted Turmeric Tilapia

Prep time: 5 minutes | Cook time: 20 minutes | Serves:4

| 4 tilapia fillets, boneless and halved | 1 tablespoon avocado oil | 1 teaspoon ground turmeric |

1. Add ground turmeric and avocado oil to the tilapia fillets. 2. Place it in the air fryer and cook for 10 minutes on each side at 185°C.
Per Serving: Calories 145, Fat 5.5g; Sodium 61mg; Carbs 0.5g; Fibre 0.2g; Sugar 0.02g; Protein 23.37g

Simple Basil Prawns

Prep time: 5 minutes | Cook time: 12 minutes | Serves: 4

| 1 teaspoon dried basil | 455g prawns, peeled | 1 tablespoon avocado oil | ½ teaspoon salt |

1. Combine salt, dried basil, and avocado oil with the prawns. 2. Layer them in the air fryer and cook for 12 minutes at 185°C.
Per Serving: Calories 145, Fat 5.05g; Sodium 1277mg; Carbs 0.08g; Fibre 0.1g; Sugar 0g; Protein 23.2g

Prawns Skewers with Rosemary

Prep time: 10 minutes | Cook time: 05 minutes | Serves: 5

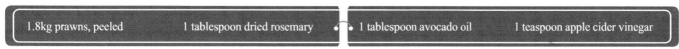

| 1.8kg prawns, peeled | 1 tablespoon dried rosemary | 1 tablespoon avocado oil | 1 teaspoon apple cider vinegar |

1. Combine the prawns with the apple cider vinegar, avocado oil, and dried rosemary. 2. After that, thread the prawns onto skewers and fried them in an air fryer. 3. Cook the prawns for 5 minutes at 200°C.
Per Serving: Calories 389, Fat 7.76g; Sodium 3157mg; Carbs 0.19g; Fibre 0.1g; Sugar 0.1g; Protein 74.11g

Cod with Heavy Cream Sauce

Prep time: 5 minutes | Cook time: 15 minutes | Serves: 2

| 1 teaspoon garlic powder | 2 cod fillets, boneless | 60g heavy cream |
| 1 teaspoon butter, softened | ½ teaspoon cayenne pepper | 1 teaspoon ground black pepper |

1. Combine heavy cream, cayenne pepper, garlic powder, and black pepper in a mixing bowl. 2. Continue whisking while adding butter. 3. Then put the cod fillets in the baking pan and top with heavy cream sauce. Put the baking pan in the air fryer. 4. Cook the fish for 15 minutes at 190°C.
Per Serving: Calories 164, Fat 8.07g; Sodium 375mg; Carbs 3.93g; Fibre 0.6g; Sugar 1.65g; Protein 18.8g

Cheese Cod Fillets

Prep time: 10 minutes | Cook time:15 minutes | Serves: 4

| 1 teaspoon avocado oil | 4 cod fillets, boneless | 100g Cheddar cheese, shredded | ½ teaspoon ground black pepper |

1. Season the cod fillets with freshly ground black pepper and drizzle with avocado oil. 2. Add Cheddar cheese on top and place them in the air fryer basket. 3. Prepare the fish for 15 minutes at 185°C.
Per Serving: Calories 226, Fat 12.77g; Sodium 564mg; Carbs 0.97g; Fibre 0.1g; Sugar 0.38g; Protein 25.76g

Cod with Hot Sauce

Prep time: 5 minutes | Cook time: 15 minutes | Serves:4

4 cod fillets, boneless	1 tablespoon keto hot sauce	1 tablespoon avocado oil	½ teaspoon ground cinnamon

1. Drizzle avocado oil, ground cinnamon, and spicy sauce over the fish fillets. 2. After that, cook the fish for 15 minutes at 175°C in the air fryer basket.
Per Serving: Calories 113, Fat 3.99g; Sodium 383mg; Carbs 0.56g; Fibre 0.3g; Sugar 0.18g; Protein 17.8g

Lime Lobster Tail with Basil

Prep time: 10 minutes | Cook time: 6 minutes | Serves:4

½ teaspoon dried basil	4 lobster tails, peeled	2 tablespoons lime juice	½ teaspoon coconut oil, melted

1. Combine the lobster tails with the lime juice, coconut oil, and dried basil. 2. Cook the lobster tails in the air fryer for 6 minutes at 195°C.
Per Serving: Calories 123, Fat 1.71g; Sodium 635mg; Carbs 0.69g; Fibre 0.1g; Sugar 0.13g; Protein 23.83g

Coconut Sardines

Prep time: 15 minutes | Cook time: 10 minutes | Serves: 5

300g sardines, trimmed, cleaned	125g coconut flour 1 tablespoon coconut oil	1 teaspoon salt	

1. Before coating the sardines in coconut flour, salt them. 2. After that, coat the air fryer basket with coconut oil and add the sardines. 3. Prepare them for 10 minutes at 195°C.
Per Serving: Calories 174, Fat 10.61g; Sodium 724mg; Carbs 1.78g; Fibre 0.5g; Sugar 1.25g; Protein 17.1g

Paprika Provolone Salmon

Prep time: 5 minutes | Cook time: 15 minutes | Serves: 4

455g salmon fillet, chopped	50g Provolone, grated	1 teaspoon avocado oil	¼ teaspoon ground paprika

1. Drizzle avocado oil over the salmon fillets before placing them in the air fryer. 2. After that, top the fish with Provolone cheese and paprika powder. 3. Prepare the fish for 15 minutes at 180°C.
Per Serving: Calories 234, Fat 13.05g; Sodium 615mg; Carbs 0.38g; Fibre 0.1g; Sugar 0.09g; Protein 27.04g

Flavoured Catfish

Prep time: 5 minutes | Cook time: 15 minutes | Serves: 4

½ teaspoon apple cider vinegar	1 tablespoon ground cumin	1 tablespoon avocado oil	455g catfish fillet

1. Catfish fillets should be rubbed with ground cumin, avocado oil, and apple cider vinegar before being cooked in an air fryer for 15 minutes at 180°C .
Per Serving: Calories 145, Fat 7.03g; Sodium 51mg; Carbs 0.74g; Fibre 0.2g; Sugar 0.1g; Protein 18.84g

Salmon with Basil

Prep time: 10 minutes | Cook time: 8 minutes | Serves: 2

1 teaspoon dried basil 250g salmon fillet	½ teaspoon ground coriander 1 teaspoon ground cumin	1 tablespoon avocado oil	

1. Combine the dried basil, ground cumin, and ground coriander in a small bowl. 2. Next, drizzle avocado oil over the salmon fillet and cover with the seasonings. 3. Place the fish in the basket of the air fryer and cook for 4 minutes on each side at 200°C.
Per Serving: Calories 284, Fat 17.41g; Sodium 616 mg; Carbs 0.64g; Fibre 0.2g; Sugar 0.03g; Protein 29.51g

Scallops with Rosemary

Prep time: 10 minutes | Cook time: 6 minutes | Serves:4

| 300g scallops | 1 tablespoon dried rosemary | ½ teaspoon Pink salt | 1 tablespoon avocado oil |

1. Drizzle avocado oil, pink salt, and dried rosemary over the scallops. 2. After that, place the scallops in the air fryer basket and cook for 6 minutes at 200°C.
Per Serving: Calories 91, Fat 3.94g; Sodium 334mg; Carbs 2.92g; Fibre 0.1g; Sugar 0g; Protein 10.31g

Prawns in Italian Style

Prep time: 3 minutes | Cook time: 5 minutes | Serves:4

| 455g prawns, peeled | 1 tablespoon avocado oil | 1 tablespoon Italian seasonings |

1. Place the prawns in the air fryer basket and season with Italian seasonings and avocado oil. 2. Cook the prawns for 5 minutes at 200°C.
Per Serving: Calories 151, Fat 5.04g; Sodium 1141mg; Carbs 1.25g; Fibre 0.3g; Sugar 0.23g; Protein 23.25g

Easy Lime Salmon

Prep time: 5 minutes | Cook time: 20 minutes | Serves: 4

| 455g salmon, chopped / 1 tablespoon lime juice | 1 teaspoon avocado oil / 1 teaspoon lime zest, grated | ¼ teaspoon ground nutmeg |

1. Apply avocado oil, lime juice, ground nutmeg, and lime zest to the fish. 2. Cook the fish for 20 minutes at 180°C in the air fryer.
Per Serving: Calories 185, Fat 9.31g; Sodium 491mg; Carbs 0.5g; Fibre 0.1g; Sugar 0.09g; Protein 23.42g

Spicy Calamari

Prep time: 10 minutes | Cook time:6 minutes | Serves:2

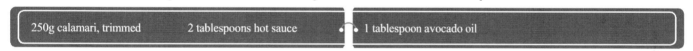

| 250g calamari, trimmed | 2 tablespoons hot sauce | 1 tablespoon avocado oil |

1. Cut the calamari into slices and drizzle with avocado oil. 2. Place the calamari in the air fryer and fry for 3 minutes on each side at 200°C. 3. After that, put the calamari on a platter for serving and top with hot sauce.
Per Serving: Calories 309, Fat 16.51g; Sodium 232mg; Carbs 1.21g; Fibre 0.3g; Sugar 0.71g; Protein 37.06g

Cod with Jalapeno

Prep time: 5 minutes | Cook time: 14 minutes | Serves: 4

| 4 cod fillets, boneless | 1 jalapeno, minced | 1 tablespoon avocado oil | ½ teaspoon minced garlic |

1. Combine the minced jalapeno, avocado oil, and minced garlic in a small bowl. 2. Arrange the cod fillets in a single layer in the air fryer basket, then top with the minced jalapeno mixture. 3. Cook the fish for 7 minutes on each side at 185°C.
Per Serving: Calories 113, Fat 3.99g; Sodium 352mg; Carbs 0.34g; Fibre 0.1g; Sugar 0.15g; Protein 17.77g

Spicy Cinnamon Cod

Prep time: 15 minutes | Cook time:9 minutes | Serves:2

| 1 chili pepper, chopped | 300g cod fillet, sliced | 1 teaspoon avocado oil | ½ teaspoon ground cinnamon |

1. Place the fish fillet in the air fryer basket after sprinkling it with avocado oil. 2. Then sprinkle ground cinnamon and chili powder on top. 3. Prepare the fish for 9 minutes at 190°C.
Per Serving: Calories 148, Fat 3g; Sodium 517mg; Carbs 2.65g; Fibre 0.7g; Sugar 1.16g; Protein 26.45g

Flavourful Tilapia Fillets

Prep time: 5 minutes | Cook time: 14 minutes | Serves: 4

| 2 tablespoons Erythritol | 4 tilapia fillets, boneless | 1 teaspoon olive oil | 1 tablespoon apple cider vinegar |

1. Combine erythritol, olive oil, and apple cider vinegar. 2. Next, coat the tilapia fillets with the sweet mixture and arrange them in a single layer in the air fryer basket. 3. Cook the fish for 7 minutes on each side at 180°C .
Per Serving: Calories 123, Fat 3.1g; Sodium 60 mg; Carbs 0.94g; Fibre 0g; Sugar 0.37g; Protein 23.3g

Lemon Crawfish

Prep time: 10 minutes | Cook time:5 minutes | Serves:4

| 455g crawfish | 1 tablespoon olive oil | 1 tablespoons lemon juice |

1. Place the crawfish in the air fryer and cook at 185°C for 5 minutes. 2. Next, take the crawfish out of the air fryer and drizzle with lemon juice and olive oil.
Per Serving: Calories 123, Fat 4.74g; Sodium 395mg; Carbs 0.53g; Fibre 0g; Sugar 0.19g; Protein 18.92g

Parmesan Mackerel

Prep time: 10 minutes | Cook time: 7 minutes | Serves:2

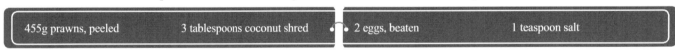

| 300g mackerel fillet | 50g Parmesan, grated | 1 teaspoon ground coriander | 1 tablespoon olive oil |

1. Place the mackerel fillet in the air fryer basket after lightly sprinkling it with olive oil. 2. Sprinkle grated Parmesan and ground coriander over the fish. 3. Prepare the fish for 7 minutes at 200°C.
Per Serving: Calories 343, Fat 11.57g; Sodium 595mg; Carbs 11.53g; Fibre 0g; Sugar 0.43g; Protein 45.84g

Delicious Coconut Prawns

Prep time: 5 minutes | Cook time: 12 minutes | Serves:4

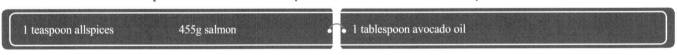

| 455g prawns, peeled | 3 tablespoons coconut shred | 2 eggs, beaten | 1 teaspoon salt |

1. Combine the salt and prawns. 2. Next, coat each prawns with coconut shred after dipping it in the eggs. 3. Add the prawns to the air fryer, and cook for 12 minutes at 190°C.
Per Serving: Calories 180, Fat 6.38g; Sodium 1631mg; Carbs 0.92g; Fibre 0.1g; Sugar 0.62g; Protein 27.72g

Spiced Salmon

Prep time: 10 minutes | Cook time: 15 minutes | Serves:4

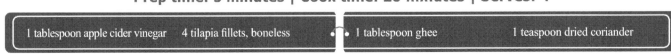

| 1 teaspoon allspices | 455g salmon | 1 tablespoon avocado oil |

1. Sprinkle avocado oil over the salmon after seasoning with all the seasonings. 2. Place the salmon in the basket of the air fryer and cook for 15 minutes at 180°C.
Per Serving: Calories 206, Fat 11.67g; Sodium 491mg; Carbs 0.34g; Fibre 0.1g; Sugar 0g; Protein 23.42g

Fresh Tilapia

Prep time: 5 minutes | Cook time: 20 minutes | Serves: 4

| 1 tablespoon apple cider vinegar | 4 tilapia fillets, boneless | 1 tablespoon ghee | 1 teaspoon dried coriander |

1. Combine the dried basil, ground cumin, and ground coriander in the small bowl. 2. Next, drizzle avocado oil over the salmon fillet and cover with the seasonings. 3. Place the fish in the basket of the air fryer and cook for 10 minutes on each side at 190°C.
Per Serving: Calories 138, Fat 4.85g; Sodium 83mg; Carbs 0.04g; Fibre 0g; Sugar 0.02g; Protein 23.32g

Coconut Cod Nuggets

Prep time:10 minutes | Cook time:10 minutes | Serves: 4

25g coconut shred	1 teaspoon salt	250g cod fillet
3 tablespoons almond flour	3 eggs, beaten	1 teaspoon avocado oil

1. Salt the cod fillets after cutting them into nuggets. 2. Next, coat the fish with almond flour after dipping it in eggs. 3. Next, coat the fish with coconut shred after dipping it once more in the eggs. 4. After that, put the nuggets in the air fryer and sprinkle with avocado oil. 5. At 190°C, cook the nuggets for 5 minutes on each side.
Per Serving: Calories 321, Fat 21.59g; Sodium 1021mg; Carbs 7.89g; Fibre 4.6g; Sugar 1.49g; Protein 23.32g

Spicy Cod Pan

Prep time: 5 minutes | Cook time: 12 minutes | Serves: 4

455g cod fillet, chopped	1 teaspoon chili flakes	1 teaspoon dried coriander
1 teaspoon coconut oil	½ teaspoon cayenne pepper	¼ teaspoon ground nutmeg

1. Rub the coconut oil, chili flakes, cayenne, dried coriander, and crushed nutmeg into the cod fillet. 2. Place the fillets in the air fryer and heat to 185°C for 6 minutes on each side.
Per Serving: Calories 250, Fat 13.86g; Sodium 82mg; Carbs 0.54g; Fibre 0.3g; Sugar 0.08g; Protein 29.17g

Coconut Salmon

Prep time: 15 minutes | Cook time: 8 minutes | Serves: 4

900g salmon fillet	25g coconut shred	1 teaspoon coconut oil
1 teaspoon Italian seasonings	2 eggs, beaten	

1. Serve the salmon fillet in pieces. 2. Next, add some Italian spice and dip the fish in the eggs. 3. Next, cover each salmon fillet with shredded coconut and place it in the air fryer. 4. Cook the fish for 4 minutes on each side at 190°C.
Per Serving: Calories 427, Fat 22.24g; Sodium 1101mg; Carbs 1.48g; Fibre 0.3g; Sugar 0.8g; Protein 51.41g

Coconut Crab Buns

Prep time: 15 minutes | Cook time: 20 minutes | Serves: 2

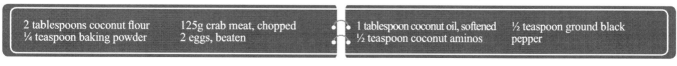

2 tablespoons coconut flour	125g crab meat, chopped	1 tablespoon coconut oil, softened	½ teaspoon ground black pepper
¼ teaspoon baking powder	2 eggs, beaten	½ teaspoon coconut aminos	

1. Combine the crab meat, eggs, coconut flour, baking powder, coconut aminos, coarsely powdered black pepper, and coconut oil in a mixing bowl. 2. Knead the silky dough and chop it up. 3. Form the crab mixture into buns and place them in the air fryer basket. 4. Bake the crab buns at 185°C for 20 minutes.
Per Serving: Calories 418, Fat 18.6g; Sodium 128 mg; Carbs 30.16g; Fibre 12.8g; Sugar 1.65g; Protein 36.33g

Tilapia with Chili and Oregano

Prep time: 5 minutes | Cook time: 20 minutes | Serves: 4

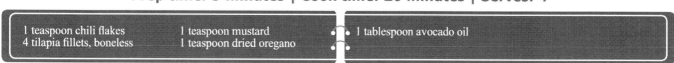

1 teaspoon chili flakes	1 teaspoon mustard	1 tablespoon avocado oil
4 tilapia fillets, boneless	1 teaspoon dried oregano	

1. Before placing the tilapia fillets in the air fryer, season them with mustard, avocado oil, dried oregano, and chili flakes. 2. At 180°C, cook it for 10 minutes on each side.
Per Serving: Calories 146, Fat 5.62g; Sodium 94mg; Carbs 0.58g; Fibre 0.4g; Sugar 0.07g; Protein 23.45g

Haddock in Cream

Prep time: 10 minutes | Cook time: 8 minutes | Serves: 4

455g haddock fillet	1 teaspoon salt	120g heavy cream
1 teaspoon cayenne pepper	1 teaspoon coconut oil	

1. Use coconut oil to coat the baking dish. 2. Next, place the haddock fillet inside and top with heavy cream, salt, and cayenne pepper. 3. Place the baking pan in the basket of the air fryer, and cook for 8 minutes at 190°C.
Per Serving: Calories 147, Fat 7.26g; Sodium 829mg; Carbs 0.67g; Fibre 0.1g; Sugar 0.47g; Protein 18.87g

Spinach Stuffed Mackerel

Prep time: 15 minutes | Cook time: 20 minutes | Serves: 5

455g mackerel, trimmed	15g spinach, chopped	1 teaspoon ground black pepper
1 pepper, chopped	1 tablespoon avocado oil	1 teaspoon tomato paste

1. Combine the pepper, spinach, tomato paste, and coarsely ground black pepper in a mixing dish. 2. Fill the mackerel with spinach mixture. 3. Next, fried the fish in the air fryer after brushing it with avocado oil. 4. Cook the fish for 20 minutes at 185°C.
Per Serving: Calories 128, Fat 4.67g; Sodium 148 mg; Carbs 1.93g; Fibre 0.4g; Sugar 1.01g; Protein 18.87g

Cheese and Olive Stuffed Salmon

Prep time: 15 minutes | Cook time:15 minutes | Serves:4

455g salmon fillet	1 teaspoon avocado oil	50g Mozzarella, shredded
4 kalamata olives, sliced	1 teaspoon Italian seasonings	

1. Cut the salmon with a pocket-shaped incision. 2. Stuff the cut fish with mozzarella and olives. 3. Use the toothpick to close the cut, then top the salmon with avocado oil and Italian spice. 4. Cook the fish in the air fryer basket for 15 minutes at 195°C.
Per Serving: Calories 210, Fat 9.67g; Sodium 691mg; Carbs 1.02g; Fibre 0.4g; Sugar 0.3g; Protein 27.95g

Simple Prawns Cakes

Prep time: 15 minutes | Cook time: 15 minutes | Serves:4

455g prawns, peeled, chopped	1 egg, beaten	1 teaspoon avocado oil
3 tablespoons coconut flour	1 courgette, grated	

1. Combine grated courgette, coconut flour, and chopped prawns in a bowl, stir well. 2. Brush avocado oil on the air fryer basket. 3. Then, in the air fryer, prepare the prawns cakes. 4. Cook them for 15 minutes at 190°C.
Per Serving: Calories 158, Fat 5.11g; Sodium 1024mg; Carbs 0.76g; Fibre 0.2g; Sugar 0.46g; Protein 25.55g

Delicious Prawns Bake

Prep time: 15 minutes | Cook time: 5 minutes | Serves: 4

350g prawns, peeled	240ml of coconut milk	½ teaspoon coconut oil
1 egg, beaten	100g Cheddar cheese, shredded	1 teaspoon ground coriander

1. Combine the prawns, egg, coconut milk, Cheddar cheese, coconut oil, and powdered coriander in a mixing dish. 2. After that, place the mixture in the baking ramekins and air fried them. 3. Cook the prawns for 5 minutes at 200°C.
Per Serving: Calories 340, Fat 22.65g; Sodium 1106mg; Carbs 2.36g; Fibre 0.7g; Sugar 1.26g; Protein 31.13g

Cheesy Mustard Tilapia

Prep time:10 minutes | Cook time:14 minutes | Serves: 4

¼ teaspoon ground cumin 100g Monterey Jack cheese,	grated 4 tilapia fillets	1 tablespoon Dijon mustard

1. Sprinkle some Dijon mustard and ground cumin on the tilapia fillets. 2. Arrange the fish in a single layer and top with the cheese in the air fryer. 3. Prepare the tilapia at 185°C for 14 minutes.
Per Serving: Calories 237, Fat 12.12g; Sodium 302mg; Carbs 0.51g; Fibre 0.2g; Sugar 0.2g; Protein 31.54g

Turmeric Cod with Chili

Prep time:10 minutes | Cook time:7 minutes | Serves: 2

1 tablespoon coconut oil, melted	300g cod fillet 1 teaspoon ground turmeric	1 teaspoon chili flakes ½ teaspoon salt

1. Combine salt, crushed turmeric, and chili flakes with coconut oil. 2. Next, combine ground turmeric with fish fillet before placing in air fryer basket. 3. Prepare the cod for 7 minutes at 195°C.
Per Serving: Calories 184, Fat 7.74g; Sodium 1136mg; Carbs 1.68g; Fibre 0.8g; Sugar 0.15g; Protein 26.3g

Salmon Cubes with Garlic

Prep time: 5 minutes | Cook time:15 minutes | Serves:4

900g salmon, cubed 1 teaspoon minced garlic	½ teaspoon garlic powder 1 tablespoon ghee, melted	½ teaspoon dried dill ½ teaspoon dried parsley

1. Combine the chopped salmon with the garlic, dry dill, parsley, and minced garlic. 2. Add fish to the ghee in the air fryer. 3. Prepare the fish for 15 minutes at 185°C. Shake the fish every 5 minutes.
Per Serving: Calories 376, Fat 19.19g; Sodium 1005mg; Carbs 0.69g; Fibre 0.1g; Sugar 0.02g; Protein 46.98g

Salmon with Chicory

Prep time: 5 minutes | Cook time: 20 minutes | Serves:4

1 tablespoon ghee 2 chicory, shredded	60g coconut cream 455g salmon fillet, chopped	1 teaspoon ground coriander

1. Place everything in the air fryer and give it a gentle shake. 2. Cook the food at 180°C for 20 minutes with the cover on. Shake the fish every five minutes.
Per Serving: Calories 251, Fat 16.24g; Sodium 518mg; Carbs 1.48g; Fibre 0.8g; Sugar 0.04g; Protein 24.15g

Erythritol Salmon with Coconut Amino

Prep time: 10 minutes | Cook time: 9 minutes | Serves:6

900g salmon fillet, chopped 1 teaspoon Erythritol	1 tablespoon coconut aminos ½ teaspoon dried basil	1 tablespoon avocado oil

1. Combine the avocado oil, dried basil, erythritol, and coconut aminos with the salmon. 2. Give the fish a 5-minute marinade. 3. After that, place the mixture in the air fryer and heat it to 180°C for 9 minutes.
Per Serving: Calories 253, Fat 13.18g; Sodium 657mg; Carbs 0.29g; Fibre 0.1g; Sugar 0.07g; Protein 31.23g

Mustard Tuna

Prep time: 10 minutes | Cook time: 12 minutes | Serves:4

| 1 tablespoon mustard | 455g tuna steaks, boneless and | 1 tablespoon apple cider |
| 1 tablespoon avocado oil | cubed | vinegar |

1. Combine mustard, apple cider vinegar, and avocado oil. 2. Next, apply the mustard mixture on the tuna steaks and place them in the air fryer basket. 3. Sear the fish for 6 minutes on each side at 180°C.
Per Serving: Calories 299, Fat 17.82g; Sodium 110mg; Carbs 0.67g; Fibre 0.2g; Sugar 0.41g; Protein 31.12g

Sweet and Sour Mussels

Prep time: 10 minutes | Cook time: 2 minutes | Serves:5

| 900g mussels, cleaned, peeled | 1 teaspoon ground cumin | 60ml apple cider vinegar |
| 1 teaspoon onion powder | 1 tablespoon avocado oil | |

1. Combine the mussels with the cumin powder, avocado oil, onion powder, and apple cider vinegar. 2. Place the mussels in the air fryer and fry for 2 minutes at 200°C.
Per Serving: Calories 190, Fat 6.98g; Sodium 520mg; Carbs 8.66g; Fibre 0.1g; Sugar 1.23g; Protein 21.73g

Cod in Tomatillos

Prep time: 10 minutes | Cook time: 15 minutes | Serves:4

| 1 tablespoon avocado oil | 1 teaspoon keto tomato paste | 455g cod fillet, roughly |
| 1 tablespoon lemon juice | 50g tomatillos, chopped | chopped |

1. Combine tomato paste and avocado oil. 2. Next, combine the tomato mixture with the fish fillet and cook in the air fryer. 3. Add tomatillos and lemon juice. 4. Prepare the fish for 15 minutes at 185°C.
Per Serving: Calories 274, Fat 16.2g; Sodium 63mg; Carbs 1.25g; Fibre 0.3g; Sugar 0.76g; Protein 29.23g

Spicy Fish Fingers

Prep time: 15 minutes | Cook time: 9 minutes | Serves:4

| 455g tilapia fillet | 2 eggs, beaten | 1 teaspoon dried oregano |
| 60g coconut flour | ½ teaspoon ground paprika | 1 teaspoon avocado oil |

1. Slice the tilapia fillets into fingers and season with dry oregano and paprika. 2. Next, coat the tilapia fingers in coconut flour after dipping them in eggs. 3. Drizzle avocado oil over fish fingers and air fry for 9 minutes at 185°C.
Per Serving: Calories 191, Fat 7.98g; Sodium 142mg; Carbs 1.95g; Fibre 0.5g; Sugar 1.15g; Protein 27.54g

Parsley Prawns with Coriander

Prep time: 5 minutes | Cook time: 12 minutes | Serves:4

| 455g prawns, peeled and | 1 teaspoon dried parsley | 1 tablespoon olive oil |
| deveined | 1 teaspoon dried coriander | ½ teaspoon salt |

1. Combine the parsley, coriander, salt, and olive oil with the prawns. 2. Fill the air fryer basket with the prawns mixture, and cook for 12 minutes at 180°C.
Per Serving: Calories 143, Fat 4.92g; Sodium 1278mg; Carbs 0.02g; Fibre 0g; Sugar 0g; Protein 23.17g

Creamy Prawns with Swiss Chard

Prep time: 10 minutes | Cook time: 10 minutes | Serves:4

455g prawns, peeled and deveined	½ teaspoon smoked paprika 20g Swiss chard, chopped	2 tablespoons apple cider vinegar	1 tablespoon coconut oil 60g heavy cream

1. Combine prawns with apple cider vinegar and smoked paprika. 2. Add coconut oil to the air fryer before adding the prawns. 3. Cook the prawns for 10 minutes at 175°C. 4. Carefully combine cooked prawns with the remaining ingredients.
Per Serving: Calories 174, Fat 7.77g; Sodium 1000mg; Carbs 1.42g; Fibre 0.2g; Sugar 1.04g; Protein 23.44g

Cheese Prawns and Lettuce Salad

Prep time: 10 minutes | Cook time: 5 minutes | Serves:4

60g mozzarella, shredded 1 tablespoon apple cider	vinegar 1 teaspoon white pepper	30g lettuce, chopped 455g prawns, peeled	1 teaspoon avocado oil 1 teaspoon chili powder

1. Combine the prawns with the apple cider vinegar and white pepper. 2. Cook the prawns in the air fryer at 200°C for 5 minutes. 3. Following that, add the prawns to the salad dish. 4. Fill the salad with the remaining ingredients and shake.
Per Serving: Calories 133, Fat 1.87g; Sodium 260mg; Carbs 1.58g; Fibre 0.8g; Sugar 0.4g; Protein 27.61g

Cajun Prawns with Mascarpone

Prep time: 10 minutes | Cook time: 6 minutes | Serves:4

455g prawns, peeled 1 teaspoon olive oil	1 teaspoon Cajun seasonings 1 teaspoon mascarpone	½ teaspoon salt

1. Combine prawns with salt, olive oil, and Cajun seasonings. 2. Place the prawns in the air fryer and fry them for 6 minutes at 200°C. 3. After that, add the mascarpone and place the prawns in the bowl.
Per Serving: Calories 126, Fat 2.67g; Sodium 1330mg; Carbs 0.42g; Fibre 0.1g; Sugar 0.08g; Protein 23.19g

Tilapia and Cauliflower Fritters

Prep time: 15 minutes | Cook time: 12 minutes | Serves:4

455g tilapia fillet, diced 3 tablespoons coconut flour	25g cauliflower, shredded 1 egg, beaten	1 teaspoon ground black pepper ¼ teaspoon ground paprika

1. Combine chopped tilapia fillet, coconut flour, cauliflower, egg, black pepper, and paprika in a mixing dish. 2. From the tilapia mixture, make fritters and place them in the air fryer in a single layer. 3. Cook the fritters for 6 minutes on each side at 185°C.
Per Serving: Calories 150, Fat 4.42g; Sodium 99mg; Carbs 2.15g; Fibre 0.5g; Sugar 1.17g; Protein 25.47g

Salmon and Courgette Fritters

Prep time: 15 minutes | Cook time: 12 minutes | Serves:4

2 tablespoons almond flour 1 courgette, grated	1 egg, beaten 150g salmon fillet, diced	1 teaspoon avocado oil ½ teaspoon ground black	pepper

1. Combine almond flour, courgette, salmon, eggs, and freshly ground black pepper. 2. Next, use the salmon mixture to form the fritters. 3. Add the fritters to the avocado oil-sprinkle-lined air fryer basket. 4. Cook the fritters for 6 minutes on each side at 190°C.
Per Serving: Calories 114, Fat 6.91g; Sodium 210mg; Carbs 1g; Fibre 0.2g; Sugar 0.48g; Protein 11.33g

Parmesan Tuna Boats

Prep time: 15 minutes | Cook time: 12 minutes | Serves:2

| 1 courgette, trimmed, halved | 150g. tuna, canned | 1 teaspoon dried parsley | 50g Parmesan, grated |

1. To create the shape of the boards, remove the courgette's flesh. 2. Next, combine the tuna with Parmesan and dry parsley. 3. Place the courgette boats in the air fryer basket after filling them with the tuna mixture. 4. Prepare the food for 12 minutes at 195°C.
Per Serving: Calories 199, Fat 1.86g; Sodium 365mg; Carbs 11.55g; Fibre 0.1g; Sugar 0.43g; Protein 32.26g

Roasted Prawns with Peppers

Prep time: 5 minutes | Cook time: 12 minutes | Serves:4

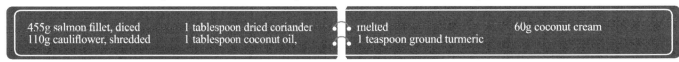

| 2 peppers, sliced | vinegar | 1 teaspoon onion powder | 455g prawns, peeled |
| 1 tablespoon apple cider | 1 teaspoon fajita seasonings | 1 tablespoon avocado oil | |

1. Combine apple cider vinegar, fajita spice, onion powder, and avocado oil in a shallow basin. 2. Next, combine the spice mixture with the prawns, and add to the air fryer. 3. Cook the prawns for 5 minutes 200°C. 4. Place the peppers on top of the prawns on the serving plate.
Per Serving: Calories 160, Fat 5.11g; Sodium 988mg; Carbs 0.34g; Fibre 0.2g; Sugar 0.01g; Protein 23.19g

Coconut Salmon with Cauliflower

Prep time: 5 minutes | Cook time: 25 minutes | Serves:4

| 455g salmon fillet, diced | 1 tablespoon dried coriander | melted | 60g coconut cream |
| 110g cauliflower, shredded | 1 tablespoon coconut oil, | 1 teaspoon ground turmeric | |

1. Combine the salmon with the cauliflower, ground turmeric, dried coriander, and coconut oil. 2. Place the salmon mixture in the air fryer, and fry the food for 25 minutes at 175°C. Every five minutes, stir the food to prevent scorching.
Per Serving: Calories 261, Fat 16.83g; Sodium 500mg; Carbs 2.84g; Fibre 1g; Sugar 0.54g; Protein 24.53g

Minty Sardines

Prep time: 10 minutes | Cook time: 16 minutes | Serves:4

| 455g sardines, trimmed | 1 teaspoon olive oil | ½ teaspoon ground black |
| 1 teaspoon dried mint | ½ teaspoon salt | pepper |

1. Add salt, pepper, olive oil, dried mint, and black pepper to the sardines. 2. Place the sardines in the air fryer basket and fry them for 8 minutes each on each side at 190°C.
Per Serving: Calories 248, Fat 14.13g; Sodium 640mg; Carbs 0.6g; Fibre 0.1g; Sugar 0.29g; Protein 28.06g

Coconut Mackerel

Prep time: 10 minutes | Cook time: 6 minutes | Serves:4

| 900g mackerel fillet | 1 teaspoon ground coriander | 1 garlic clove, peeled, chopped |
| 240g coconut cream | 1 teaspoon cumin seeds | |

1. Roughly chop the mackerel, then season it with coconut cream, cumin seeds, ground coriander, and garlic. 2. After that, cook the fish in the air fryer for 6 minutes at 200°C.
Per Serving: Calories 439, Fat 25.47g; Sodium 362mg; Carbs 4.47g; Fibre 1.4g; Sugar 0.02g; Protein 48.32g

Easy Clove Prawns

Prep time: 5 minutes | Cook time: 12 minutes | Serves:4

| 455g prawns, peeled and deveined | 1 tablespoon avocado oil | 1 teaspoon ground clove |

1. Combine prawns with ground clove and avocado oil. 2. Place the prawns in the air fryer and cook for 12 minutes at 175°C.
Per Serving: Calories 146, Fat 5.11g; Sodium 988mg; Carbs 0.34g; Fibre 0.2g; Sugar 0.01g; Protein 23.19g

French Style Trout.

Prep time: 10 minutes | Cook time: 20 minutes | Serves:4

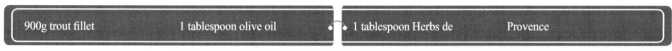

| 900g trout fillet | 1 tablespoon olive oil | 1 tablespoon Herbs de Provence |

1. Sprinkle some olive oil on the trout and rub some Herbs de Provence on it. 2. Place the fish in the air fryer basket and fry for 10 minutes on each side at 190°C.
Per Serving: Calories 366, Fat 18.37g; Sodium 118mg; Carbs 0.01g; Fibre 0g; Sugar 0g; Protein 47.11g

Roasted Fennel Tilapia

Prep time: 15 minutes | Cook time: 10 minutes | Serves:4

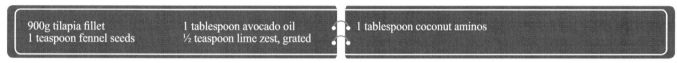

| 900g tilapia fillet | 1 tablespoon avocado oil | 1 tablespoon coconut aminos |
| 1 teaspoon fennel seeds | ½ teaspoon lime zest, grated | |

1. Combine the fennel seeds, avocado oil, lime zest, and coconut aminos in a shallow basin. 2. After that, add the tilapia fillet to the air fryer and sprinkle with fennel seeds. 3. Prepare the fish for 10 minutes at 195°C.
Per Serving: Calories 251, Fat 7.44g; Sodium 112mg; Carbs 0.45g; Fibre 0.2g; Sugar 0.11g; Protein 45.65g

Creamy Salmon

Prep time: 5 minutes | Cook time: 12 minutes | Serves:4

| 455g salmon fillet | 120g heavy cream | ½ teaspoon dried rosemary |
| 50g spring onions | 1 teaspoon ground black pepper | ¼ teaspoon salt |

1. Combine salt, black pepper, and dried rosemary with the salmon fillet. 2. Next, add heavy cream to the air fryer basket with the fish. 3. Cook the fish at 195°C for 10 minutes. 4. Add the spring onions, and simmer the food for an additional two minutes.
Per Serving: Calories 234, Fat 13.74g; Sodium 645mg; Carbs 2.54g; Fibre 0.6g; Sugar 1.32g; Protein 24.19g

• Chapter 6 Snack and Starter Recipes •

Cheese Apple Rollups

Prep time: 10 minutes | Cook time: 5 minutes | Serves:8

2 tablespoons butter, melted	8 slices whole wheat sandwich	½ small apple, chopped
100g Colby Jack cheese, grated	bread	

1. Trim the bread's crusts, then use a rolling pin to flatten the slices. Do not be delicate. Press firmly to make the bread very thin. 2. Evenly distribute the cheese and apple pieces on top of the bread slices. 3. Tightly roll up each slice and fasten it with one or two toothpicks. 4. Apply melted butter to the rolls' outside. 5. Put the food in the air fryer basket and cook for 4 to 5 minutes at 200°C, or until the outside is crisp and beautifully browned.
Tip: If you detest wasting food, like we do, freeze the discarded bread crusts and use them for homemade bread crumbs or stuffing later. Try finely chopped ham instead of apple as a variation. You will need about 3 tablespoons of cubed ham to make 8 rollups. Together, ham and apple taste fantastic. Just remember not to overfill them or they won't roll easily.
Per Serving: Calories 214, Fat 9.93g; Sodium 268mg; Carbs 25.3g; Fibre 3g; Sugar 2.81g; Protein 7.29g

Asian Five-Spice Chicken Wings

Prep time: 1 hours 10 minutes | Cook time: 15 minutes | Serves:4

120ml Asian-style salad dressing	2 tablespoons Chinese five-spice powder	900g chicken wings

1. Wing tips can be removed, discarded, or frozen for stock. At the junction, divide the remaining wing parts in half. 2. Put the wing parts in a sizable bag that can be sealed. The Asian dressing should be added, the bag should be sealed, and the wings should be thoroughly covered. Place in the fridge for at least an hour. 3. Take the wings out of the bag, pour off any excess marinade, and put them in the air fryer basket. 4. Cook for 13–15 minutes at 180°C, or until juices run clear. For more consistent cooking, shake the basket or stir the wings halfway through the cooking period. 5. Transfer cooked wings in a single layer to a platter. Then flip the wings and season the opposite side with the remaining Chinese five-spice powder.
Tip: For this dish, we advise utilizing Newman's Own Sesame Ginger Dressing.
Per Serving: Calories 294, Fat 8.45g; Sodium 225mg; Carbs 1.06g; Fibre 0.1g; Sugar 0.57g; Protein 50.03g

Asian Rice Logs with Orange Marmalade Dipping

Prep time: 30 minutes | Cook time: 5 minutes | Serves:8

1 egg, beaten	rice	2 teaspoons five-spice powder	160g all-natural orange
35g plain breadcrumbs	2 tablespoons sesame seeds	1 tablespoon tamari sauce	marmalade
1 teaspoon sesame oil	2 teaspoons water	**Orange Marmalade Dipping**	
80g panko breadcrumbs	2 teaspoons diced shallots	**Sauce**	
300g cooked jasmine or sushi	¼ teaspoon salt	1 tablespoon soy sauce	

1. Make the rice as directed on the packet. Make the dipping sauce by combining the marmalade and soy sauce, then set it aside while the rice cooks. 2. Combine the salt, five-spice powder, shallots, and tamari sauce with the cooked rice. 3. Separate the rice into 8 equal portions. Create a log shape for each piece using your somewhat damp hands. Cool in the refrigerator for 10 to 15 minutes. 4. In a small bowl, combine the egg, sesame oil, and water. 5. Place the plain breadcrumbs on a sheet of wax paper. 6. Combine the panko breadcrumbs and sesame seeds, and then spread them out on a different piece of wax paper. 7. After dipping the rice logs in egg wash, panko, and sesame seeds, roll them in plain breadcrumbs. 8. Cook the logs until golden brown, about 5 minutes, at 200°C. 9. Let the dish cool a little before dipping it in orange marmalade.
Per Serving: Calories 192, Fat 13.83g; Sodium 174mg; Carbs 17.9g; Fibre 6.3g; Sugar 2.96g; Protein 7.29g

Crispy Avocado Fries

Prep time: 5 minutes | Cook time: 10 minutes | Serves:4

2 tablespoons flour	Oil for misting or cooking	1 egg	1 large avocado
⅛ teaspoon hot sauce	spray	1 tablespoon lime juice	
40g polenta	80g panko breadcrumbs	¼ teaspoon salt	

1. Combine the egg, lime juice, and spicy sauce in a small bowl. 2. Spread a piece of wax paper with flour. 3. Combine the panko, polenta, and salt. Spread the mixture on another wax paper sheet. 4. Halve the avocado and remove the pit. Avocado halves can be peeled or removed from the skin with a spoon. 5. Slice an avocado into 2.5 cm-thick pieces lengthwise. Each is coated with flour, followed by an egg wash and a panko mixture. 6. Mist with oil or cooking spray and cook at 200°C for 10 minutes, until crust is brown and crispy.
Per Serving: Calories 182, Fat 10.27g; Sodium 211mg; Carbs 18.9g; Fibre 4g; Sugar 1.1g; Protein 4.95g

Simple Cheese Sandwich

Prep time: 5 minutes | Cook time: 5 minutes | Serves: 2

100g Cheddar cheese slices	4 slices bread	2 teaspoons butter or oil

1. Lay the four cheese slices on two of the bread slices and top with the remaining two slices of bread. 2. Spread butter or oil on both sides of the sandwiches before cutting them into square half. 3. Place in air fryer basket and cook for 5 minutes at 200°C or until cheese is melted and the outside is crunchy.
Per Serving: Calories 240, Fat 10.22g; Sodium 851mg; Carbs 25.84g; Fibre 1.1g; Sugar 6.27g; Protein 11.18g

Tasty Bagel Chips

Prep time: 10 minutes | Cook time: 4 minutes | Serves:2½ cups

Sweet	1 teaspoon ground cinnamon	1 large plain bagel
1 large plain bagel	Butter-flavoured cooking spray	1 teaspoon Italian seasoning
2 teaspoons sugar	Savoury	½ teaspoon garlic powder

1. Turn on air fryer and heat to 200°C. 2. Slice the bagel into ½ cm or thinner pieces. 3. Combine the seasonings. 4. Arrange the slices on a plate, brush with cooking spray or oil, and sprinkle with half the ingredients. 5. Flip it over and repeat to season and coat the other side with oil or frying spray. 6. Place there and cook for two minutes in an air fryer basket. Cook for additional one to two minutes, stirring or shaking the basket occasionally, or until toasty golden and crispy.
Note: Although the bagel can be cut into rounds, it might be challenging to cut pieces that are all the same thickness. We find that laying the bagel flat and slicing it vertically is considerably easier. Chips of all sizes are produced, but it is considerably simpler to cut them all to the same thickness. Unsplit bagels can be sliced into rounds by cutting them crosswise. Due of the bagel's curvature, each slice will be a different width, but this variation won't affect cooking.
Variation: Try flavoured bagels like blueberry, cinnamon, or "everything," as a variation. They only need to be sprayed with cooking spray or misted with oil to taste seasoning. Use frying spray with a butter flavour for delicious bagels.
Per Serving: Calories 191, Fat 1.3g; Sodium 349mg; Carbs 37.9g; Fibre 1.7g; Sugar 7.33g; Protein 7.14g

Beef Sliders with Horseradish Mayonnaise Sauce

Prep time: 8 minutes | Cook time: 20 minutes | Serves: 8

455g top sirloin steaks, about 2 cm thick	1 tablespoon extra-light olive oil	**Horseradish Mayonnaise**	2 teaspoons Worcestershire sauce
salt and pepper	8 slider buns	240g light mayonnaise	1 teaspoon coarse brown mustard
2 large onions, thinly sliced		4 teaspoons prepared horseradish	

1. Steak should be cooked for six minutes at 200°C in an air fryer basket. For medium rare, turn the food over and cook it for an additional 5 to 6 minutes. Continue cooking for an additional 2 to 3 minutes if you like your steak medium. 2. Make the horseradish mayonnaise by combining all the ingredients while the steak is cooking. 3. After the steak has finished cooking, remove it from the air fryer, season with salt and pepper, and place it somewhere to rest. 4. Place the onion slices in the air fryer basket after tossing with oil. Cook onion rings for 5 to 7 minutes at 200°C, or until they are tender and caramelized. 5. Make very thin steak slices. 6. Place the meat and onions on top of the slider buns after spreading them with horseradish mayo. Serve with any leftover horseradish sauce on the side for dipping.
Tip: Purchase top-notch beef, ideally grass-fed, for premium flavour. It's worth the investment if you value outstanding steak flavour!
Per Serving: Calories 533, Fat 34.93g; Sodium 515mg; Carbs 37.17g; Fibre 2g; Sugar 19.33g; Protein 16.95g

Cinnamon Pita Chips

Prep time: 5 minutes | Cook time: 6 minutes | Serves: 4

2 whole 15 cm pitas, whole grain or white	2 teaspoons cinnamon	spray
	Oil for misting or cooking	2 tablespoons sugar

1. Cinnamon and sugar should be combined. 2. Cut each pita in half and each half into 4 wedges. Break apart each wedge at the fold. 3. Spray oil or cooking spray on the cut side of the pita wedges. Add half of the cinnamon sugar to each of them. 4. After flipping the wedges over, drizzle oil or frying spray on the opposite side and top with the remaining cinnamon sugar. 5. Put pita wedges in the air fryer basket and fry for 2 minutes at 165°C. 6. Shake the basket, then cook for two more minutes. Reshake and heat for a further 1-2 minutes, or until crisp, as necessary. They will cook quickly at this point, so keep an eye on them.
Tip: The smooth side will seem darker after cooking than the rough side. Additionally, as they cool, the chips will get a little crispier.
Per Serving: Calories 503, Fat 4.81g; Sodium 808mg; Carbs105.15g; Fibre 14.2g; Sugar 5.43g; Protein 17.89g

Crispy Cheddar Cheese Wafers

Prep time: 4 hours 10 minutes | Cook time: 5 minutes | Serves: 48

100g sharp Cheddar cheese, grated	55g butter 65g flour	¼ teaspoon salt 20g crisp rice cereal	Oil for misting or cooking spray

1. Cream the butter and grated cheese together. You can do it by hand, but using a stand mixer is faster and easier. 2. Combine flour and salt in a sieve. Blend it thoroughly after adding it to the cheese mixture. 3. Add cereal and mix. 4. Roll the dough into a long log with a diameter of about 2.5 cm and place it on wax paper. Wax paper should be used to wrap tightly. Chill for at least 4 hours. 5. Set the air fryer to 180°C and get ready to cook. 6. Slice the cheese roll into ½ cm thick pieces. 7. Spray air fryer basket with oil or cooking spray and place slices in a single layer, close but not touching. 8. Cook until golden brown, about 5 to 6 minutes. Place them on paper towels to cool after finished. 9. To cook the remaining cheese bites, repeat the previous step.
Tips: Follow steps 1 through 4 above, slice the cheese roll, and arrange the slices in a single layer on a baking sheet. The raw cheese pieces should be kept in airtight containers or bags after being placed on the cookie sheet and frozen for about an hour. The cooking time will be the same whether you cook these straight from the freezer without first thawing them (5 to 6 minutes or until golden brown).
Per Serving: Calories 19, Fat 1.19g; Sodium 47mg; Carbs1.49g; Fibre 0g; Sugar 0.2g; Protein 0.48g

Fried Chicken Wings

Prep time: 1 hour 20 minutes | Cook time:19 minutes | Serves: 4

900g chicken wings **Marinade** ½ teaspoon salt	240ml buttermilk ½ teaspoon black pepper Coating	2 tablespoons poultry seasoning 125g flour 2 teaspoons salt	Oil for misting or cooking spray 110g panko breadcrumbs

1. Remove the wings' tips. Save for stock or discard. To create two pieces per wing, split the remaining wing portions at the joint. In a sizable bowl or plastic bag, put the wings. 2. Combine all the marinade ingredients, then pour it over the wings. Refrigerate for at least 1 hour but for no more than 8 hours. 3. Set the air fryer to 180°C. 4. In a plate or on wax paper, combine all the coating ingredients. 5. Shake off excess marinade from the wings before rolling them in the coating mixture. 6. Apply oil or cooking spray to both sides of each wing. 7. Arrange wings in an air fryer basket in a single layer, keeping them near together but not crammed. Cook the chicken for 17 to 19 minutes, or until the juices flow clear. 8. To cook the remaining wings, repeat step 7.
Tip: The second wing joint cooks more quickly than the meatier drum joint. Cook the drum joints in one batch before cooking the second batch of joints. When ready to serve, you can rewarm the first batch if necessary by placing it back in the air fryer for a minute.
Per Serving: Calories 456, Fat 9.4g; Sodium 1794mg; Carbs 32.8g; Fibre 1.4g; Sugar 3.56g; Protein 56.11g

Cheese Crab Toasts

Prep time: 10 minutes | Cook time:5 minutes | Serves: 18

25g shredded Parmesan cheese 1 loaf artisan bread, French bread, or baguette, cut into	slices ¾ cm thick 1 teaspoon Worcestershire sauce	25g shredded sharp Cheddar cheese 1 150g can flaked crabmeat,	well drained 3 tablespoons light mayonnaise ½ teaspoon lemon juice

1. Mix together all ingredients except the bread slices. 2. Apply a thin layer of the crabmeat mixture to each slice of bread. (You will need approximately 12 spoonful of the crab mixture for each piece of bread measuring 5 x 3.5 cm. 3. Place in the air fryer basket in a single layer and cook for 5 minutes at 180°C, or until the toast is crispy and the tops are browned. 4. To cook the remaining crab toasts, repeat step 3.
Note: Crabmeat must be well drained. When combining the filling ingredients, throw away any liquid that gathers at the bottom of the dish.
Tip: You should freeze these as a make-ahead snack. Once prepared, freeze uncooked crab toasts on a cookie sheet by following steps 1 and 2 above. Until ready to use, store in freezer bags or airtight containers. Don't defrost. Cook frozen crab toasts as described above in an air fryer, but add an extra two minutes to the total frying time.
Per Serving: Calories 63, Fat 4g; Sodium 86mg; Carbs 6.07g; Fibre 1g; Sugar 3.6g; Protein 1.11g

Cheddar Cheese Crisps

Prep time: 15 minutes | Cook time: 12 minutes | Serves:2

50g shredded Cheddar cheese 1 egg white	

1. Turn the air fryer on at 200°C. Put some parchment paper in the air fryer basket's bottom. 2. Stir the cheese and egg white with a fork in a medium bowl until well blended. 3. Fill the air fryer basket with a single layer of little cheese mixture scoops (2.5 cm apart). 4. Spread the mixture as thinly as you can use the fork. Crisps should be golden brown after 10 to 12 minutes in the air fryer. 5. Before moving them to a platter, allow to cool for a few minutes. 6. Keep at room temperature in an airtight container for up to three days.
Per Serving: Calories 123, Fat 9.58g; Sodium 209mg; Carbs 0.5g; Fibre 0g; Sugar 0.2g; Protein 8.59g

Cumin Aubergine Fries

Prep time: 10 minutes | Cook time:8 minutes | Serves: 4

Oil for misting or cooking spray	1 teaspoon garlic powder	1 teaspoon ground coriander	breadcrumbs
	½ teaspoon salt	2 tablespoons water	1 large egg
1 teaspoon cumin	1 medium aubergine	110g crushed panko	

1. Peel the aubergine and slice it into 1.5 to 2.5 cm-thick fat fry. 2. Turn the air fryer on at 200°C. 3. Combine the coriander, cumin, garlic, and salt in a small cup. 4. In a shallow plate, mix 1 teaspoon of the spice mix with the panko crumbs. 5. Add the remaining seasoning to the bowl with the aubergine fries and toss to incorporate. 6. Combine eggs and water and pour over french fries made from aubergine. Stir to coat. 7. Shake off excess egg wash from the aubergine before rolling it in panko crumbs. 8. Spray with oil. 9. Fill the air fryer basket with half the fries. It's okay if they slightly overlap, but you should only have one layer. 10. Cook for five minutes. Shake the basket, lightly spritz with oil, and cook for an additional 2 to 3 minutes, or until crispy and golden. 11. To cook the remaining aubergine, repeat step 10.
Per Serving: Calories 72, Fat 1.73g; Sodium 410mg; Carbs 13.43g; Fibre 5.4g; Sugar 7.55g; Protein 3.23g

Buffalo Cheese Chicken Bites

Prep time: 15 minutes | Cook time: 12 minutes | Serves: 16

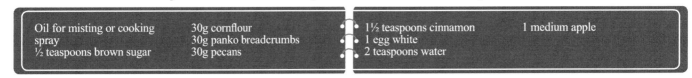

1 tablespoon maple syrup	sauce	50g Gruyère cheese, cut into 16 cubes
8 tablespoons buffalo wing	455g chicken mince	

1. Combine all of the chicken mince with 4 tablespoons of buffalo wing sauce. 2. Log the chicken and cut it into 16 equal pieces. 3. Form each piece of chicken into a hard ball by wrapping it around a cheese cube with slightly damp fingertips. Place the eight meatballs you've just formed in the air fryer basket. 4. Cook for about 5 minutes at 200°C. Shake the basket, lower the heat to 180°C, and continue to cook for an additional 5 to 6 minutes. 5. Form the leftover chicken and cheese into 8 additional meatballs while the first batch is cooking. 6. To cook the second batch of meatballs, repeat step 4. 7. Combine the maple syrup and the remaining 4 tablespoons of buffalo wing sauce in a medium bowl. Add and coat with all of the cooked meatballs. 8. To set the glaze, place the meatballs back into the air fryer basket and cook at 200°C for 2 to 3 minutes. Use a toothpick to skewer each before serving.
Tip: For this dish, we advise using Frank's Red Hot Buffalo Wings Sauce.
Per Serving: Calories 118, Fat 8.23g; Sodium 174mg; Carbs 2.47g; Fibre 0.1g; Sugar 1.05g; Protein 8.29g

Crispy Apple Wedges

Prep time: 10 minutes | Cook time:8 minutes | Serves: 4

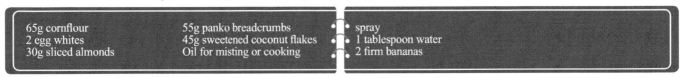

Oil for misting or cooking spray	30g cornflour	1½ teaspoons cinnamon	1 medium apple
	30g panko breadcrumbs	1 egg white	
½ teaspoons brown sugar	30g pecans	2 teaspoons water	

1. Combine brown sugar, cinnamon, pecans, and panko in a food processor. Process to make small crumbs. 2. Put cornflour in a lidded basin or plastic bag. Beat the egg white and water in a small bowl until just frothy. 3. Set the air fryer to 200°C. 4. Slicing an apple into tiny wedges. The thickest edge shouldn't be any thicker than 1–1.5 cm. Peel the fruit but do not remove the core. 5. Place apple wedges in a basin or bag of cornflour, close it, and shake to coat. 6. Roll wedges in the crumbs after dipping them in egg wash and shaking off the excess. Spray some oil on. 7. Arrange the apples in a single layer and cook them in the air fryer basket for 5 minutes. Shake the basket and separate any clumped-together apples. 8. Lightly mist with oil and cook for a further 3 to 4 minutes, or until crispy.
Per Serving: Calories 117, Fat 4.7g; Sodium 26mg; Carbs 18.09g; Fibre 2.3g; Sugar 6.85g; Protein 1.87g

Almond Banana Sticks

Prep time: 10 minutes | Cook time:8 minutes | Serves: 4

65g cornflour	55g panko breadcrumbs	spray
2 egg whites	45g sweetened coconut flakes	1 tablespoon water
30g sliced almonds	Oil for misting or cooking	2 firm bananas

1. Almonds, coconut, and panko are combined in a food processor. Process to make small crumbs. 2. Fill a dish with cornflour. Beat the egg whites and water until just frothy in another shallow bowl. 3. Set the air fryer to 200°C. 4. Halve bananas crosswise. To make 16 "sticks," quarter each half lengthwise. 5. After coating banana sticks with cornflour, tap the excess off. Bananas are then coated with egg wash and rolled in a crumb mixture. Spray some oil on. 6. Arrange bananas in a single layer in the air fryer basket and cook for 4 minutes. Spray oil on any areas that have not yet turned brown. Cook for a further 2 to 4 minutes, or until crispy and golden. 7. Repeat step 6 to prepare the rest of the bananas.
Per Serving: Calories 183, Fat 3.45g; Sodium 81mg; Carbs 35.9g; Fibre 2.9g; Sugar 11.49g; Protein 3.22g

Fried Green Tomatoes with Horseradish Sauce

Prep time: 18 minutes | Cook time:15 minutes | Serves: 8

50g breadcrumbs	spray	**Horseradish Drizzle**	60g mayonnaise
¼ teaspoon salt	675g firm green tomatoes, cut	⅛ teaspoon black pepper	60g sour cream
60ml buttermilk	in ¾ cm slices	½ teaspoon Worcestershire	2 teaspoons prepared
80g polenta	2 eggs	sauce	horseradish
Oil for misting or cooking		½ teaspoon lemon juice	

1. Mix all ingredients for Horseradish Drizzle together and chill while you prepare the green tomatoes. 2. Turn the air fryer on at 200°C. 3. In a small bowl, combine the buttermilk and eggs. 4. Combine polenta, breadcrumbs, and salt in a shallow dish or plate. 5. Roll 4 tomato slices in the breadcrumb mixture after dipping them in the egg mixture. 6. Mist one side with oil and arrange in a single layer in the air fryer basket, oil-side down. 7. Spray some oil on the top. 8. Cook until crispy and golden for 10 to 15 minutes, flipping once. 9. To prepare the remaining tomatoes, repeat steps 5 through 8. 10. Just before serving, drizzle horseradish sauce over the tomatoes.
Tip: For a flavourful side salad that pairs well with grilled steak, scatter a few fried green tomatoes over chopped romaine lettuce.
Per Serving: Calories 126, Fat 6.13g; Sodium 217mg; Carbs 13.05g; Fibre 1.2g; Sugar 1.04g; Protein 4.94g

Crispy Peaches

Prep time: 15 minutes | Cook time:8 minutes | Serves: 4

2 tablespoons brown sugar	40g crisp rice cereal	30g cornflour	Oil for misting or cooking
½ teaspoon almond extract	2 medium, very firm peaches,	1 tablespoon water	spray
2 egg whites	peeled and pitted	30g sliced almonds	

1. Turn the air fryer on at 200°C. 2. In a shallow bowl, whisk egg whites and water together. 3. Combine the almonds, brown sugar, and almond extract in a food processor. Processing is needed to thoroughly blend the ingredients and finely chop the nuts. 4. Add the cereal and pulse just long enough to smash it. Place crumb mixture on a platter or in a shallow dish. 5. Divide each peach into eighths and put them in a lidded container or plastic bag. Add cornflour, then shake to coat after sealing. 6. Take the peach slices out of the bag or container and give them a firm shake to remove any excess cornflour. Roll in crumbs after dipping in egg wash. Spray some oil on. 7. Place in air fryer basket and cook for 5 minutes. Shake basket, separate any that have stuck together, and spritz a little oil on any spots that aren't browning. 8. Cook for a further 1 to 3 minutes, or until golden and crispy.
Tip: Fresh summer peaches that are overflowing with taste and juice won't work well, and that's okay. If you're lucky enough to find those, take advantage of them just as they are.
Per Serving: Calories 112, Fat 0.47g; Sodium 64mg; Carbs 24.32g; Fibre 1.3g; Sugar 11.13g; Protein 2.99g

Spicy Fried Pickles

Prep time: 10 minutes | Cook time:15 minutes | Serves: 2 cups

75g breadcrumbs	1 tablespoon milk	spray	drained
1 egg	Oil for misting or cooking	310g sliced dill pickles, well	¼ teaspoon hot sauce

1. Turn the air fryer on at 200°C. 2. Beat together egg, milk, and hot sauce in a bowl large enough to hold all the pickles. 3. Add pickles to the egg wash and stir well to coat. 4. Put the breadcrumbs in a sizable lidded plastic bag or container. 5. Remove the pickles from the egg wash and put them in a bag with the breadcrumbs. Shake to coat. 6. Arrange pickles in a basket for the air fryer and drizzle with oil. 7. Continue to cook. Spray oil into basket after shaking it. 8. Continue cooking for 5 more minutes. Shake again and spray. Pickles that have clumped together should be separated, and any missed areas should be misted. 9. Cook for a further 1 to 5 minutes, or until crisp and rich golden brown.
Per Serving: Calories 106, Fat 5.64g; Sodium 191mg; Carbs 7.57g; Fibre 0.4g; Sugar 1.53g; Protein 5.92g

Turkey and Pineapple Burgers

Prep time: 10 minutes | Cook time: 7 minutes | Serves:8

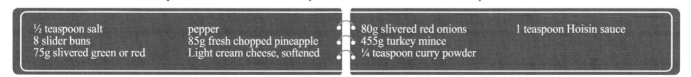

½ teaspoon salt	pepper	80g slivered red onions	1 teaspoon Hoisin sauce
8 slider buns	85g fresh chopped pineapple	455g turkey mince	
75g slivered green or red	Light cream cheese, softened	¼ teaspoon curry powder	

1. Thoroughly combine the turkey, curry powder, Hoisin sauce, and salt. 2. Create 8 little patties out of the turkey mixture. 3. Put the patties in the air fryer basket and cook for 5 to 7 minutes at 180°C, or until they are thoroughly cooked and the juices flow clear. 4. Place each patty on the bottom half of a slider bun and top with onions, peppers, and pineapple. Spread the remaining bun halves with cream cheese to taste, place on top, and serve.
Per Serving: Calories 593, Fat 43.57g; Sodium 395mg; Carbs 35.43g; Fibre 1.1g; Sugar 19.17g; Protein 14.17g

Crispy Avocado Fries with Cheese

Prep time: 10 minutes | Cook time: 15 minutes | Serves:6

Salsa, for serving (optional)	2 teaspoons ground cumin	2 large eggs	Parmesan cheese for
Fresh chopped coriander	1 teaspoon chili powder	3 firm, barely ripe avocados,	vegetarian)
leaves, for garnish (optional)	1 teaspoon paprika	halved, peeled, and pitted (see	2 teaspoons fine sea salt
2 teaspoons ground black	½ teaspoon garlic powder	Tip)	
pepper	½ teaspoon onion powder	200g parmesan (or powdered	

1. Spray avocado oil on the air fryer basket. Set the air fryer to 200°C for frying. 2. Cut the avocados into thick slices to resemble French fries. 3. Combine the seasonings, salt, pepper, and parmesan in a bowl. 4. Beat the eggs in a separate shallow basin. 5. After shaking off any excess, dip the avocado fries in the beaten eggs, then coat them with the parmesan mixture. Press the parmesan into each fry with your hands. 6. Spray the fries with avocado oil, then arrange them in a single layer with space between them in the air fryer basket. Work in batches if there are too many fries to fit in a single layer. Cook in the air fryer for 13 to 15 minutes, flip after 5 minutes, until golden brown. 7. Garnish with freshly cut coriander, if preferred, and serve with salsa, if wanted. Fresh food is preferred. 8. You can keep leftovers in the refrigerator for up to 5 days if they are sealed tightly. Reheat for three minutes, or until thoroughly heated, in an air fryer set to 200°C.

Tip: Although baking avocado fries gives them a texture similar to french fries, avocados may appear like an unusual substitute for potatoes. To make slicing the avocados for this recipe easier, pick firm avocados.

Per Serving: Calories 260, Fat 18.9g; Sodium 818mg; Carbs 10.7g; Fibre 7.4g; Sugar 0.82g; Protein 14.7g

Garlic Chicken Wings

Prep time: 1 hour 20 minutes | Cook time:15 minutes | Serves: 4

Cooking spray	**Marinade**	240ml buttermilk	150g grated Parmesan cheese
900g chicken wings	1 teaspoon Worcestershire	2 cloves garlic, mashed flat	75g breadcrumbs
Oil for misting	sauce	**Coating**	½ teaspoon salt
	1 bay leaf	1½ tablespoons garlic powder	

1. Combine all of the marinade ingredients. 2. Cut off the wing tips (the third joint) and freeze them for stock or discard them. The remaining wings should be split down the middle and tossed into the marinade. Stir to thoroughly coat. Place in the refrigerator for at least an hour but no more than eight. 3. Place all coating ingredients in a shallow dish. 4. Shake off excess marinade from the wings before rolling them in the coating mixture. To make the coating adhere well, press it into the wings. Apply oil to the wings. 5. Cooking spray the air fryer basket. Put one layer of wings in the basket, close together but not touching. 6. Cook the chicken for 13 to 15 minutes at 180°C, or until the juices run clear. 7. Cook the remaining wings by repeating the previous process.

Tip: The second wing joint cooks more quickly than the meatier drum joint. Cook the drum joints in one batch before cooking the second batch of joints. When ready to serve, you can rewarm the first batch if necessary by placing it back in the air fryer for a minute.

Per Serving: Calories 504, Fat 19.53g; Sodium 1316mg; Carbs 15.01g; Fibre 0.6g; Sugar 3.58g; Protein 63.81g

Berry Granola

Prep time: 10 minutes | Cook time:10 minutes | Serves: 4

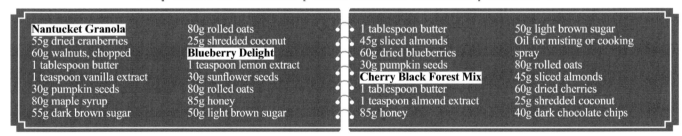

Nantucket Granola	80g rolled oats	1 tablespoon butter	50g light brown sugar
55g dried cranberries	25g shredded coconut	45g sliced almonds	Oil for misting or cooking
60g walnuts, chopped	**Blueberry Delight**	60g dried blueberries	spray
1 tablespoon butter	1 teaspoon lemon extract	30g pumpkin seeds	80g rolled oats
1 teaspoon vanilla extract	30g sunflower seeds	**Cherry Black Forest Mix**	45g sliced almonds
30g pumpkin seeds	80g rolled oats	1 tablespoon butter	60g dried cherries
80g maple syrup	85g honey	1 teaspoon almond extract	25g shredded coconut
55g dark brown sugar	50g light brown sugar	85g honey	40g dark chocolate chips

1. Brown sugar, butter, and syrup or honey should be combined in a microwave-safe basin or small saucepan. Just heat and swirl to melt the butter and dissolve the sugar. Stir in the extract. 2. Add all remaining dry ingredients to a sizable basin. (The chocolate chips have not yet been added to the Cherry Black Forest Mix.) 3. Stir the oat mixture until it is thoroughly coated with the melted butter mixture. 4. Lightly mist a baking pan with cooking spray or oil. 5. Add the granola to the pan and heat for 5 minutes at 200°C. Stir. When the food is golden brown, cook it for a further 2 to 5 minutes, stirring every minute or so. Keep a watchful eye. The mixture will cook fast once it starts to become brown. 6. Take the granola out of the pan and lay it out on wax paper. As it cools, it will become crispier. 7. After the granola has completely cooled, whisk in the chocolate chips for the Cherry Black Forest Mix. 8. Keep the container airtight.

Note: The cooking process is the same for all three recipes. Simply select a version and adhere to the instructions.

Make the Cherry Black Forest Mix recipe as directed above for a wonderful trail mix. Stir up to 100g of small pretzels into the mixture once it has totally cooled.

Per Serving: Calories 289, Fat 14.74g; Sodium 62mg; Carbs 42.43g; Fibre 4.9g; Sugar 23g; Protein 7.94g

Per Serving (Blueberry Delight): Calories 278, Fat 13.15g; Sodium 49mg; Carbs 43.96g; Fibre 5.4g; Sugar 24.94g; Protein 8.59g

Per Serving (Cherry Black Forest Mix): Calories 183, Fat 5.95g; Sodium 47mg; Carbs 38.15g; Fibre 4.4g; Sugar 21.18g; Protein 4.9g

Pita Chips with Garlic and Herbs

Prep time: 5 minutes | Cook time:5 minutes | Serves: 4

¼ teaspoon marjoram	¼ teaspoon ground thyme	grain or white	¼ teaspoon dried basil
¼ teaspoon ground oregano	¼ teaspoon salt	Oil for misting or cooking	
¼ teaspoon garlic powder	2 whole 15 cm pitas, whole	spray	

1. Combine all seasonings. 2. 4 wedges should be cut from each pita half. wedges should be split at the fold. 3. Oil the outside of the pita wedges. Add half of the seasoning mix. 4. The other side of the pita wedges should be sprayed with oil before being sprinkled with the remaining seasonings. 5. Pita wedges should be cooked in an air fryer basket for two minutes at 165°C. 6. Cook for two more minutes after shaking the basket. Shake once more, and if necessary, heat until crisp for a further 1 to 2 minutes. They will cook quickly at this point, so keep an eye on them.
Tip: The smooth side will appear a little bit darker after cooking than the rough side. Additionally, when the chips cool, they will get crispier.
Per Serving: Calories 486, Fat 4.8g; Sodium 954mg; Carbs 100.38g; Fibre 13.6g; Sugar 1.5g; Protein 17.9g

Hummus Olive Tacos

Prep time: 10 minutes | Cook time: 3 minutes | Serves: 8

8 small flour tortillas (10 cm diameter)	cheese	(optional)
4 tablespoons crumbled feta	4 tablespoons chopped kalamata or other olives	Olive oil for misting
		8 tablespoons hummus

1. Each tortilla should have a tablespoon of hummus or tapenade in the centre. If using, sprinkle 1 teaspoon of chopped olives and 1 teaspoon of feta crumbles over top. 2. Apply water to the tortilla's edges all over with your finger or a tiny spoon. 3. Fold the tortilla in half to form a half-moon. Gently press the middle. After that, firmly press the sides to enclose the filling. 4. Spray olive oil on both sides. 5. Pack the air fryer basket tightly, but try to avoid overlapping the items. 6. Cook for 3 minutes at 200°C, or just until crispy and lightly browned.
Tips: In order for the tortillas to fold without breaking, make sure they are at room temperature. Depending on the power of your microwave, microwave tortillas wrapped in damp paper towels for 30 to 60 seconds, or just long enough to mildly reheat them and make them pliable enough to fold without breaking.
Per Serving: Calories 192, Fat 6.24g; Sodium 524mg; Carbs 28g; Fibre 1.9g; Sugar 2.17g; Protein 5.74g

Cheese Pear Sandwich

Prep time: 10 minutes | Cook time:5 minutes | Serves: 4

200g Brie	8 slices oat nut bread	into 1 cm-thick slices
2 tablespoons butter, melted	1 large ripe pear, cored and cut	

1. Four slices of bread should each have a quarter of the Brie spread on them. 2. Place the remaining 4 pieces of bread on top of the Brie, followed by thick slices of pear. 3. Use melted butter to lightly brush each sandwich on both sides. 4. Cook sandwiches in an air fryer basket, two at a time, for 5 to 6 minutes at 180°C, or until the cheese melts and the outside is golden brown.
Tip: Opt for any dense whole-grain or artisan bread if you can't locate or don't like oat nut bread. Slices should be larger than normal sandwich bread, with the same thickness.
Per Serving: Calories 459, Fat 25.04g; Sodium 723mg; Carbs 35.87g; Fibre 6.1g; Sugar 5.5g; Protein 22.79g

Italian Rice Balls with Olives

Prep time: 20 minutes | Cook time:10 minutes | Serves: 8

8 pitted black olives	100g mozzarella cheese cut into tiny sticks (small enough to stuff into olives)	Oil for misting or cooking spray	80g panko breadcrumbs
300g cooked sticky rice		¾ teaspoon salt	
½ teaspoon Italian seasoning blend	2 eggs, beaten	35g Italian breadcrumbs	

1. Turn the air fryer on at 200°C. 2. Combine the cooked rice with the Italian spice and ½ teaspoon salt. 3. Insert a piece of mozzarella cheese into each black olive. 4. Shape the rice into a log and divide into 8 equal pieces. Each quantity of rice should be moulded around an olive and shaped into a hard ball with slightly damp palms. Chill in freezer for 10 to 15 minutes or until the outside is cold to the touch. 5. Prepare 3 shallow plates for dipping: one with beaten eggs, one with Italian breadcrumbs, and one with a mixture of panko crumbs and the remaining salt. 6. After dipping each rice ball in the beaten egg, roll it in the panko crumbs. 7. Oil-spraying all surfaces. 8. Cook for 10 minutes, or until the outside is crispy and light golden brown.
Tip: Although these are wonderful on their own, serving them with pizza or spaghetti sauce for dipping will give them an extra taste boost.
Per Serving: Calories 123, Fat 7.97g; Sodium 318mg; Carbs 13.26g; Fibre 4.9g; Sugar 0.64g; Protein 6.29g

Cheese Stuffed Peppers

Prep time: 60 minutes | Cook time: 5 minutes | Serves: 20

30g panko breadcrumbs	1 tablespoon lime juice	25g plain breadcrumbs	100g cream cheese
½ teaspoon salt	Oil for misting or cooking	**Filling**	¼ teaspoon salt
30g cornflour	spray	1 teaspoon grated lime zest	⅛ teaspoon garlic powder
1 egg	225g jalapeño peppers	¼ teaspoon chile powder	

1. Combine all filling ingredients in small bowl and mix well. Refrigerate while preparing peppers. 2. Slice jalapenos lengthwise into 4 cm pieces. To get rid of the seeds and veins, use a little, sharp knife. 3. Remove the seeds and veins for mild appetizers. 4. Finely cut the seeds and veins for hot appetizers. When the filling is the right temperature for you, add a small quantity, taste it, and add more as needed. 5. Stuff each pepper slice with filling. 6. Fill a dish with cornflour. 7. Combine the egg and lime juice in another shallow dish. 8. Add salt and breadcrumbs to a third shallow dish and mix to combine. 9. Coat each slice of pepper with cornflour, shake off extra, and then cover with egg mixture. 10. Coat with breadcrumbs by rolling in them and pressing firmly. 11. Freeze pepper slices for 30 minutes after placing them in a single layer on a platter. 12. Set the air fryer to 200°C. 13. Use frying spray or oil to coat frozen peppers. Cook for 5 minutes after placing in a single layer in the air fryer basket.
Tip: For this dish, avoid using low-fat cream cheese. It is far more prone to melt and drip out before the peppers are fully cooked since it is so soft. Additionally, when handling the peppers, we strongly advise using gloves made for handling food.
Per Serving: Calories 55, Fat 3.89g; Sodium 127mg; Carbs 3.7g; Fibre 0.5g; Sugar 1.05g; Protein 1.78g

Cheese Eggrolls

Prep time: 10 minutes | Cook time:5 minutes | Serves: 8

8 mozzarella string cheese "sticks"	1 egg	8 eggroll wraps	
	1 tablespoon water	Sauce for dipping	

1. In a small bowl, whisk the egg and water together. 2. Spread the eggroll wraps out and apply egg wash to the edges. 3. Near one end of each wrap, put a slice of string cheese. 4. To roll up the eggroll, fold the sides over the cheese's ends. 5. Apply egg wash to the wrap's exterior and gently press to seal. 6. Put in a single layer in the air fryer basket and cook at 200°C for five minutes. If necessary, cook for an additional 1 to 2 minutes to achieve a golden brown and crispy texture. 7. Provide your preferred dipping sauce on the side.
Per Serving: Calories 365, Fat 12.89g; Sodium 1196mg; Carbs 28.8g; Fibre 2.4g; Sugar 4.47g; Protein 32.58g

Tasty Muffuletta Sliders

Prep time: 10 minutes | Cook time:5 minutes | Serves: 8

Olive oil for misting	1 tablespoon sesame seeds	**Olive Mix**	pimentos
115g thin-sliced pastrami	115g thin-sliced deli ham	1 teaspoon red wine vinegar	35g chopped kalamata olives
100g low-fat mozzarella	8 slider buns	35g sliced black olives	¼ teaspoon basil
cheese, grated or sliced thin		65g sliced green olives with	⅛ teaspoon garlic powder

1. Combine all the ingredients for the olive mix in a small bowl. 2. Separate the cheese and meats into eight equal parts. To assemble sliders, stack in this order: bottom bun, ham, pastrami, 2 tablespoons olive mix, cheese, top bun. 3. Lightly grease the tops of the sliders. Sprinkle sesame seeds on top. 4. To melt cheese and heat through, place sliders in the air fryer basket four at a time, and cook for 5 to 7 minutes at 180°C .
Note: The olive mixture is a tasty salad topping as well. To create a great Italian chopped salad, chop the lettuce, tomatoes, and Olive Mix into small pieces.
Per Serving: Calories 441, Fat 29.28g; Sodium 385mg; Carbs 32.6g; Fibre 1.3g; Sugar 16.79g; Protein 12.06g

Crispy Potatoes Chips

Prep time: 15 minutes | Cook time:15 minutes | Serves: 2

Salt and pepper	2 medium potatoes	spray	
2 teaspoons extra-light olive oil	Oil for misting or cooking		

1. Potatoes must be peeled. 2. Shave potatoes into thin slices with a mandoline or paring knife, putting each slice into a dish of water as you go. 3. Using paper towels or a fresh dish towel, completely dry the potatoes. Toss the oil with the potato slices to evenly coat them. 4. Add potato slices to the cooking spray-coated air fryer basket. 5. Stir and separate with a fork. 6. Cook for five minutes at 200°C. Separate and stir potato slices. Cook for 5 more minutes. Potatoes are again separated and stirred. Cook another 5 minutes. 7. Add spices to taste.
Tip: Some potato chips will still have white centres after they've completed cooking but will have crispy outer edges. One of the delicious variations that make these chips so alluring is this one. Remove the browned chips from the basket and keep frying the other chips until the centres are all totally browned if you want them all to be brown.
Per Serving: Calories 335, Fat 5.02g; Sodium 109mg; Carbs 66.73g; Fibre 8.6g; Sugar 4.48g; Protein 7.79g

Prawns Pirogues

Prep time: 15 minutes | Cook time: 5 minutes | Serves: 8

150g small, peeled, and deveined raw prawns	crushed	each approximately 15 cm long	2 tablespoons plain yogurt
1 teaspoon dried dill weed,	Salt	75g cream cheese, room	1 teaspoon lemon juice
	4 small hothouse cucumbers,	temperature	

1. Fill the air fryer drawer's bottom with 4 tablespoons of water. 2. Arrange the prawns in a single layer in the air fryer basket and cook at 200°C for 4 to 5 minutes, or just until done. Watch the prawns carefully since it cooks quickly and becomes rough if overcooked. 3. Cut prawns into chunks no bigger than 1 cm. Refrigerate while mixing the remaining ingredients. 4. Whip and mash the cream cheese with a fork until it is smooth. 5. Add the yoghurt and beat until well combined. Add the chopped prawns, lemon juice, and dill to the dish. 6. Examine for seasoning. If more salt is desired, add ¼ to ½ teaspoon. 7. Keep in the fridge until you're ready to serve. 8. Split cucumbers lengthwise and wash and dry them when you're ready to serve. Cucumbers should be seeded and then placed upside-down on paper towels to dry for ten minutes. 9. Dry off the cucumber centres just before filling. Slice the pirogues in half crosswise after spooning the prawns filling inside. Serve right away.
Tips: For a delicious tea sandwich, spread the dilled prawns mixture over pumpernickel bread. Additionally, it is a delectable addition to crackers or toast points.
Per Serving: Calories 49, Fat 3.37g; Sodium 99mg; Carbs 3.2g; Fibre 0.9g; Sugar 2.24g; Protein 1.63g

Bacon Rumaki

Prep time: 1 hour 15 minutes | Cook time:12 minutes | Serves: 24

60ml low-sodium teriyaki sauce	12 slices turkey bacon	250g raw chicken livers	drained
	Toothpicks	1 can sliced water chestnuts,	

1. Slice the livers into 2.5 cm-thick chunks, removing any hard veins as you go. 2. In a small lidded container, combine livers, water chestnuts, and teriyaki sauce. To ensure that the livers are covered, if necessary, add one more tablespoon of teriyaki sauce. Refrigerate for one hour. 3. When ready to cook, split each piece of bacon in half across. 4. Wrap one slice of water chestnut and one piece of liver in each bacon strip. Use a toothpick to secure. 5. After you've wrapped half of the livers, arrange them in a single layer in the air fryer basket. 6. Cook the liver and bacon at 200°C for 10 to 12 minutes, or until they are fully cooked. 7. Wrap the remaining livers while the first batch of livers cooks. To cook your second batch, repeat step 6.
Per Serving: Calories 81, Fat 5.85g; Sodium 70 mg; Carbs 3.16g; Fibre 0.5g; Sugar 0.26g; Protein 3.81g

Fried String Beans

Prep time: 15 minutes | Cook time: 5 minutes | Serves:6

4 teaspoons water	(optional)	50g breadcrumbs	pepper
65g white flour	Oil for misting or cooking	¼ teaspoon salt	225g fresh string beans
¼ teaspoon dry mustard	spray	¼ teaspoon ground black	2 eggs

1. Turn on the air fryer to 180°C. 2. Trim the string bean stem ends, wash them, and pat them dry. 3. Beat eggs and water together until thoroughly combined in a shallow bowl. 4. In a second shallow dish, add flour. 5. In a third shallow dish, stir together the breadcrumbs, salt, pepper, and dry mustard if using. 6. Dip each string bean in egg mixture, flour, egg mixture again, then breadcrumbs. 7. Open the air fryer and put the string beans in the basket once you have coated all of them. 8. Cook for three minutes. 9. Stop and sprinkle oil or cooking spray on the string beans. 10. Cook the string beans for an additional 2 to 3 minutes, or until they are crispy and beautifully browned.
Per Serving: Calories 115, Fat 4.32g; Sodium 270mg; Carbs 13.4g; Fibre 1.6g; Sugar 1.39g; Protein 5.42g

Cheese Ham Stuffed Mushrooms

Prep time: 15 minutes | Cook time: 12 minutes | Serves:16

70g diced ham	1 to 2 teaspoons olive oil	¼ teaspoon ground oregano	100g mozzarella cheese
¼ teaspoon ground black pepper	2 tablespoons breadcrumbs	16 fresh, small mushrooms	
	½ teaspoon garlic powder	2 green onions	

1. Wash and remove stems from mushroom caps. 2. Chop cheese and green onions into small pieces and add to food processor. 3. Combine minced items with the ham, breadcrumbs, garlic powder, oregano, and pepper. 4. Add just enough olive oil to the food processor while it is running to create a thick paste. 5. Distribute the stuffing among the mushroom caps and lightly tuck them in. 6. Arrange the packed mushrooms in a single layer in the air fryer basket, and cook for 12 minutes at 200°C, or until the tops are golden brown and the mushrooms are soft. 7. To cook the remaining mushrooms, repeat step 6.
Tip: Check out the next recipe, Stuffed Mushrooms, for a similar quick and simple meal.
Per Serving: Calories 25, Fat 0.46g; Sodium 80mg; Carbs 2.42g; Fibre 0.4g; Sugar 0.56g; Protein 3.05g

Prosciutto-Wrapped Onion Rings

Prep time: 10 minutes | Cook time: 10 minutes | Serves:6

3 large sweet onions	free if needed)	½ teaspoon dried parsley	softened
24 slices prosciutto or beef bacon	**Ranch Dressing (makes: about 1½ cups)**	¼ teaspoon garlic powder	120ml chicken or beef stock
240ml Ranch Dressing, for serving (optional; use dairy-	½ teaspoon dried chives	¼ teaspoon onion powder	⅛ teaspoon ground black
	½ teaspoon dried dill weed	⅛ teaspoon fine sea salt	pepper
		1 (200g) package cream cheese,	

1. For the ranch dressing: Mix all the ingredients together thoroughly in a blender or with a hand mixer and a big basin. 2 hours of refrigeration and protection before serving (it will thicken up as it rests). 2. Spray avocado oil on the air fryer basket. Set the air fryer to 200°C for frying. 3. Make slices of onion that are 5 – 8 cm thick, which are simple to wrap with prosciutto; save the small inner rings for other uses. 4. Tightly encase each onion ring in prosciutto. Cook the prosciutto-wrapped onion rings in the air fryer for 10 minutes, or until crisp. If preferred, serve with ranch dressing. 5. You can keep leftovers in the fridge for up to 5 days if they are sealed in a container. Reheat for 5 minutes, or until thoroughly heated, flipping halfway through in an air fryer set to 200°C.
Per Serving: Calories 898, Fat 13.6g; Sodium 1780mg; Carbs 22.07g; Fibre1.6g; Sugar 13.1g; Protein 23.3g

Cheese Stuffed Mushrooms with Thyme

Prep time: 10 minutes | Cook time: 8 minutes | Serves:12

Ground dried thyme	small pieces (about 1 cm)	stems removed	6 fresh mozzarella cheese balls
¼ roasted red pepper cut into	200g white mushroom caps,	Salt	

1. Add salt to taste within the mushroom caps. 2. Halve the mozzarella balls. 3. Place a half of a mozzarella cheese ball inside each cap. Thyme should be sparingly sprinkled. 4. Place a thin piece of roasted red pepper on top of each mushroom, gently pressing it into the cheese. 5. If you like your mushrooms softer, cook them at 200°C for 8 minutes or longer.
Tip: We used 2.5 cm-diameter mozzarella cheese balls, which paired beautifully with 6 -8 cm mushroom caps. Use smaller cheese balls for mushrooms that aren't as big, or slice larger ones into smaller pieces to fit within the caps.
Per Serving: Calories 26, Fat 0.1g; Sodium 140mg; Carbs 1.57g; Fibre 0.7g; Sugar 0.69g; Protein 4.92g

Bacon-Wrapped Dates with Almonds

Prep time: 10 minutes | Cook time: 7 minutes | Serves:16

16 whole almonds	6 to 8 strips turkey bacon	16 whole, pitted dates

1. Insert an entire almond into each date. 2. Divide or thirdize bacon strips according to the size of the stuffed dates. Each strip needs to be long enough to round a date completely. 3. Use toothpicks to wrap each date in a strip of bacon with the ends overlapping. 4. Place in air fryer basket and cook for 5 to 7 minutes at 200°C, or until bacon is the desired crispiness. 5. Drain and place wire rack or paper towels. Whether hot or cool, serve.
Per Serving: Calories 52, Fat 2.43g; Sodium 114mg; Carbs 6.17g; Fibre 0.8g; Sugar 4.83g; Protein 2.13g

Spicy Cauliflower with Blue Cheese Sauce

Prep time: 5 minutes | Cook time: 11 minutes | Serves:4

1 small head cauliflower, cut into 2.5 cm bites	Blue Cheese Dressing (see below), for serving	sweetener	60ml beef bone stock
60ml hot sauce	**Blue Cheese Dressing**	1 tablespoon MCT oil	60g full-fat sour cream
25g powdered Parmesan cheese	**(makes: about 2 cups (2**	1 clove garlic, peeled	60ml red wine vinegar or
2 tablespoons unsalted butter,	**tablespoons per serving))**	200g crumbled blue cheese,	coconut vinegar
melted	1½ tablespoons powdered	plus more if desired for a	
		chunky texture	

1. For Blue Cheese Dressing: In a food processor, combine all the ingredients and pulse until completely smooth. Place in a jar. If desired, stir in additional blue cheese chunks. Keep in the fridge for up to five days. 2. Turn the air fryer on at 200°C. Use avocado oil to coat a baking dish that will fit inside your air fryer. 3. In a sizable bowl, combine the butter, Parmesan, and spicy sauce. Cauliflower should be added and thoroughly coated. 4. Place the baked cauliflower that has been coated in the pan. 11 minutes of cooking in the air fryer, with a halfway stir. With blue cheese dressing, serve. 5. You can keep leftovers in the fridge for up to 4 days if they are sealed in a container. Reheat for three minutes, until well cooked and crispy, in a 200°C oven.
Per Serving: Calories 407, Fat 30.17g; Sodium 1302mg; Carbs 14.43g; Fibre 1.6g; Sugar 7.66g; Protein 20.46g

Spicy Chicken Wings

Prep time: 15 minutes | Cook time: 40 minutes | Serves:4

1 tablespoon paprika	½ teaspoon dried oregano	black pepper	removed
1 tablespoon Sweetener sugar replacement	½ teaspoon garlic powder	½ teaspoon cayenne	
	½ teaspoon freshly ground	455g chicken wings, tips	

1. Mix the paprika, Sweetener, oregano, garlic powder, black pepper, and cayenne in a big basin. Add the chicken wings and stir to coat completely. Cover and chill for at least an hour and up to eight hours. 2. Turn the air fryer on at 200°C. 3. Place the wings in the air fryer basket in a single layer, working in batches if required. Spray lightly with olive oil. Air fried the wings for 35 to 40 minutes, turning them over halfway through cooking, or until they are browned and crispy and a thermometer inserted into the thickest section reads 75°C.
Per Serving: Calories 159, Fat 4.9g; Sodium 93mg; Carbs 3.66g; Fibre 0.8g; Sugar 2.17g; Protein 25.3g

Tasty Kale Chips

Prep time: 5 minutes | Cook time: 10 minutes | Serves:8 cups

½ teaspoon dried parsley	¼ teaspoon onion powder	pepper
¼ teaspoon garlic powder	¼ teaspoon fine sea salt	½ teaspoon dried chives
2 large bunches kale	⅛ teaspoon ground black	½ teaspoon dried dill weed

1. Spray avocado oil on the air fryer basket. Set the air fryer temperature to 180°C. 2. In a small bowl, combine the spices, salt, and pepper. 3. Thoroughly dry the kale after washing it. After removing the thick inner stems with a sharp knife, spritz the leaves with avocado oil, then top them with the spice mixture. 4. After adding the kale leaves to the air fryer, spread them out evenly. Cook for 10 minutes, flipping and stirring the chips halfway through. Put the crisped-up cooked chips on a baking sheet to cool fully. The remaining kale should be repeated. If desired, season the served chips with salt after they have cooled. 5. Kale chips should be consumed within three days, but they can be kept at room temperature for up to a week in an airtight container.
Per Serving: Calories 67, Fat 1.25g; Sodium 90mg; Carbs 11.9g; Fibre 4.9g; Sugar 3.08g; Protein 5.79g

Pickle Poppers Wrapped in Bacon

Prep time: 10 minutes | Cook time: 10 minutes | Serves:24

12 medium dill pickles	100g shredded sharp cheddar cheese	lengthwise
1 (200g) package cream cheese, softened	12 slices bacon, sliced in half	Ranch Dressing or Blue Cheese Dressing, for serving (optional)

1. Spray avocado oil on the air fryer basket. Set the air fryer to 200°C for frying. 2. Cut the dill pickles in half lengthwise, then scoop out the centres with a spoon. 3. In a small bowl, combine the cheddar and cream cheese by stirring well. 4. Distribute an equal amount of the cream cheese mixture among the pickles by spooning it into their hollowed-out centres. Wrap each filled pickle with a slice of bacon and secure the bacon with toothpicks. 5. Put the bacon-wrapped pickles in the air fryer basket seam side down and cook for 8 to 10 minutes, flipping halfway through, or until the bacon is crispy. If desired, serve warm with ranch or blue cheese dressing. 6. Fresh food is best. Keep leftovers in the refrigerator in an airtight container for up to five days. Reheat for three minutes, or until thoroughly heated, in an air fryer set to 200°C.
Tip: One of my recipe testers neglected to use toothpicks to hold the bacon in place, which caused the filling to leak out when she flipped the poppers. Don't forget to do it.
Per Serving: Calories 94, Fat 8.47g; Sodium 163mg; Carbs 1.7g; Fibre 0.4g; Sugar 1.14g; Protein 3.08g

Berbere Chicken Wings

Prep time: 5 minutes | Cook time: 32 minutes | Serves:12

1 dozen chicken wings	2 teaspoons berbere spice	**For Serving (Omit for Egg-Free):**	¼ teaspoon berbere spice
1 tablespoon coconut oil or bacon fat, melted	1 teaspoon fine sea salt	2 hard-boiled eggs	¼ teaspoon dried chives
		½ teaspoon fine sea salt	

1. Spray avocado oil on the air fryer basket. Set the air fryer's temperature to 195°C. 2. In a big bowl, arrange the chicken wings. Pour the oil over them, then rotate them to evenly coat. Salt and berbere should be applied liberally to the chicken. 3. Put the chicken wings in the air fryer and cook for 25 minutes, turning the wings over after 15 minutes. 4. After 25 minutes, raise the heat to 200°C and continue cooking for an additional 6 to 7 minutes, or until the skin is browned and crisp. 5. While the chicken cooks, prepare the hard-boiled eggs (if using): Peel the eggs, slice them in half, and season them with the salt, berbere, and dried chives. Serve the chicken and eggs together. 6. You may keep leftovers in the fridge for up to 4 days if they are sealed in a container. Reheat the chicken for five minutes, or until well heated, in an air fryer set to 200°C.
Per Serving: Calories 214, Fat 13.6g; Sodium 837mg; Carbs 3.27g; Fibre 0.7g; Sugar 1.91g; Protein 18.47g

Chicken Wings with Tomato Tamari Sauce

Prep time: 10 minutes | Cook time: 32 minutes | Serves:8

900g chicken wings or drummies	¼ teaspoon grated fresh ginger	120ml chicken stock	**For Garnish (Optional):**
½ teaspoon fine sea salt	1 clove garlic, smashed to a paste	15g powdered sweetener	Chopped green onions
Sauce	1 tablespoon apple cider vinegar	60ml tomato sauce	Sesame seeds
¾ teaspoon red pepper flakes		60ml wheat-free tamari	

1. Spray avocado oil on the air fryer basket. Set the air fryer's temperature to 195°C. 2. Season the chicken wings on all sides with the salt and place them in the air fryer. Cook for 25 minutes, flipping after 15 minutes. After 25 minutes, increase the temperature to 200°C and cook for 6 to 7 minutes more, until the skin is browned and crisp. 3. Prepare the sauce while the wings cook by combining all the ingredients in a sizable sauté pan. Simmer for 10 minutes or until reduced and thickened. 4. Apply the sauce to the cooked chicken wings. If preferred, garnish with sesame seeds and green onions. Extra sauce should be served on the side for dipping. 5. You can keep leftovers in the fridge for up to 4 days if they are sealed in a container. Reheat for five minutes in an air fryer that has been warmed to 175°C, then raise the heat to 200°C and continue to cook for three to five more minutes, or until hot and crispy.
Per Serving: Calories 206, Fat 5.31g; Sodium 452mg; Carbs 8.52g; Fibre 1.5g; Sugar 3.22g; Protein 29.4g

Sour Pork Belly Strips

Prep time: 5 minutes | Cook time: 12 minutes | Serves:4

455g slab pork belly (see Tip)	Fine sea salt	**For Serving (Optional):**	Pico de Gallo
120ml apple cider vinegar		Guacamole	

1. Cut the pork belly into strips that are ½ cm thick, and put the strips in a shallow dish. Pour the vinegar over the pork belly and swirl to coat. Place in the refrigerator for 30 minutes of marinating. 2. Spray avocado oil on the air fryer basket. Set the air fryer to 200°C for frying. 3. Take the pork belly out of the vinegar and arrange the strips in a single layer with space between them in the air fryer basket. Cook in the air fryer for 10 to 12 minutes, turning after 5 minutes, until crispy. Sprinkle with salt after removing from the air fryer. If preferred, serve with guacamole and pico de gallo. 4. Fresh food is best. Keep leftovers in the refrigerator in an airtight container for up to five days. Reheat for 5 minutes, or until thoroughly heated, flipping halfway through in an air fryer set to 200°C.
Tip: Trader Joe's sells fully cooked pork belly; you only need one packet for this recipe.
Per Serving: Calories 602, Fat 60.1g; Sodium 136mg; Carbs 3.55g; Fibre 0.1g; Sugar 3g; Protein 10.63g

Asparagus Wrapped in Bacon

Prep time: 5minutes | Cook time: 10 minutes | Serves:4

455g asparagus, trimmed (about 24 spears)	4 slices bacon	serving	chives, for garnish
	120ml Ranch Dressing, for	2 tablespoons chopped fresh	

1. Spray avocado oil on the air fryer basket. Set the air fryer to 200°C for frying. 2. Cut the bacon into long, thin strips by slicing it in half. 3 asparagus spears are wrapped in 1 slice of bacon; the ends are held together with toothpicks. Continue with the remaining asparagus and bacon. 3. Arrange the asparagus bundles in a single layer in the air fryer. (If a smaller air fryer is being used, cooking in batches may be necessary.) Cook the asparagus until the ends are just barely browned and the bacon is crisp, about 8 minutes for thin stalks and 10 minutes for medium to thick stalks. 4. Add ranch dressing and chives as garnish. Fresh food is preferred. Keep leftovers in the refrigerator in an airtight container for up to five days. Reheat for three minutes, or until thoroughly heated, in an air fryer set to 200°C.
Per Serving: Calories 255, Fat 23.7g; Sodium 395mg; Carbs 6.4g; Fibre 2.4g; Sugar 3.78g; Protein 6.2g

Cheese Avocado Fries

Prep time: 10 minutes | Cook time: 8 minutes | Serves: 4

4 lime wedges, for garnish (optional)	½ teaspoon smoked paprika	25g almond flour	total)
25g grated Parmesan cheese	¼ teaspoon garlic powder	Flesh of 3 avocados, each sliced into 8 pieces (24 wedges	Salt and freshly ground black pepper
	2 eggs		

1. Turn the air fryer on at 200°C. 2. Combine the almond flour, Parmesan cheese, paprika, and garlic powder in a small basin. 3. Whisk the eggs in a separate shallow basin. 4. Working with one avocado wedge at a time, dip it first in the egg, then lightly press it to coat it with the almond flour mixture. Put the avocado fries on a platter that has been covered in parchment paper. 5. Place the avocado fries in the air fryer basket in a single layer, making sure they don't touch, working in batches if required. 6. Spray olive oil liberally. Fry the fries in the air fryer for 7 to 8 minutes, turning the fries over halfway through frying, or until the coating is crisp and golden. With the lime wedges, serve (if desired).
Per Serving: Calories 347, Fat 28.79g; Sodium 176mg; Carbs 18.6g; Fibre 10.6g; Sugar 2.11g; Protein 9.61g

Cheese Calamari Rings

Prep time: 10 minutes | Cook time: 15 minutes | Serves:4

½ teaspoon garlic powder	garnish (optional)	cheese (or parmesan for dairy-free; see here)	Lemon slices, for serving (optional)
½ teaspoon onion powder	240ml marinara sauce, for serving (optional)	35g coconut flour	
455g calamari, sliced into rings (see Tip)	2 large egg yolks	3 teaspoons dried oregano leaves	
Fresh oregano leaves, for	100g powdered Parmesan		

1. Spray avocado oil on the air fryer basket. Set the air fryer to 200°C for frying. 2. Whip the egg yolks in a small dish. Combine the Parmesan, coconut flour, and spices in a separate bowl. 3. After coating the calamari rings thoroughly in the cheese mixture, dip them in the egg yolks and tap out any excess. If necessary, press the coating onto the calamari with your hands. Spray avocado oil on the coated rings. 4. After spacing them out, add the calamari rings to the air fryer and cook for 15 minutes, or until golden brown. Serve with marinara sauce for dipping and lemon slices and garnish with fresh oregano if desired. 5. Fresh food is best. Keep leftovers in the refrigerator in an airtight container for up to five days. Reheat for three minutes, or until thoroughly heated, in an air fryer set to 200°C.
Tip: The coating adheres better to the calamari rings when only egg yolks are used.
Busy Family Tip: To make this recipe even simpler, I buy frozen calamari rings from a nearby seafood shop.
Per Serving: Calories 290, Fat 11.3g; Sodium 987mg; Carbs 10.7g; Fibre 1.9g; Sugar 3.39g; Protein 35.7g

Blooming Onion

Prep time: 10 minutes | Cook time: 35 minutes | Serves:8

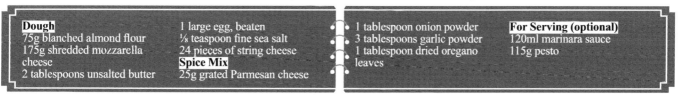

¼ teaspoon cayenne pepper	in diameter)	1 teaspoon garlic powder	**For Serving (optional):**
¼ teaspoon fine sea salt	2 large eggs	**For Garnish (optional):**	Prepared yellow mustard
¼ teaspoon ground black pepper	1 tablespoon water	Fresh parsley leaves	Ranch Dressing
1 extra-large onion (about 8 cm	50g powdered Parmesan cheese	Powdered Parmesan cheese	Reduced-sugar or sugar-free ketchup
	2 teaspoons paprika		

1. Spray avocado oil on the air fryer basket. Set the air fryer to 175°C for frying. 2. Using a sharp knife, cut the top 1 cm off the onion and peel off the outer layer. You want the onion to stay intact at the base, so cut it into 8 equal slices, stopping 2.5 cm from the bottom. The "petals" or parts should be gently spread apart. 3. Crack the eggs into a big bowl, then whisk in the water. Put the onion in the dish and thoroughly cover it with the egg. Coat the onion's interior and all of its petals with a spoon. 4. Combine the Parmesan, spices, salt, and pepper in a small bowl. 5. Put the onion in a casserole or pie dish with a 15 cm diameter. Use your fingers to massage the seasoning mixture into the onion's petals after sprinkling it all over the onion. Spray avocado oil on the onion. 6. Loosely wrap the onion with foil and parchment paper. The dish should be placed in the air fryer. Once it has finished cooking for 30 minutes, remove it from the air fryer and raise the temperature to 200°C. 7. Take off the foil and paper and re-apply avocado oil to the onion. Transfer the onion to the air fryer basket while wearing oven-safe gloves or a tea towel to protect your hands. Cook for a further 3 to 5 minutes, or until crispy and light brown. 8. If wanted, garnish with chopped fresh parsley and Parmesan. If preferred, top with ketchup, ranch dressing, and mustard before serving. 9. You can keep leftovers in the refrigerator for up to 4 days if they are sealed tightly. Reheat for 3 to 5 minutes, until warm and crispy, in an air fryer that has been warmed to 200°C.
Per Serving: Calories 46, Fat 3.15g; Sodium 197mg; Carbs 1.94g; Fibre 0.3g; Sugar 0.18g; Protein 2.69g

Fried Cheese Sticks

Prep time: 15minutes | Cook time: 14 minutes | Serves:24

Dough	1 large egg, beaten	1 tablespoon onion powder	**For Serving (optional)**
75g blanched almond flour	¼ teaspoon fine sea salt	3 tablespoons garlic powder	120ml marinara sauce
175g shredded mozzarella cheese	24 pieces of string cheese	1 tablespoon dried oregano leaves	115g pesto
2 tablespoons unsalted butter	**Spice Mix**		
	25g grated Parmesan cheese		

1. Prepare the dough: In a sizable microwave-safe bowl, combine the mozzarella and butter. Microwave for 1 to 2 minutes, or until the cheese is completely melted, stir well. 2. Add the egg and thoroughly incorporate with a hand mixer set to low. With the mixer running, add the salt and almond flour. 3. Place the dough on a sheet of parchment paper that has been spread out on the tabletop. It should take three minutes to knead; the dough should be thick but malleable. (Note: Chill the dough in the fridge for an hour or overnight if it's too sticky.) 4. Scoop up three tablespoons of the dough and press it into a thin rectangle that is 8 by 5.5 cm. Use your hands to press the dough firmly around the central piece of string cheese after placing it. Repeat with the remaining dough and string cheese. 5. Combine the components for the spice mixture in a small dish. Place a piece of string cheese that has been wrapped in the dish, roll it up, and press down to create a good crust. Continue with the remaining string cheese pieces. Place for two hours in the freezer. 6. Spray the air fryer basket with avocado oil ten minutes prior to air frying, and prepare the air fryer to 220°C. 7. Insert the frozen mozzarella sticks into the air fryer basket, spacing them apart, and cook for 9 to 12 minutes, or until golden brown. Remove from the air fryer and, if preferred, serve with pesto and marinara sauce. 8. You can keep leftovers in the freezer for up to a month or in the fridge for up to three days if you store them in an airtight container. Reheat for 4 minutes, or until thoroughly heated, in an air fryer set to 220°C.
busy family tip: I make a triple batch of these because my kids adore them so much and freeze the extras!
Per Serving: Calories 202, Fat 15.9g; Sodium 328mg; Carbs 3.8g; Fibre 0.9g; Sugar 0.8g; Protein 11.63g

Prosciutto Wrapped Onion Rings with Guacamole

Prep time: 10 minutes | Cook time: 6 minutes | Serves: 8

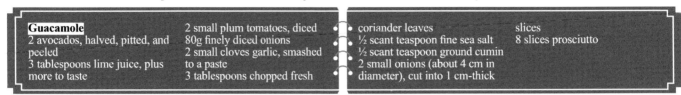

Guacamole	2 small plum tomatoes, diced	coriander leaves	slices
2 avocados, halved, pitted, and peeled	80g finely diced onions	½ scant teaspoon fine sea salt	8 slices prosciutto
3 tablespoons lime juice, plus more to taste	2 small cloves garlic, smashed to a paste	½ scant teaspoon ground cumin	
	3 tablespoons chopped fresh	2 small onions (about 4 cm in diameter), cut into 1 cm-thick	

1. To make the guacamole, mash the avocados with a fork in a large bowl with the lime juice until it has the consistency you like. Stir to thoroughly blend before adding the tomatoes, onions, garlic, coriander, salt, and cumin. If desired, taste and add extra lime juice. For serving, set aside half of the guacamole. (Note: If making guacamole ahead of time, place it in a sizable, resealable plastic bag, press out any excess air, and seal it. When kept in the refrigerator in this manner, it can last up to three days.) 2. Arrange the onion slices on a tray that will fit in your freezer. Cut the slices into 8 rings before placing them there. Add about 2 tablespoons of guacamole to each ring. Place the tray in the freezer for two hours. 3. Spray avocado oil on the air fryer basket. Set the air fryer to 200°C for frying. 4. Take the rings out of the freezer and wrap one piece of prosciutto around each one. If you're using a smaller air fryer, you may need to cook them in batches. Place them in the air fryer basket with room between them, and cook for 6 minutes, flipping once halfway through. The rings should be taken out of the air fryer using a spatula. Serve with the guacamole that has been set aside. 5. You can keep leftovers in the fridge for up to 4 days if they are sealed in a container. Reheat for about 3 minutes, or until thoroughly heated, in an air fryer set to 200°C.
Per Serving: Calories 130, Fat 9g; Sodium 252mg; Carbs 10.69g; Fibre 4g; Sugar 4.36g; Protein 3.91g

Bacon-Wrapped Jalapeno Poppers with Cheese

Prep time: 10 minutes | Cook time: 20 minutes | Serves: 4

8 jalapeño peppers, halved lengthwise and seeded	100g cream cheese, softened	1 teaspoon garlic powder	cut in half
	1 tablespoon hot sauce	8 slices reduced-sodium bacon,	

1. Mix the cream cheese, spicy sauce, and garlic powder in a small bowl. 2. Equal portions of the cream cheese mixture should be placed inside each pepper half. Then, each pepper should be snugly wrapped with a half-piece of bacon to seal in the ingredients. Make sure the bacon ends are on the bottom of the peppers for optimal results. 3. Place the peppers in the air fryer basket in a single layer, cut-side up. When the bacon is crisp and the peppers are tender, set the air fryer to 175°C and air fry for 15 to 20 minutes. Before serving, allow it cool somewhat.
Per Serving: Calories 335, Fat 28.72g; Sodium 406mg; Carbs 10.8g; Fibre 1.5g; Sugar 6.21g; Protein 10.53g

Roasted Curry Chickpeas

Prep time: 5 minutes | Cook time:15 minutes | Serves: 1 cup

¼ teaspoon salt	1 (375g) can chickpeas, drained	2 teaspoons curry powder	1 tablespoon olive oil

1. Chickpeas should be fully drained and then put on paper towels in a single layer. To remove additional moisture, cover with another paper towel and press lightly. Avoid pressing too firmly to avoid crushing the chickpeas. 2. Combine salt and curry powder. 3. Put the spices and chickpeas in a medium bowl. A good stir will coat. 4. Add the olive oil and mix it in again. 5. Cook for 15 minutes at 200°C, stopping to shake the basket halfway through. 6. Allow to fully cool before storing in an airtight container.
Tips: Try seasoning with any herbs, spices, or blends that you enjoy instead of curry powder, such as garlic, rosemary, Italian seasoning, chili powder, or smoky paprika.
Per Serving: Calories 724, Fat 25.84g; Sodium 1630mg; Carbs 98.05g; Fibre 29.3g; Sugar 17.16g; Protein 30.56g

Courgette Fries with Marinara Sauce

Prep time: 10 minutes | Cook time: 10 minutes | Serves: 4

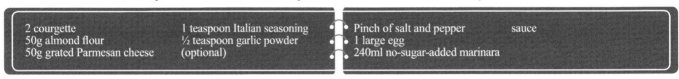

2 courgette	1 teaspoon Italian seasoning	Pinch of salt and pepper	sauce
50g almond flour	½ teaspoon garlic powder	1 large egg	
50g grated Parmesan cheese	(optional)	240ml no-sugar-added marinara	

1. Set the air fryer to 200°C for frying. 2. Cut the courgette in half lengthwise, then into sticks that are 10 cm long and about a cm thick. 3. Almond flour, Parmesan, Italian seasoning, garlic powder (if used), salt, and pepper should all be combined in a small basin. 4. With a fork, lightly beat the egg in another shallow basin. 5. After dipping it in the egg mixture, coat the courgette with the almond flour mixture. Make careful to arrange the pieces in the air fryer basket so that they don't touch (work in batches if necessary). Spray the courgette with olive oil liberally. 6. Crispy food should be air-fried for 10 minutes, flipping halfway through and adding more oil as needed. Warm up the marinara in the meantime using a microwave. Along with the marinara sauce, serve the courgette sticks.
Per Serving: Calories 95, Fat 4.85g; Sodium 782mg; Carbs 8.29g; Fibre 1.6g; Sugar 3.49g; Protein 5.68g

Garlic Kale Chips with Cajun Spice

Prep time: 10 minutes | Cook time: 10 minutes | Serves: 2

1 large bunch kale, stems removed and torn into chip-size	pieces 2 tablespoons olive oil	1 teaspoon garlic powder 1 teaspoon cajun seasoning	

1. Set the air fryer to 180°C. 2. Combine the kale, olive oil, garlic powder, and cajun seasoning in a sizable bowl. Kale should be fully coated after tossing. 3. Fill the air fryer basket with an even layer of around 60g of kale while working in batches. (Let the mixture continue to be as fluffy as possible to promote airflow in the basket.) Air fried for 8 to 10 minutes, shaking the basket halfway through. 4. To totally cool, spread out the kale chips on a baking pan. The remaining kale should be repeated. Keep at room temperature in an airtight container for up to two days.
Per Serving: Calories 133, Fat 13.59g; Sodium 109mg; Carbs 2.69g; Fibre 0.6g; Sugar 0.38g; Protein 0.66g

Crispy Mozzarella Sticks

Prep time: 5 minutes | Cook time: 5 minutes | Serves: 4

25g almond flour 25g grated Parmesan cheese	½ teaspoon Italian seasoning ¼ teaspoon garlic powder	1 egg 6 part-skim mozzarella sticks,	cut in half

1. Combine the almond flour, Parmesan, Italian seasoning, and garlic powder in a small basin. 2. Whisk the egg in a separate shallow basin. 3. Roll the mozzarella sticks in the almond flour mixture after dipping them in the egg wash, coating them completely. Put the mozzarella sticks on a platter that has been covered in parchment paper. For 30 minutes, freeze. 4. Set the air fryer's temperature to 200°C. 5. Place the mozzarella sticks in the air fryer basket in a single layer. Spray olive oil liberally. The coating needs to be air-fried for 5 minutes to brown. Before transferring to a plate, let stand for 1 minute.
Per Serving: Calories 169, Fat 10.9g; Sodium 427mg; Carbs 2.67g; Fibre 0.1g; Sugar 0.69g; Protein 14.4g

Bacon and Egg Bites

Prep time: 40 minutes | Cook time: 15 minutes | Serves: 4

Salt and freshly ground black pepper Flesh of ½ avocado, chopped 2 tablespoons unsalted butter,	softened 2 tablespoons mayonnaise 150g (about 9 slices) reduced-sodium bacon	2 hard-boiled eggs, chopped Juice of ½ lime 1 jalapeño pepper, seeded and finely chopped	2 tablespoons chopped fresh coriander

1. Place the bacon in the air fryer basket in a single layer; it's fine if some of the bacon hangs over the sides. Cook for 10 minutes at 175°C in the air fryer. If necessary, cook for 2 to 3 minutes more after checking for crispiness. Place the bacon on a plate covered with paper towels and allow to cool completely. 2 tablespoons of the bacon grease from the air fryer basket's bottom should be set aside. Chop the bacon into tiny, shallow pieces, and set aside. 2. Combine the eggs, avocado, butter, mayonnaise, jalapenos, coriander, and lime juice in a sizable bowl. Use a fork or potato masher to crush the food into a paste. Use salt and pepper to taste to season. 3. Combine the egg mixture with the bacon fat that was set aside by giving it a gentle toss. Cover and chill the mixture for 30 minutes, or until the mixture is stiff. 4. Form the mixture into 12 equal sections by dividing it into equal portions. To completely cover, roll the balls in the chopped bacon bites.
Per Serving: Calories 344, Fat 31.4g; Sodium 314mg; Carbs 4.94g; Fibre 2g; Sugar 1.58g; Protein 11.28g

Sausage Cheese Bites

Prep time: 20 minutes | Cook time: 30 minutes | Serves: 12

1 teaspoon garlic powder ½ teaspoon baking powder ½ teaspoon smoked paprika	½ teaspoon dried oregano 3 eggs 60ml coconut oil, melted	120g sour cream 455g Italian sausage 50g almond flour	35g coconut flour 200g shredded Cheddar cheese

1. In the basket of the air fryer, shred the sausage into small pieces. Air fry until golden for 10 to 15 minutes at 200°C in the air fryer. Put the sausage in a bowl and reserve. Drain the fat, then wash the air fryer basket once it is cold enough to handle. 2. In the meantime, combine the paprika, oregano, garlic powder, coconut flour, baking powder, and almond flour in a small bowl. 3. Combine the eggs, coconut oil, and sour cream in a sizable bowl. 4. Combine the egg mixture with the flour mixture. Gently fold the ingredients using a silicone spatula until well incorporated (do not overmix). Add the Cheddar and the sausage that was set aside. Give the batter five minutes to rest. 5. Using a small cookie scoop, shape the dough into 24 balls and arrange them on a rimmed baking sheet. Refrigerate for 10 minutes. 6. Set the air fryer's temperature to 185°C. 7. Place the balls in a single layer in the air fryer basket while working in batches (about 2.5 cm apart). Spray olive oil liberally. Air fry the food for 10 to 12 minutes, shaking the basket halfway through, until golden brown.
Per Serving: Calories 307, Fat 27.3g; Sodium 457mg; Carbs 2.04g; Fibre 0.1g; Sugar 0.4g; Protein 13.36g

Homemade Prosciutto Pierogi

Prep time: 15 minutes | Cook time: 20 minutes | Serves:4

1 tablespoon unsalted butter (or lard or bacon fat for dairy-free), melted	Pinch of fine sea salt 50g shredded sharp cheddar cheese	8 slices prosciutto Fresh oregano leaves, for garnish (optional)	110g chopped cauliflower 2 tablespoons diced onions

1. Set the air fryer's temperature to 175°C. Prepare a 18 cm pie plate or a casserole dish that will fit inside your air fryer by lightly greasing it. 2. To prepare the filling, put the onion and cauliflower in the pan. Salt should be added, then drizzled with melted butter. Mix everything with your hands, making sure the cauliflower is completely covered in butter. 3. After adding the cauliflower mixture to the air fryer, cook it for 10 minutes, stirring once, until it is soft to the fork. 4. Pour the cauliflower mixture into a high-speed blender or food processor. Spray some avocado oil in the air fryer basket and raise the temperature to 200°C. 5. Use the food processor to pulse the cauliflower mixture until it is smooth. Add the cheese and mix. 6. Assemble the pierogis by placing 1 slice of prosciutto on a parchment-lined baking sheet with the short end facing you. On top of it, place a second slice of prosciutto at a right angle to create a cross. Place two heaping tablespoons of filling in the cross's middle. 7. Ensure that the filling is completely covered by folding each prosciutto cross arm over it to form a square. To smooth out the square form, press down with your fingers all over the filling. Continue by using the remaining prosciutto and stuffing. 8. After applying avocado oil to the pierogi, put them in the air fryer basket. Cook until crispy for 10 minutes. 9. If preferred, garnish with oregano before serving. Keep leftovers in the refrigerator in an airtight container for up to 4 days. Reheat for three minutes, or until thoroughly heated, in an air fryer set to 200°C.

Per Serving: Calories 67, Fat 5.4g; Sodium 345mg; Carbs 3.59g; Fibre 0.7g; Sugar 1.61g; Protein 6.16g

Bacon-Wrapped Pickles

Prep time: 5 minutes | Cook time: 13 minutes | Serves: 4

60ml ranch dressing	4 dill pickles	8 slices reduced-sodium bacon, cut in half

1. Cut each pickle lengthwise into four spears. Each pickle spear is encircled by a slice of bacon. 2. Arrange the pickles in the air fryer basket in a single layer, seam-side down. Air fried for 10 minutes at 175°C. 3. If necessary, cook for 2 to 3 minutes more after checking for crispiness. Ranch dressing should be available for dipping.

Per Serving: Calories 291, Fat 27.51g; Sodium 1477mg; Carbs 4.55g; Fibre 1.4g; Sugar 2.58g; Protein 7.39g

Chapter 7 Dessert Recipes

Easy Lime Bars

Prep time: 10 minutes | Cook time: 35 minutes | Serves: 10

3 tablespoons coconut oil, melted	3 tablespoons lime juice 3 tablespoons Splenda	150g coconut flour 3 eggs, beaten	1 teaspoon lime zest, grated

1. Place baking paper on the air fryer basket's bottom. 2. Next, combine Splenda with coconut flour, eggs, lime juice, coconut oil and zest in a mixing bowl. 3. Add the mixture to the air fryer basket and gently press it down. 4. Prepare the food for 35 minutes at 175°C. 5. After a brief period of cooling, cut the prepared food into bars.
Per Serving: Calories 83, Fat 7.05g; Sodium 69mg; Carbs 2.34g; Fibre 0.4g; Sugar 1.46g; Protein 2.97g

Delicious Macadamia Nut Bars

Prep time: 15 minutes | Cook time: 30 minutes | Serves: 10

3 tablespoons butter, softened 1 teaspoon baking powder 1 teaspoon apple cider vinegar	150g coconut flour 3 tablespoons sweetener 1 teaspoon vanilla extract	2 eggs, beaten 50g macadamia nuts, chopped Cooking spray

1. Spray the air fryer basket with cooking spray. 2. After that, combine all of the additional ingredients in the mixing bowl and whisk until the mixture is homogeneous. 3. Fill the air fryer basket with the mixture, and cook for 30 minutes at 175°C. 4. Slice the cooked mixture into bars and place them on serving plates.
Per Serving: Calories 106, Fat 9.78g; Sodium 86mg; Carbs 2.98g; Fibre 0.9g; Sugar 1.43g; Protein 2.54g

Flavoured Vanilla Scones

Prep time: 20 minutes | Cook time: 10 minutes | Serves: 6

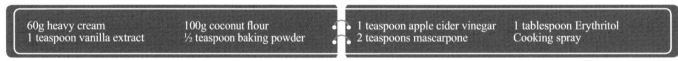

60g heavy cream 1 teaspoon vanilla extract	100g coconut flour ½ teaspoon baking powder	1 teaspoon apple cider vinegar 2 teaspoons mascarpone	1 tablespoon Erythritol Cooking spray

1. Coconut flour, baking powder, apple cider vinegar, mascarpone, heavy cream, vanilla extract, and erythritol should all be combined in a bowl. 2. Cut the dough into scones after kneading it. 3. After that, put them in the air fryer basket with cooking spray on them. 4. Bake the vanilla scones at 185°C for 10 minutes.
Per Serving: Calories 24, Fat 1.93g; Sodium 22mg; Carbs 1.23g; Fibre 0.2g; Sugar 0.8g; Protein 0.24g

Courgette Bread

Prep time: 10 minutes | Cook time: 40 minutes | Serves: 12

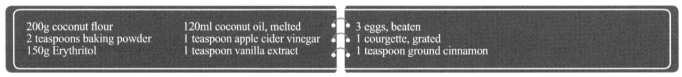

200g coconut flour 2 teaspoons baking powder 150g Erythritol	120ml coconut oil, melted 1 teaspoon apple cider vinegar 1 teaspoon vanilla extract	3 eggs, beaten 1 courgette, grated 1 teaspoon ground cinnamon

1. Combine baking powder, erythritol, coconut oil, apple cider vinegar, vanilla extract, eggs, courgette, and ground cinnamon in a bowl with the coconut flour. 2. Spread the ingredients out into the shape of bread in the air fryer basket. 3. Bake the bread for 40 minutes at 175°C.
Per Serving: Calories 121, Fat 11.58g; Sodium 68mg; Carbs 2.42g; Fibre 0.6g; Sugar 1.3g; Protein 2.56g

Lime Almond Pie

Prep time: 10 minutes | Cook time: 35 minutes | Serves: 8

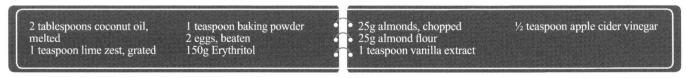

2 tablespoons coconut oil, melted 1 teaspoon lime zest, grated	1 teaspoon baking powder 2 eggs, beaten 150g Erythritol	25g almonds, chopped 25g almond flour 1 teaspoon vanilla extract	½ teaspoon apple cider vinegar

1. Mix all ingredients in the mixing bowl and whisk until smooth. 2. Then pour the mixture into the baking pan and flatten gently. 3. Put the baking pan in the air fryer and cook the pie at 185°C for 35 minutes.
Per Serving: Calories 85, Fat 7.6g; Sodium 26mg; Carbs 1.48g; Fibre 0.5g; Sugar 0.43g; Protein 3g

Simple Mint Pie

Prep time: 15 minutes | Cook time: 25 minutes | Serves:2

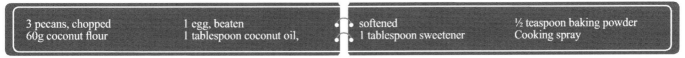

1 tablespoon instant coffee 2 tablespoons almond butter, softened	2 tablespoons Erythritol 1 teaspoon dried mint 3 eggs, beaten	1 teaspoon spearmint, dried 4 teaspoons coconut flour Cooking spray

1. Spray the air fryer basket with cooking spray. 2. Next, incorporate each ingredient into the mixing bowl. 3. Place the mixture in the air fryer basket once it is smooth. Gently press it flat. 4. Bake the pie for 25 minutes at 185°C.
Per Serving: Calories 302, Fat 23.51g; Sodium 202mg; Carbs 6.28g; Fibre 1.9g; Sugar 2.24g; Protein 17.14g

Sweet Sage Muffins

Prep time: 10 minutes | Cook time: 20 minutes | Serves:8

3 tablespoons coconut oil, softened 1 teaspoon dried sage	3 tablespoons mascarpone 1 egg, beaten 100g Erythritol	25g almond flour ½ teaspoon baking soda Cooking spray

1. Spray the muffin tins with cooking spray. 2. After that, combine everything in the mixing bowl and stir until it is smooth. 3. Fill the muffin tins with the mixture, and then place them in the air fryer. 4. Bake the muffins for 20 minutes at 175°C.
Per Serving: Calories 61, Fat 6.33g; Sodium 91mg; Carbs 0.19g; Fibre0g; Sugar 0.08g; Protein 1.14g

Pecan Tarts

Prep time: 10 minutes | Cook time: 10 minutes | Serves:5

3 pecans, chopped 60g coconut flour	1 egg, beaten 1 tablespoon coconut oil,	softened 1 tablespoon sweetener	½ teaspoon baking powder Cooking spray

1. Spray the air fryer basket with cooking spray. 2. Next, combine the egg, coconut oil, sweetener, and baking powder with the coconut flour. 3. Once the batter is smooth, pour it into the air fryer basket, gently press it down, and sprinkle pecans on top. 4. Bake the tart for 10 minutes at 190°C.
Per Serving: Calories 507, Fat 51.81g; Sodium 46mg; Carbs 10.4g; Fibre 6.6g; Sugar 3.35g; Protein 7.96g

Raspberry Tart

Prep time: 5 minutes | Cook time: 20 minutes | Serves: 8

150g coconut flour 1 teaspoon lime zest, grated	1 teaspoon baking powder 80ml coconut oil, melted	75g raspberries 5 egg whites	65g Erythritol Cooking spray

1. Combine baking powder, coconut oil, coconut flour, erythritol, and lime zest in an egg mixture. 2. Smooth up the mixture by whisking it. 3. After that, pour the batter into the air fryer basket that has been coated with cooking spray. 4. Place raspberries on top of the batter and bake for 20 minutes at 180°C .
Per Serving: Calories 103, Fat 9.18g; Sodium 82mg; Carbs 3.44g; Fibre 1.2g; Sugar 1.8g; Protein 2.7g

Coffee Cake Muffins

Prep time: 10 minutes | Cook time: 11 minutes | Serves: 6

50g Erythritol 1 teaspoon vanilla extract	125g coconut flour 4 tablespoons coconut oil	1 egg, beaten 1 teaspoon instant coffee	1 teaspoon baking powder

1. Combine baking powder, vanilla extract, instant coffee, egg, and erythritol with the coconut flour and coconut oil. 2. Place the mixture in the muffin tins and bake for 11 minutes at 190°C in the air fryer.
Per Serving: Calories 111, Fat 10.76g; Sodium 60mg; Carbs 3.44g; Fibre 0.5g; Sugar 1.2g; Protein 1.8g

Hand pies with coconut

Prep time: 20 minutes | Cook time: 26 minutes | Serves: 6

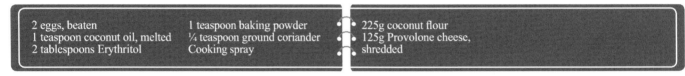

2 eggs, beaten
1 tablespoon almond butter, melted

1 tablespoon almond meal
200g coconut flour
2 tablespoons coconut shred

Cooking spray
1 teaspoon vanilla extract
2 tablespoons Sweetener

1. Combine coconut flour, almond meal, almond butter, Sweetener, vanilla essence, and eggs. 2. Roll the dough up after kneading it. 3. Cut the dough into squares and top with shredded coconut. 4. Form the squares into pies and place them in the basket of the air fryer. 5. Sprinkle the pies with cooking spray and cook at 175°C for 13 minutes per side.
Per Serving: Calories 71, Fat 4.92g; Sodium 85 mg; Carbs 2.57g; Fibre 0.8g; Sugar 1.6g; Protein 3.9g

Coconut Cheese Balls

Prep time: 15 minutes | Cook time: 4 minutes | Serves:10

2 eggs, beaten
1 teaspoon coconut oil, melted
2 tablespoons Erythritol

1 teaspoon baking powder
¼ teaspoon ground coriander
Cooking spray

225g coconut flour
125g Provolone cheese, shredded

1. Combine eggs, erythritol, baking powder, cinnamon, Provolone cheese, coconut oil, and coconut flour in a bowl. 2. Create the balls and place them in the basket of the air fryer. 3. Cook the balls for 4 minutes at 200°C after spraying with cooking spray.
Per Serving: Calories 85, Fat 6.23g; Sodium 172mg; Carbs 1.69g; Fibre 0.3g; Sugar 0.88g; Protein 5.61g

Almond Cookies

Prep time: 5 minutes | Cook time: 15 minutes | Serves: 8

100g almond flour
50g. almonds, grinded

2 tablespoons Erythritol
½ teaspoon baking powder

5 tablespoons coconut oil, softened

½ teaspoon vanilla extract

1. Combine almonds, erythritol, baking powder, coconut oil, and vanilla extract with the almond flour. Work the dough. 2. Prepare the tiny cookies and put them in the basket of the air fryer. 3. Bake the cookies for 15 minutes at 175°C.
Per Serving: Calories 116, Fat 12.12g; Sodium 0mg; Carbs 1.74g; Fibre 0.9g; Sugar 0.35g; Protein 1.53g

Coconut Muffins

Prep time: 5 minutes | Cook time: 25 minutes | Serves: 5

2 tablespoons coconut oil
2 eggs, beaten

60g coconut flour
2 tablespoons cocoa powder

3 tablespoons Erythritol
1 teaspoon baking powder

45g coconut shred

1. Mix all ingredients in a large bowl. 2. After that, pour the mixture into the muffin moulds and place them in the air fryer basket. 3. Bake the muffins for 25 minutes at 175°C.
Per Serving: Calories 114, Fat 9.68g; Sodium 93mg; Carbs 4.52g; Fibre 1.2g; Sugar 1.55g; Protein 4.32g

Crispy Coconut Almond Cookies

Prep time: 15 minutes | Cook time:9 minutes | Serves: 6

2 teaspoons coconut oil, softened

1 tablespoon Erythritol
1 egg, beaten

50g coconut flour
25g almonds, chopped

1. In a mixing dish, combine all the ingredients. Work the dough. 2. Then use the batter to bake cookies and place them in the air fryer basket. 3. Bake the cookies for 9 minutes at 185°C.
Per Serving: Calories 66, Fat 5.51g; Sodium 38mg; Carbs 1.93g; Fibre 0.8g; Sugar 0.84g; Protein 2.64g

Low-Carb Hot Chocolate

Prep time: 10 minutes | Cook time: 7 minutes | Serves: 3

¼ teaspoon vanilla extract 480ml organic almond milk	1 teaspoon coconut oil 1 tablespoon cocoa powder	2 tablespoons Erythritol

1. In the air fryer basket, combine all the ingredients. 2. The mixture should be well-combined. 3. Cook the dessert for 7 minutes at 190°C.
Per Serving: Calories 98, Fat 3.74g; Sodium 114mg; Carbs 16.1g; Fibre 1.2g; Sugar 14.08g; Protein 1.33g

Raspberry Jam

Prep time: 10 minutes | Cook time: 20 minutes | Serves:12

50g Erythritol	175g raspberries	1 tablespoon lime juice	60ml of water

1. Fill the air fryer with all the ingredients and gently mix. 2. Cook the jam for 20 minutes at 175°C. Stir the jam every 5 minutes to avoid burning.
Per Serving: Calories 9, Fat 0.11g; Sodium 0mg; Carbs 2.4g; Fibre 1.1g; Sugar 0.75g; Protein 0.2g

Cream Egg Custard

Prep time: 5 minutes | Cook time: 30 minutes | Serves: 6

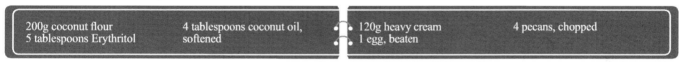

6 eggs, beaten	480g heavy cream	100g Erythritol	1 teaspoon vanilla extract

1. Blend all the ingredients, then pour them into the air fryer basket. 2. Cook the custard at 175°C for 30 minutes. 3. Next, properly cool it.
Per Serving: Calories 270, Fat 24.44g; Sodium 117mg; Carbs 2.22g; Fibre 0g; Sugar 1.86g; Protein 9.79g

Coconut Pecan Bars

Prep time: 5 minutes | Cook time: 40 minutes | Serves: 12

200g coconut flour 5 tablespoons Erythritol	4 tablespoons coconut oil, softened	120g heavy cream 1 egg, beaten	4 pecans, chopped

1. Combine coconut oil, heavy cream, egg, erythritol, and coconut flour. 2. Fill the air fryer basket with the batter, then evenly spread it out. 3. Pecans should be sprinkled on top before the meal is cooked for 40 minutes at 175°C. 4. Cut the prepared food into bars.
Per Serving: Calories 326, Fat 33.4g; Sodium 52mg; Carbs 6.74g; Fibre 3.9g; Sugar 2.68g; Protein 4.47g

Cinnamon Cocoa Muffins

Prep time: 15 minutes | Cook time: 10 minutes | Serves: 2

1 tablespoon cocoa powder 1 tablespoon Erythritol	1 egg, beaten 1 tablespoon coconut oil,	softened 2 tablespoons almond flour	1 teaspoon ground cinnamon

1. Combine the egg with the coconut oil, almond flour, cocoa, erythritol, and cinnamon powder. 2. Fill the muffin tins with the batter. 3. Bake the muffins at 190°C for 10 minutes.
Per Serving: Calories 139, Fat 12.59g; Sodium 52mg; Carbs 3.39g; Fibre 1.6g; Sugar 0.45g; Protein 5.28g

Poppy Seed Muffins

Prep time: 10 minutes | Cook time: 10 minutes | Serves: 5

1 teaspoon baking powder 2 tablespoons Erythritol	125g coconut flour 5 tablespoons coconut oil,	softened 1 egg, beaten	1 teaspoon vanilla extract 1 tablespoon poppy seeds

1. In the mixing bowl, mix coconut oil with egg, vanilla extract, poppy seeds, baking powder, Erythritol, and coconut flour. 2. When the mixture is homogenous, pour it into the muffin molds and transfer it to the air fryer basket. 3. Cook the muffins for 10 minutes at 185°C.
Per Serving: Calories 165, Fat 16.36g; Sodium 72mg; Carbs 3.05g; Fibre 0.9g; Sugar 1.54g; Protein 2.46g

Coconut Pie

Prep time: 10 minutes | Cook time: 40 minutes | Serves: 8

120ml coconut cream	125g coconut flour	melted	1 teaspoon baking powder
3 eggs, beaten	1 tablespoon coconut oil,	1 tablespoon vanilla extract	3 tablespoons sweetener

1. Combine coconut flour, coconut oil, sweetener, baking powder, and coconut cream with the other ingredients. 2. Next, put the mixture in the air fryer basket and gently press it down. 3. Bake the pie for 40 minutes at 180°C.
Per Serving: Calories 124, Fat 10.58g; Sodium 71mg; Carbs 2.99g; Fibre 0.7g; Sugar 1.23g; Protein 4.12g

Almonds Doughnuts

Prep time: 15 minutes | Cook time: 14 minutes | Serves: 6

200g almond flour	1 egg, beaten	softened	1 teaspoon baking powder
2 tablespoons Erythritol	2 tablespoons almond butter,	100g heavy cream	

1. Combine almond flour, erythritol, egg, almond butter, heavy cream, and baking powder in a mixing dish. Work the dough. 2. Using the cutter, roll up the dough and cut out the donuts. 3. Place the doughnuts in the air fryer basket and fry for 7 minutes on each side at 185°C.
Per Serving: Calories 339, Fat 30.44g; Sodium 37mg; Carbs 10.24g; Fibre 5.3g; Sugar 2.61g; Protein 11g

Baked Nutmeg Donuts

Prep time: 20 minutes | Cook time: 6 minutes | Serves: 4

1 teaspoon ground nutmeg	50g almond flour	1 egg, beaten	softened
½ teaspoon baking powder	1 tablespoon Sweetener	1 tablespoon coconut oil,	Cooking spray

1. Spray cooking spray onto the air fryer basket. 2. Next, combine all the ingredients and knead the dough. 3. Prepare the dough to make the donuts, then air fry them. 4. Cook the doughnuts for three minutes on each side at 200°C. .
Per Serving: Calories 67, Fat 6.15g; Sodium 26mg; Carbs 0.87g; Fibre 0.1g; Sugar 0.19g; Protein 2.31g

Fluffy Turmeric Cookies

Prep time: 10 minutes | Cook time: 20 minutes | Serves:12

2 eggs, beaten	3 tablespoons coconut oil,	2 teaspoons ground turmeric	250g coconut flour
1 tablespoon coconut cream	melted	1 teaspoon vanilla extract	2 tablespoons Erythritol

1. In the mixing bowl, combine all the ingredients. 2. Work the dough and use the cutter to make the cookies. 3. Cook the cookies in the air fryer basket for 20 minutes at 175°C.
Per Serving: Calories 67, Fat 5.56g; Sodium 70mg; Carbs 2.49g; Fibre 0.7g; Sugar 1.47g; Protein 1.95g

Coconut Saffron Cookies

Prep time: 10 minutes | Cook time: 15 minutes | Serves:12

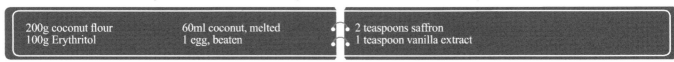

200g coconut flour	60ml coconut, melted	2 teaspoons saffron
100g Erythritol	1 egg, beaten	1 teaspoon vanilla extract

1. Mix all ingredients in the bowl and knead the dough. 2. Make the cookies and put them in the air fryer basket in one layer. 3. Cook the cookies at 180°C for 15 minutes.
Per Serving: Calories 21, Fat 0.9g; Sodium 56mg; Carbs 1.87g; Fibre 0.5g; Sugar 1.27g; Protein 1.08g

Coconut Vanilla Shortcake

Prep time: 15 minutes | Cook time: 30 minutes | Serves:4

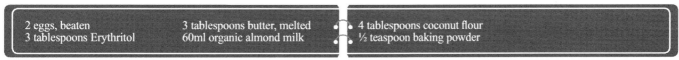

| 1 teaspoon vanilla extract | 3 eggs, beaten | 2 teaspoons sweetener | ½ teaspoon baking powder |
| 120ml coconut cream | 50g almond flour | Cooking spray | |

1. Spray cooking oil on the air fryer basket. 2. Then combine the eggs, baking powder, sweetener, vanilla extract, and coconut cream with the almond flour. 3. Pour the smoothed-out mixture into the air fryer basket and use the spatula to gently press it flat. 4. Cook the shortcake for 30 minutes at 180°C.
Per Serving: Calories 201, Fat 17.77g; Sodium 79mg; Carbs 3.23g; Fibre 0.7g; Sugar 0.63g; Protein 7.85g

Easy Raspberry Cream

Prep time: 10 minutes | Cook time: 20 minutes | Serves: 6

| 60g raspberries | 2 tablespoons water | ¼ teaspoon ground cinnamon |
| 1 tablespoon lime juice | 3 tablespoons Erythritol | |

1. Blend the raspberries and combine with water, erythritol, lime juice, and crushed cinnamon. 2. Fill the air fryer with the mixture, and cook for 20 minutes at 175°C.
Per Serving: Calories 20, Fat 0.03g; Sodium 1mg; Carbs 5.23g; Fibre 0.8g; Sugar 4.32g; Protein 0.19g

Almond milk Pie

Prep time: 10 minutes | Cook time: 20 minutes | Serves: 8

| 2 eggs, beaten | 3 tablespoons butter, melted | 4 tablespoons coconut flour |
| 3 tablespoons Erythritol | 60ml organic almond milk | ½ teaspoon baking powder |

1. Combine all ingredients in a mixer bowl and blend until thoroughly combined. 2. Spoon the mixture into the air fryer basket, and cook for 20 minutes at 185°C.
Per Serving: Calories 76, Fat 6.84g; Sodium 73mg; Carbs 1.39g; Fibre 0.1g; Sugar 1.02g; Protein 2.39g

Chia-Cocoa Pudding

Prep time: 40 minutes | Cook time: 10 minutes | Serves: 3

| 1 teaspoon vanilla extract | 480ml coconut cream | 1 tablespoon Erythritol |
| 3 tablespoons chia seeds | 1 teaspoon of cocoa powder | |

1. Fill the air fryer with the coconut cream. 2. Add erythritol, vanilla essence, and chocolate powder. Smoothen the liquid by stirring it. 3. After that, bake it for 10 minutes at 175°C. 4. Add the chia seeds, thoroughly combine the dessert, and then give it 40 minutes to rest.
Per Serving: Calories 606, Fat 60.18g; Sodium 9mg; Carbs 17.48g; Fibre 8.9g; Sugar 0.19g; Protein 8.4g

Muffins with Pumpkin Spice

Prep time: 15 minutes | Cook time: 10 minutes | Serves: 6

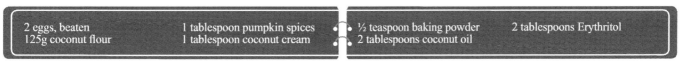

| 2 eggs, beaten | 1 tablespoon pumpkin spices | ½ teaspoon baking powder | 2 tablespoons Erythritol |
| 125g coconut flour | 1 tablespoon coconut cream | 2 tablespoons coconut oil | |

1. Mix all ingredients in the mixing bowl. 2. When the batter is smooth, pour it into the muffin molds and transfer to the air fryer basket. 3. Cook the muffins at 185°C for 10 minutes.
Per Serving: Calories 102, Fat 8.81g; Sodium 77mg; Carbs 2.83g; Fibre 0.6g; Sugar 1.33g; Protein 3.42g

Homemade Butter Cookies

Prep time: 15 minutes | Cook time: 10 minutes | Serves: 5

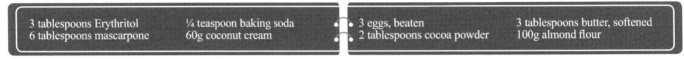

| 4 tablespoons butter, softened | 4 teaspoons Splenda | 1 egg, beaten | 125g coconut flour |

1. Combine the butter, Splenda, egg, and coconut flour in a mixing bowl. 2. Make the balls by kneading the dough (cookies). 3. Cook them for 10 minutes at 185°C in the air fryer.
Per Serving: Calories 116, Fat 11.24g; Sodium 144mg; Carbs 1.99g; Fibre 0.5g; Sugar 1.39g; Protein 2.24g

Mascarpone Brownies

Prep time: 10 minutes | Cook time: 25 minutes | Serves: 6

| 3 tablespoons Erythritol | ¼ teaspoon baking soda | 3 eggs, beaten | 3 tablespoons butter, softened |
| 6 tablespoons mascarpone | 60g coconut cream | 2 tablespoons cocoa powder | 100g almond flour |

1. In a mixing bowl, combine all the ingredients and blend well. 2. After that, put the baking paper inside the air fryer basket and add the brownie batter inside. 3. Cook the food for 25 minutes at 180°C. 4. After cooling slightly, slice the dessert into brownies.
Per Serving: Calories 154, Fat 14.38g; Sodium 152mg; Carbs 2.27g; Fibre 0.8g; Sugar 0.37g; Protein 5.27g

Almond Chia Balls

Prep time: 15minutes | Cook time:10 minutes | Serves: 4

4 teaspoons chia seeds	1 tablespoon Erythritol	1 teaspoon almond flakes
1 tablespoon coconut oil, softened	½ teaspoon vanilla extract	1 egg, beaten
	1 tablespoon almond flour	Cooking spray

1. Spray the air fryer basket with cooking spray. 2. Next, combine the remaining ingredients in a mixing dish and stir to combine well. 3. Form the mixture into balls and arrange them in a single layer in the air fryer. 4. Chia balls should be baked for 10 minutes at 185°C.
Per Serving: Calories 84, Fat 7.24g; Sodium 26mg; Carbs 1.94g; Fibre 1.3g; Sugar 0.26g; Protein 2.95g

Baked Avocado Cream

Prep time: 10 minutes | Cook time: 30 minutes | Serves:5

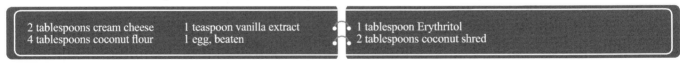

| 1 egg, beaten | 240g coconut cream | chopped | 1 tablespoon butter, softened |
| 2 tablespoon Erythritol | 1 avocado, peeled, pitted, | ½ teaspoon ground nutmeg | |

1. The avocado, egg, erythritol, coconut cream, butter, and grated nutmeg are all blended. 2. Transfer the smooth liquid into the ramekins. 3. The ramekins should be placed in the air fryer basket and cooked for 30 minutes at 175°C.
Per Serving: Calories 270, Fat 26.85g; Sodium 43mg; Carbs 6.93g; Fibre 3.8g; Sugar 0.4g; Protein 4.38g

Coconut Cream Cheese Bombs

Prep time: 10 minutes | Cook time: 5 minutes | Serves:2

| 2 tablespoons cream cheese | 1 teaspoon vanilla extract | 1 tablespoon Erythritol |
| 4 tablespoons coconut flour | 1 egg, beaten | 2 tablespoons coconut shred |

1. Combine the coconut flour, vanilla extract, egg, erythritol, and coconut shred with the cream cheese. 2. Form the mixture into balls and place them in the air fryer basket. 3. Bake the cheese bombs for five minutes at 200°C.
Per Serving: Calories 124, Fat 9.2g; Sodium 164mg; Carbs 2.97g; Fibre 0.5g; Sugar 2.29g; Protein 5.87g

Coconut Cream Cups

Prep time: 5 minutes | Cook time: 10 minutes | Serves:2

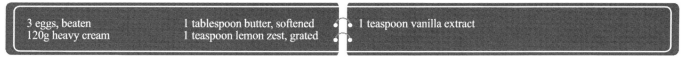

| 240g coconut cream
4 egg yolks | 2 tablespoons Erythritol
1 tablespoon coconut flour | 1 teaspoon vanilla extract |

1. Combine the coconut cream, erythritol, and egg yolks in a bowl. 2. Next, incorporate vanilla essence and coconut flour. Blend the mixture with a whisk. 3. Spoon the mixture into the baking cups, then place them in the basket of the air fryer. 4. Prepare the cups for 10 minutes at 200°C.
Per Serving: Calories 513, Fat 50.6g; Sodium 29mg; Carbs 9.74g; Fibre 2.7g; Sugar 0.65g; Protein 9.8g

Lemon Cream Pudding

Prep time: 10 minutes | Cook time: 35 minutes | Serves:2

| 3 eggs, beaten
120g heavy cream | 1 tablespoon butter, softened
1 teaspoon lemon zest, grated | 1 teaspoon vanilla extract |

1. In a mixing bowl, whisk each ingredient until it is well combined. 2. Place the baking pan with the mixture inside, then place the basket inside the air fryer. 3. Cook the custard at 170°C for 35 minutes.
Per Serving: Calories 355, Fat 31.32g; Sodium 211mg; Carbs 2.81g; Fibre 0g; Sugar 2.15g; Protein 14.14g

Courgette with Sweet Cream Cheese

Prep time: 10 minutes | Cook time: 15 minutes | Serves:4

| 60g heavy cream
2 tablespoons Erythritol | 1 teaspoon butter
4 teaspoons cream cheese | 1 courgette, grated |

1. Combine cream cheese, butter, Erythritol, heavy cream, and grated courgette. 2. Place the mixture in the basket of the air fryer and gently press down. 3. Prepare the food for 15 minutes at 180°C.
Per Serving: Calories 50, Fat 5.17g; Sodium 32mg; Carbs 0.47g; Fibre 0g; Sugar 0.38g; Protein 0.59g

Coconut Cookie with Sesame Seeds

Prep time: 15 minutes | Cook time: 10 minutes | Serves:8

| 2 eggs, beaten
1 teaspoon baking powder | 10g Splenda
3 tablespoons sesame seeds | 100g almond flour
2 tablespoons coconut shred | 1 tablespoon coconut oil,
softened |

1. Combine all the ingredients in a bowl and knead the dough. 2. Form the dough into balls and gently press them into the shape of cookies. 3. Layer the cookies in the air fryer basket and cook them at 180°C for 10 minutes.
Per Serving: Calories 68, Fat 6.03g; Sodium 31mg; Carbs 1.1g; Fibre 0.4g; Sugar 0.31g; Protein 2.91g

● Conclusion ●

If you're like most people, you probably use your air fryer to make quick and easy meals. But what about when you want to make a big batch of food? Is your air fryer up to the task? The answer is, it depends. Some air fryers are better suited for large batches than others. If you're not sure if your air fryer can handle a big batch, it's best to check the manual or contact the manufacturer. In general, though, most air fryers can handle a big batch of food if you're careful. Here are a few tips to help you make the most of your air fryer:

● Preheat the air fryer. This will help ensure that the food cooks evenly.

● Use a cooking spray or oil. This will help prevent the food from sticking to the air fryer.

● Don't overcrowd the air fryer. This will prevent the food from cooking evenly.

Appendix 1 Measurement Conversion Chart

WEIGHT EQUIVALENTS

US STANDARD	METRIC (APPROXIMATE)
1 ounce	28 g
2 ounces	57 g
5 ounces	142 g
10 ounces	284 g
15 ounces	425 g
16 ounces (1 pound)	455 g
1.5pounds	680 g
2pounds	907 g

VOLUME EQUIVALENTS (LIQUID)

US STANDARD	US STANDARD (OUNCES)	METRIC (APPROXIMATE)
2 tablespoons	1 fl.oz	30 mL
¼ cup	2 fl.oz	60 mL
½ cup	4 fl.oz	120 mL
1 cup	8 fl.oz	240 mL
1½ cup	12 fl.oz	355 mL
2 cups or 1 pint	16 fl.oz	475 mL
4 cups or 1 quart	32 fl.oz	1 L
1 gallon	128 fl.oz	4 L

VOLUME EQUIVALENTS (DRY)

US STANDARD	METRIC (APPROXIMATE)
⅛ teaspoon	0.5 mL
¼ teaspoon	1 mL
½ teaspoon	2 mL
¾ teaspoon	4 mL
1 teaspoon	5 mL
1 tablespoon	15 mL
¼ cup	59 mL
½ cup	118 mL
¾ cup	177 mL
1 cup	235 mL
2 cups	475 mL
3 cups	700 mL
4 cups	1 L

TEMPERATURES EQUIVALENTS

FAHRENHEIT (F)	CELSIUS(C) (APPROXIMATE)
225 °F	107 °C
250 °F	120 °C
275 °F	135 °C
300 °F	150 °C
325 °F	160 °C
350 °F	180 °C
375 °F	190 °C
400 °F	205 °C
425 °F	220 °C
450 °F	235 °C
475 °F	245 °C
500 °F	260 °C

Appendix 2 Air Fryer Cooking Chart

Frozen Foods	Temp (℉)	Time (min)
Onion Rings (12 oz.)	400	8
Thin French Fries (20 oz.)	400	14
Thick French Fries (17 oz.)	400	18
Pot Sticks (10 oz.)	400	8
Fish Sticks (10 oz.)	400	10
Fish Fillets (½-inch, 10 oz.)	400	14

vegetables	Temp (℉)	Time (min)
Asparagus (1-inch slices)	400	5
Beets (sliced)	350	25
Beets (whole)	400	40
Bell Peppers (sliced)	350	13
Broccoli	400	6
Brussels Sprouts (halved)	380	15
Carrots(½-inch slices)	380	15
Cauliflower (florets)	400	12
Eggplant (1½-inch cubes)	400	15
Fennel (quartered)	370	15
Mushrooms (¼-inch slices)	400	5
Onion (pearl)	400	10
Parsnips (½-inch chunks)	380	5
Peppers (1-inch chunks)	400	15
Potatoes (baked, whole)	400	40
Squash (½-inch chunks)	400	12
Tomatoes (cherry)	400	4
Zucchni (½-inch sticks)	400	12

Meat	Temp (℉)	Time (min)
Bacon	400	5 to 7
Beef Eye Round Roast (4 lbs.)	390	50 to 60
Burger (4 oz.)	370	16 to 20
Chicken Breasts, bone-in (1.25 lbs.)	370	25
Chicken Breasts, boneless (4 oz.)	380	12
Chicken Drumsticks (2.5 lbs.)	370	20
Chicken Thighs, bone-in (2 lbs.)	380	22
Chicken Thighs, boneless (1.5 lbs.)	380	18 to 20
Chicken Legs, bone-in (1.75 lbs.)	380	30
Chicken Wings (2 lbs.)	400	12
Flank Steak (1.5 lbs.)	400	12
Game Hen (halved, 2 lbs.)	390	20
Loin (2 lbs.)	360	55
London Broil (2 lbs.)	400	20 to 28
Meatballs (3-inch)	380	10
Rack of Lamb (1.5-2 lbs.)	380	22
Sausages	380	15
Whole Chicken (6.5 lbs.)	360	75

Fish and Seafood	Temp (℉)	Time (min)
Calamari (8 oz.)	400	4
Fish Fillet (1-inch, 8 oz.)	400	10
Salmon Fillet (6 oz.)	380	12
Tuna Steak	400	7 to 10
Scallops	400	5 to 7
Shrimp	400	5

● Appendix 3 Recipes Index ●

Printed in Great Britain
by Amazon

15649443R00066